DEACCESSIONED

The Urban Idea
in Colonial America

The Urban Idea
in Colonial America

Sylvia Doughty Fries

Temple University Press

Philadelphia

Temple University Press, Philadelphia 19122
© 1977 by Temple University. All rights reserved
Published 1977
Printed in the United States of America
International Standard Book Number: 0-87722-103-0
Library of Congress Number: 77-81333

For my
Mother and Father

"I understand," he said; "you mean the city whose establish-ment we have described, the city whose home is in the ideal; for I think it can be found nowhere on earth." "Well," said I, "perhaps there is a pattern of it laid up in heaven for him who wishes to contemplate it and so beholding to constitute himself its citizen. But it makes no difference whether it exists now or ever will come into being. The politics of this city only will be his and of none other."

The Republic IX 592 (Paul Shorey, trans.)

✥

I'd even choose
a desert isle,
Myself, to midtown Rome.

You'd call our forefathers' ancestors
happy, and happy besides
Those times that long ago, under
kings and tribunes, in pride
Saw Rome with only a single jail
well satisfied.
Juvenal, Satire III
(Hubert Creekmore, trans.)

Contents

✻

✻

Illustrations

✥

Preface

❦

Ever since that urbane sage of Monticello likened cities to sores on the human body, American attitudes toward the city have been characterized by their ambivalence, if not outright hostility. In a pioneering work Morton and Lucia White placed Thomas Jefferson at the beginning of an intellectual tradition which, while occasionally acknowledging the cultural stimulation available in cities, nevertheless found them lacking. The nineteenth-century American writer's response to the city was rarely innocent of prior attachments to values which affected his critical response to the urban landscape. The romantic voices of Ralph Waldo Emerson and Henry David Thoreau criticized the city for smothering the individual, who could find greater self-fulfillment within the embrace of nature. Significantly, that self-fulfillment was transcendental rather than material. Inasmuch as the rise of the city occurred at that moment in the course of American thought when sentiment, intoxicated with Romantic values and harkening to the heroism of yeoman rustics and frontiersmen, was least receptive to the achievements of factory and countinghouse, it is small wonder that American thought since the dawn of the new republic seemed "antiurban."

Post-Civil War intellectuals, on the other hand, disliked the city not because they favored the wilderness and not because the city represented over-rationalized constraints of civilization, but because the nineteenth-century American city appeared not civilized enough. For Henry Adams, cities like Chicago, San Francisco, or New York had been injected with moral anesthesia by businessmen and the polyglot seekers of new fortunes. Robert E. Park, Jane Addams, and John Dewey bemoaned a perceived loss of community in the transience and anonymity of urban life. The modern city's most steadfast critic, Lewis Mumford, has intoned against the alleged barbarizing and dehumanizing affects of "megalopolis."[1] So persuasive have been America's various agrarian myths—be they of America as an edenic garden or the frontier as the wilderness testing place of virtue and virility—that much of what is modern, and especially the worlds of technology and the city, has been received primarily as it appears to alter the natural or bucolic landscape.[2] And yet the response of the American imagination to the city can not be simply described as antiurban.

It is true that many of those who helped to weave the fabric of American colonial society were conscious of the fact that they were frontiersmen of sorts and that the wilderness was having no small impact on their enterprise. Here is Bishop George Berkeley heralding the westward sway of empire; there is Jonathan Edwards, adjusting the schedule of the coming millenium to coincide with the march of Protestantism down the village lanes of New England. Prescience received the confirmation of hindsight when Frederick Jackson Turner, one of the first American historians to be a true child of the west, invoked the frontier as the single most formative factor in American history. However, no less important than new environments to the formation of a society, and especially of its self-perception, is the role of memory and expectations formed of the past. Turner might argue that democratic civilization was successively reborn of the frontier, but for Englishmen in the new world, however much they might claim to yearn for "rural retirement," civilization was nourished and manifest in cities. The symbolic American landscape has included not only the edenic garden but the New Jerusalem.

Studies of the city in American thought extending the scope of the Whites' work have found the response of nineteenth- and twentieth-century writers to the city to have been complex and varied. Especially when the city itself has been the primary setting of imaginative literature it has been portrayed as a dynamic force capable of shaping the experience and identity of fictional characters. It can inspire dreams as well as defeat them, as it does in Theodore Dreiser's *Sister Carrie* (1900). Its capacity to effect isolation and personal dissociation can not be separated from its power to stimulate, educate, and define the personality.[3] Reliance upon imaginative literature as documentary evidence of American attitudes toward the city, however, has its perils, not the least of which is in our approach to literature itself and thus inevitably our understanding of what the writer intends to reveal of himself and his world. If references to the city are read only as descriptive of objective reality for the writer, one can overlook the use of the city as a symbol or metaphor for experiences which are essentially independent of the landscape. The city of some American poets and novelists thus interpreted has been found to serve as a metaphor for the individual's encounter with the miraculous, or the surrender of himself to knowledge, form, and personal destiny.[4] Moreover, one risks the presumption of projecting upon those who are not literary figures or intellectuals by avocation the experiences and perceptions of those who are. When one turns to the effusions of newspaper editorialists, real estate promoters, civic boosters, travelers' accounts, and popular fiction, one finds considerable diversity in attitude toward and enthusiasm for the city. American cities become distinguishable by their age or regional location, for instance, and are often valued as places of opportunity, social and economic mobility, culture, and social progress.[5]

Explorations into the role of the city in American thought have been typically delimited by two conceptual tendencies. The "city" being studied has been largely that of the industrial era and thus perceptions of it have been confused with responses to the mechanization and rationalization of an industrial economy. Thus Robert E. Park could attribute to the city a rationalized mentality, distinctive for its inclination "to think in deterministic and mechanistic terms," the "embodiment" of which "is the tool, the machine, in which all the parts are manifestly designed to achieve a perfectly intelligible end."[6] However, much of the American urban experience has been of the preindustrial city, which has a landscape that differs in many significant ways from the industrial urban landscape. The dark, seething tenements which, for example, evoked the dismay of a Jacob Riis were only secondarily urban phenomena. Secondly, interpretations of American attitudes toward the city have been drawn almost entirely from verbal expression to the neglect of graphic documentation, thus assuming that what we say can not only be equated with what we make, but alone adequately mirrors our conception of the world. The architect or urban planner, however, can not, like the writer of imaginative or discursive literature, deny the constructed world of the city for a wholly natural landscape. By the very nature of his work he is engaged in an attempt to give material form to the city and thus to define creatively what it is or ought to become. Thus if we are to grasp fully a society's conception of the city we must examine as well the statements that inhere in the formal design of the man-made urban landscape.

The chapters that follow are in part an attempt to extend in time and through the use of graphic sources the conceptual framework of our understanding of the origin of American ideas of the city. Their purpose is to explore the idea of the city in American civilization, not from the perspective of what it became, but of whence it came. What did the city, and life in the city, mean to late seventeenth- and early eighteenth-century Englishmen as they undertook that westward adventure, the English colonization of North America? We have sought to answer that question through an examination of promotional literature, legislation, diaries and correspondence, and the architectural record.

An attempt to identify every possible concept of the city that might have underlain every European settlement in North America during the first periods of colonization would be beyond the reach of a single study. If we had limited our scope by beginning with a precise modern definition of the city—weighted as it must inevitably be toward more familiar demographic and economic characteristics—we might have rather obscured than clarified the urban expectations of societies whose views could only have been based upon what they then understood of cities and city life. Moreover, a modern statistical or functional definition could lead one to overlook the more visionary or imaginative elements which in fact emerge as central to seventeenth- and early eighteenth-century views of the city. We therefore confined our exploration to several communities which, in their diversity, might reflect a sufficiently wide and representative range of possibilities in the expectations and design of the city among the English colonies of North America. The foundings of Boston, Philadelphia, Williamsburg, and Savannah together represent the variety in origins of the English colonial enterprise. Moreover, each of these cities was planned in terms of its physical appearance, as well as social organization, before actual settlement took place. In confining our attention to the English colonies we are not unmindful that the aboriginal and pre-Columbian peoples of North America, as well as the French and the Spanish, have made contributions to the diverse American tradition of city-building which deserve more thorough discussion than could be provided here.[7]

It soon became apparent that one could not examine ideas of the city extracted from their relevant contexts of social, religious, economic, and political perceptions and aspirations. For example, Virginia, as much as Williamsburg, must be the focus of a search for urban concepts in the Tidewater region because the conception of urban life that prevailed in that area was the possession of a newly forming gentry for whom urban living was particularly a cultural and social style. Their "urbanity" was cultivated on the plantation, dependent to a degree upon slavery, and only then manifest at Williamsburg. Consideration of town and city planning has been directed less toward the genealogy of the plans themselves—an exploration which has been more than adequately accomplished by John W. Reps and Anthony N. B. Garvan, among others[8]—but toward an appreciation of the underlying conceptions of the city which may have produced those plans. Thus the appearance of a grid plan, for instance, as in the case of Philadelphia, invites consideration not only of possible precedents for Thomas Holme's layout, but of the historic purposes of the grid. The baroque plan—such as what we find in the design of Williamsburg—originates in a relatively greater emphasis upon a celebrative civic aesthetic than does an orthogonal plan which reflects the accommodation of urban space to a multitude of small settings for undisturbed private domesticity. Many considerations, of course, entered into the selection of one plan over another, or of a combination of plans. The needs of trade or security were among the most important. But such material considerations were not the exclusive determinants of the intended physical character of early colonial towns.

While the founders of Boston, Philadelphia, Williamsburg, and Savannah drew upon a substantial heritage of ideas of the city, a heritage which we have attempted to review in Chapter 1, their expectations of the city were affected by their own perceived circumstances. Their principal objective in social and architectural design of the city was the assurance of harmony and stability. Carl Bridenbaugh, in his lively portrait of the English people during the half century which embraced the migrations across the Atlantic, suggests that an era of "change and challenge"— brought about by economic dislocation, moral disorder, and social and geographic mobility—produced a society of "vexed and troubled Englishmen."[9] What most characterizes the expectations of the city manifest by these Englishmen, as they set out to re-create societies in North America, is a reactionary attempt to *reconstruct* society as well. The city became for them an instrument of that reconstruction.

This subtle transformation in the expectations held of urban places was informed by a moral critique of the alterations taking place in English society on the eve of each episode in colonization. Because the countryside, with its rural economy, was seen by men and women apprehensive of social disorder as a place where traditional social structures and moral control could be best maintained, the colonial American city was designed to preserve values and a way of life ultimately rural in character. The roots of American ideas of the city are thus to be found not in the romantic revolt against the industrial city, but in the search for order which was the psychological accompaniment of the experience of dislocation shared by those English men and women who, with a variety of purposes, ventured into the American wilderness.

This study was begun several years ago with the financial and invaluable collegial support of the Council of Humanities at Southern Methodist University. The American Philosophical Society provided funds to help defray the costs of research. The staffs of the Massachusetts Historical Society, Historical Society of Pennsylvania, Colonial Williamsburg Foundation, and the Georgia Historical Society, as well as various university libraries have contributed much in their cheerful and tireless help. Charles Albro Barker and Thomas Parke Hughes have read portions of the manuscript and tendered valuable criticisms, while Agatha Hughes has provided unfailing encouragement. This undertaking has had a faithful friend since its inception in Kenneth L. Arnold. Finally, Russell I. Fries has shared in the trials of authorship and listened patiently throughout, responding with the critical insights of a gifted historian and the expertise of a seasoned surveyor. To them and to those teachers who have offered the author in the past the priceless gift of intellectual friendship, this book is offered with affectionate gratitude.

S. D. F.

The Urban Idea
in Colonial America

1

Introduction

❦

The Englishmen who first embarked in the early years of the seventeenth century for the westward Atlantic crossing no longer as explorers but as true migrants were, no less than the great queen's servants themselves, Elizabethans. The world they knew had only begun to undergo the many social, political, and intellectual transformations which would characterize the seventeenth century. Few among them had experienced urban life as the Englishmen of Hanoverian England would. While they might think of London as the Court, or as the city of guilds and trades, and a very few among them might have known of the wealth and intellectually open climate of the great cities of the Low Lands, the vast majority of them came from the farms of the West Country, East Anglia, Lincolnshire, and Yorkshire. Thus, apart from the smaller proportion of skilled tradesmen who joined them from London, the first English settlers in North America were husbandmen and yeomen whose accustomed world was a world of farms and villages.[1] The land and a rural economy based on identiture and freehold served as the principal material bases of their social and economic values and expectations.

As Elizabethans their religion was Protestant, their politics nationalistic, and their cosmology hierarchical. Their limited experience of the cultural and social ambiance of the city was counterpoised with a visionary conception of the city—the New Jerusalem—which symbolized the apocalyptic world view alike of Dissenter and Conformist, Puritan and courtier. This vision, articulated in John Foxe's *Book of Marytrs* (1554; first English edition, 1563) and documented, as it were, in the English Bible, was a view of church and national history which placed the England of Elizabeth in the vanguard of the chiliastic struggle between Christ and Antichrist. Throughout the seventeenth century questions of church and national polity would be measured against medieval imperatives of history which, as variously interpreted by Anglican, Puritan, Presbyterian,

3

or Independent, could be traced to Augustine, Eusebius, and ultimately the Book of Revelation. The history of the world was the history of the never-relaxed struggle between two cities—the City of God and the City of the World, the New Jerusalem and Babylon.[2]

The earliest idealization of the city was the Athenian city-state, so eloquently described in the Periclesian orations of Thucydides' *The Peloponnesian War.* (c. 411 B.C.). The decline of the Periclesian ideal in the face of imperial strivings first in the eastern Mediterranean and then in Italy yielded ultimately to a universalized conception of the city. As Rome underwent the transition from republic to empire the idea of the city as an exclusive, self-sufficient, aggregation of citizens was gradually displaced by the idea of the city as the fatherland of mankind, the focus of universal order and the source of human justice and human good.[3]

In the closing passages of the *Commonwealth* (51 B.C.) Cicero introduced the idea of a celestial sphere to which man's true self, his soul, ultimately belongs. By so doing he implied that the earthly city might be conceived merely as a temporal manifestation of a perfect and eternal heavenly state. Drawing upon Platonic concepts of the transcendent city and upon the Hebrew visions of the humiliation of the proud and the New Jerusalem, Philo of Alexandria (c. 30 B.C.–A.D. 45) proclaimed a great universal city in which citizenship is a matter of the spirit. The prophet Isaiah had told of the fall of Babylon (Isaiah 13) and the psalmist had sung of Zion (Psalm 87). The promise of a new city, emerging from the ruins of the old, was nowhere more compelling than in the closing passages of the Revelation of St. John. The struggling Christian community, with its own lively sense of history and its new conception of the church, came to see the events of the early fifth century as analogous to the biblical prophecies; the corruption and collapse of Rome was readily likened to the fall of Babylon.

It was Augustine, Bishop of Hippo, who in his *City of God,* begun three years after Alaric entered Rome (410), combined Platonic, Hebrew and early Christian conceptions of the city in historical time into a theology of history which was to dominate Western thought for over ten centuries. The city was no longer one single aspect of human experience; rather, all of human experience can be located in Two Cities. These Two Cities are not simply the dwelling places of a chosen people; they are the earthly and spiritual communities outside of which all mankind knows no being. Their origin is in the very origin of the universe. In the beginning the angels were separated into two societies of light and darkness, "the one enjoying God, the other, swelling with pride."[4] Cicero's ideal city, the Roman republic, could not serve as an ideal city for Augustine for it was not, to begin with, a true republic. Even if we accept the view that a true republic is an "assemblage associated by a common acknowledge-

4

ment of right," he argued, then the republic must be "administered" with true justice. But if true justice is giving to each his due, then the Roman republic was not a true republic because it did not give to God his due: "Where, then, is the justice of man, when he deserts the true God and yields himself to impure demons?"[5]

Augustine's account of the Two Cities throughout history culminates in the eschatological vision which, quite aside from being necessitated by faith, was a logical consequence of his solution to one of the most persistent questions of Christian theology—the origins of sin, or pride, or evil. In the twelfth book of the *City of God* Augustine explained that evil—whether in men or angels—is due not to their natures, since God created them and "the things which He made are indeed good because of Him," but to an evil will which does not require an "efficient cause." An evil will, which is the true source of evil acts, originates neither in the nature of angels or men, nor in eternity, but in its own corruption by "wickedly and inordinately desiring an inferior thing." This desire is not "effective" but "defective." Defections of the will "are not towards things that are in themselves evil, but because [they are] contrary to the order of nature, . . . an abandonment of that which has supreme being for that which has less."[6] The existence of the earthly city, then, is contrary to nature. The heavenly city, on the other hand, is consonant with man's true nature as created by God. Because the restoration of paradise to the elect is the destiny of the world, realization of the heavenly city is the true end of all human history.

In the *City of God* justice, the end of the ideal city for Plato and Aristotle, is replaced by peace. "Jerusalem" means, Augustine reminds us, "Vision of Peace."

> [In the heavenly city] the peace of heaven . . . alone can be truly called and esteemed the peace of reasonable creatures, consisting as it does in the perfectly ordered and harmonious enjoyment of God and of one another in God.[7]

That eternal peace found in life after death we are helpless to know in this life because the "vision of it is reserved as the reward of our faith."[8] The requisite knowledge and power are reserved to him unto whom we will be joined only after the last judgment.

And yet the Augustinian philosophy of history, dominated as it was by the transcending vision of the City of God, was not without application to the secular world. It was possible to interpret the City of God not only as the eternal city of the Trinity, loyal angels, and the eternally saved among the human race, but as having an institutional representation on earth in the church. Prefigured in the Hebrew nation, the church was

5

composed of those who love God and, in the Middle Ages, came to be symbolized by the "church militant." The city of the earth too was represented in secular time—by the state. Although Augustine rejected the Ciceronian idealization of the Roman republic, he nonetheless distinguished between the imperial state, founded upon domination and too large to be held morally accountable, and the "commonwealth." The later might become a morally good polity, but only in so far as it was sustained by the harmony of individuals who love God—by the tranquility of order, or the peace that results from yielding to God his due. What matters ultimately is that Augustinian historical and political thought rejected the classical idealization of the secular city; the good Christian citizen must live in the world, but he could not be of it.[9]

It would be difficult to demonstrate that the English Puritans who emigrated to Massachusetts Bay perceived themselves in terms of the Augustinian paradigm of the Two Cities. Yet much of the Christian theology in which their pastors had been schooled was Augustinian in origin. This much is certain: Augustine's Two Cities would have clear and distinct echoes in Massachusetts Bay, most especially in the pervasive conception of the church as an aggregate of visible saints, and in the New England Puritans' stress on the state as a commonwealth morally justified in its unifying love of God and aspiration toward a tranquil order derived from the justice of giving God his due. When John Winthrop wrote of Christian liberty as the liberty to serve God, he wrote from an Augustinian perspective on the secular world in sacred time.[10]

Throughout the sixteenth and first half of the seventeenth centuries, Augustine's eschatological view of human history was axiomatic to all Protestant Englishmen. Until Civil War erupted in 1641, Puritans and Anglicans alike accepted Foxe's identification of the English monarchs with the Christian emperor who would lead the English nation in victory over the Roman Antichrist and all the forces of Satan. Through Foxe, the Englishmen who first settled on the North American shores identified the political destiny of the English nation with the spiritual destiny of the elect.[11] The history of the English people became the story of John Bunyan's pilgrim (1678), struggling against mighty Satan as he made his way through the city of this world in vigilant anticipation of the coming of the City of God.

The political and religious controversies which consumed England between 1603 and 1660 resulted in the eventual abandonment of the vision of the holy city as the unique destiny of the English people. The disappearance of that vision came about not because the end was disputed, but because of confusion over means. Until 1641 Anglican and Non-Separating Congregationalist alike subscribed to Foxe's millenarian promise that a new Christian emperor, the "Godly Prince," would lead the nation in righteous preparation for the coming of the New Jerusalem. But the events leading to 1641 discredited both Crown and episcopacy as leaders of a national regeneration and it appeared both to Puritans and Independents that the burden must lie with a "Godly People."[12] Those means, too, were destined for failure. The policy of national spiritual reformation through public discipline was abandoned with the Restoration. Meanwhile a strengthening, not weakening, Calvinism reproached its adherents with the impiety of presuming to schedule the divine program for redemption. Both Roger Williams and Oliver Cromwell shared in a theological scepticism which, by reaffirming Calvinist doctrine, denied that the road to the City could be traveled by any route other than that of the private conscience. Public discipline might bring about a *moral* reformation, but godly rule could not ensure spiritual regeneration. As the righteous were warned not to "catch at the spiritual privileges of New Jerusalem before it comes down from heaven"[13] the holy city itself eluded the temporal strivings of the English nation.

But not so in New England. The emigrating Puritans who carried their quest for godly rule to the American wilderness were able to escape the dispiriting political realities of the interregnum. By drawing upon the typological example of the Israelites "goinge to the land of promise and fixing thear" and Nehemiah's rebuilding of Jerusalem, the Puritans of Massachusetts Bay found justification for their attempt to reconstruct a biblical commonwealth in terms more literal than the English situation would allow. At Boston and at New Haven, as we shall see, the vision that became clouded in the religious and political controversies of the Protectorate and Restoration survived to produce to a remarkable degree an enactment of the secular and spiritual cities of Augustine.

Every student of American history soon comes upon the woodcut of George Sandys, accompanying his 1626 translation of Ovid's *Metamorphosis,* in which the Elizabethan is portrayed meditating on a Virginia beach in contemporary dress with a copy of the Latin poet's work held open before him. The woodcut, like the numerous "rhetorical adornments" from classical literature and mythology which embellished colonial discourse, are a reminder that pagan antiquity was second only to the Christian tradition as a source of colonial intellectual life. Aristotle and Polybius, Ovid and Virgil, along with numerous other classical authors, added to the vocabulary of learned Englishmen in America and hence the intellectual means for the apprehension and interpretation of their experiences. Classical analogy vied with biblical allegory as a means of explanation and justification, even in theocratic New England where such classically educated Puritan divines as John Cotton were alert enough to the authority of antiquity to caution against over reliance on classical illustrations, rather than scriptural citations, in sermons and other forms of persuasion and discourse. The importance of antiquity in the political thinking of the last quarter of the eighteenth century is widely recognized;[14] but the worlds of Greece and Rome were never absent from the memories of educated Englishmen in America, even during the mid-seventeenth century when only the theological zeal of that age prevented the more general recasting of contemporary experience in the classical models of the following century.[15]

The Western conception of the city as *civitas* originates on the shores of the Aegean where, in the century after the Greek victory over Persia at Salamis (480 B.C.), the Athenians identified their city with an ideal of public life. It was then that the city first supplanted the individual, the family, the tribe, or the seat of an individual ruler as the primary object of loyalty and service and, in turn, source of human well-being. Writing from the wistful perspective of exile, Thucydides bequeathed to us an eloquent affirmation of the idea of the city in the age of Pericles in *The Peloponnesian War* (c. 411 B.C.). It was not with encomiums of glorious ancestry or even more glorious destinies that Pericles, in the Funeral Oration, chose to arouse the patriotism of the Athenians; it was rather by acknowledging the quality of life in the Athens of the present. And what was that quality? It was one of community in which all participate in the deliberations of a government which "favors the many instead of the few." Involvement in the affairs of the city was the principal means by which individuals transcend their own private concerns and, more importantly, differences in "social standing," "class," wealth, or "obscurity of . . . condition." And yet the security with which Athenians could enjoy their democratic institutions required more than the right laws. Pericles reminded the Athenians that harmonious and constructive participation in public affairs is possible only when concord precedes the making of the written law. Civic concord consists in intimacy and openness, a willingness to "throw open our city to the world . . . trusting less in system and policy than to the native spirit of our citizens."[16]

As Thucydides himself had feared, however, the great struggle for Athenian hegemony in the Aegean world was not compatible with the survival of the vision of political intimacy, moderation, and harmony with which Pericles sought to inspire his countrymen. Conquest abroad in combination with instability and civil conflict at home—these were the forces which finally exhausted the moral vitality of the Athenian city. "For tyrants and imperial cities nothing is unreasonable if expedient," an Athenian envoy announced to the Syracusan Hermocrates; "friendship or enmity is everywhere an affair of time and circumstance."[17] The Greeks developed no practical substitute for the city-state when their own expansion raised the question of political control over areas too large for direct participation in government. As a result subsequent Greco-Roman political thought until the Age of Augustus can be characterized by the attempt to revive the tradition of the functionally divided and balanced polity of the city-state, representing all classes and existing for the well-being of the "people."[18]

Plato, who came to maturity during the final hours of the Athenian city-state, provided the West with its first speculative excursion into utopia in search of a city most worthy of man. Again and again—from the Revelation of St. John to Augustine's *City of God*, from the *Republic* of Plato to Thomas More's *Utopia*—the consequence of the failure of one's city to affirm one's ideals will be the tendency to separate experience into the two realms of the heavenly and the now corrupt earthly cities. Plato was twenty-four years old when Sparta's humiliation of Athens (404 B.C.) marked the beginning of a half century of turmoil throughout the Aegean, ended only by Philip of Macedon's triumph over Athens and Thebes in 338 B.C. His best known work stood in part as an indictment of the city which condemned and executed in 399 B.C. his teacher Socrates, and in general of those twin scourges of the dying *polis*, materialism and individualism.

The ideal city of the *Republic* is predicated upon the Platonic theory of knowledge. It is remote from the apparent world of day-to-day social and political experience, but its remoteness is the measure of its perfection. Plato's philosophy of knowledge is critical to the character of his ideal city in two respects: in the first place, it requires that the city be built upon an abstract, hierarchical model of Platonic "realities" rather than upon the lessons of actual political and social experience; in the second place, his philosophy presupposes a conception of man which, when made analogous to society, precluded the development of either the constitutional principle or political practice of full citizen participation as essential to the vitality of the city. The human soul is composed of three elements, explained Socrates, those of reason, desire, and passion (IV, 439).[19] If society is compared to the individual (and this comparison is made throughout Book IV) then the desired supremacy of rational intelligence over self-interest and passion in the individual requires, analogously, for society, the maintenance of social order as an over-ruling objective.

The four virtues which Plato assigns to the ideal state—wisdom, courage, temperence, and justice (IV, 427–434)—serve to impose an artificial unity and stratified harmony upon society. Wisdom in government is knowledge "about the whole" of the state, a wisdom beyond the capacities of mere carpenters, farmers, smiths, and the like. It is in the very nature of Plato's conception of knowledge that wisdom cannot be "common," for the development of the Platonic soul is upward, not outward. Courage, or valor, is again a virtue denied to the commonality for courage, according to Plato, is the power to preserve "true opinion in conformity with law about real and false dangers." Valor, in short, must be educated; it cannot be simply the spontaneous manifestation of loyalty from ordinary citizens. The third virtue of his ideal city, temperence, or "the rule of the better part over the worse," becomes in the *Republic* a principle by which the many are to be distinguished from the few who "are the best born and best educated"—and must submit to them (IV, 431). Lastly, justice, the fourth virtue of the Platonic city, like the others becomes less a quality than a rule for the imposition of rank and order on society. Justice in the ideal city exists when each contents himself with the station and tasks in life for which he is best suited, or when "trades, the auxiliary, and the guardian each do their own business" (IV, 434).

Ultimately the well-being of the ideal city depends upon education—not only upon the education of a ruling class which rules by virtue of its "wisdom"—but upon the education of the citizens. Civic virtue has ceased to be a generally accessible attribute, both source and consequence of common participation in the affairs of the city; it has become a special attribute denied to the many. When the majority of the residents of the city are reduced to wards of a small intelligentsia, the city and the citizen as Pericles conceived of them have ceased to exist.

Until the early Christian era the prevailing attitude toward the city was essentially political. So long as justice was considered the highest possible achievement of man, the just state, whose realization was by nature a problem of politics, would remain the ideal conception of the city. The pre-Roman conception of the ideal city which would prevail belonged, however, to Aristotle. The very familiarity of Aristotle's views—the "naturalness" of the state, the maxim of balance, the necessity for constitutional government and rule of law—is sufficient indication of the influence of his *Politics*. Aristotle's contribution was to construct an ideal city which would be removed from its purely ethical and idealistic Platonic framework and restored to the real world of actual experience.

To Plato the nature of a thing could be arrived at only by first distinguishing the apparent particular from its ideal ("real") essence. The further one ascended from the world of appearances into the realm of pure, or mathematical, objects, the more did the intelligence apprehend the true nature of a thing. Thus the distance between the rational apprehension of the good and the just, and the day-to-day world of public business, was great indeed; one could not hope to perfect public life unless daily experience had been thus transcended. But for Aristotle the nature of a thing is simply "what each thing is when fully developed" (I).[20]

He wrote as a natural scientist rather than a mathematician, inhabiting a world of material and ever-changing realities; and therein lay the difference between them. Aristotle's entire system was an attempt to integrate both speculative and empirical knowledge into a philosophy of science. Just as his concept of the nature of things was dynamic, so did he grant to the world of action, motion and material things the same importance as the speculative world of ideas. Significantly the science of ethics belonged for him among the practical sciences. Hence, the determination of virtue is a problem in the analysis of habits, rather than the definition of essences. Likewise politics is concerned with forms of human association, the understanding of which, in turn, will lead us toward the purpose of political science: knowledgeable action, or the formation of the good state.

"A state," wrote Aristotle, "is not made up only of so many men, but of different kinds of men." The fully developed community must be self-sufficient which, in turn, required a plurality of diverse elements. Thus "what is said to be the greatest good of cities [viz., unity] is in reality their destruction; . . . surely the good of things must be that which preserves them" (II, 2). Aristotle's idea of the good state was predicated upon the necessary diversity of mature societies. The attributes most appropriate to "the city" are government by all men—and the invention of some means, such as rotation in office, by which this can be accomplished; the premise that the art of politics is accessible to all, irrespective of occupation; and acknowledgement that in the city the citizens are by nature (as citizens) equal. Here we are closer to the Periclesian ideal of full participation as the essence of a vital civic life than we are to the *Republic* where an ideal of harmony based upon a static occupational hierarchy is the primary concern.

What, then, was Aristotle's ideal city? The city—which is in Hellenic thought the same as the state—exists when one can identify "a partnership of citizens in a constitution" (III, 3). It is to be distinguished in the same manner that all elements are to be differentiated, viz., by its composition, or its constitution. Citizenship is not a mere matter of residence; resident aliens, for example, are not citizens, nor are slaves or members of the artisan class who "in ancient times" were foreigners if not slaves. "He is a citizen in the highest sense who shares in the honors of the state, . . . who has the power to take part in the deliberative or judicial administration of any state" (III, 2, 6).

Unlike Plato's remote ideal, the constitution of Aristotle's ideal city was meant not as a pure philosophical abstraction but as the best *possible* constitution, one which could serve as a model upon which other actual states might be constructed. Its purpose was to promote the moral virtue of the state, virtues which are not natural to man, as Aristotle pointed out in the *Nicomachean Ethics*, but are acquired and perfected by habit. Developed through practice, moral virtue becomes the ability to identify and to choose the mean between "excess" and "defect."[21] If laws are made to promote civic virtue, the effect of justice will be to bring about a life of balance and moderation through lawfulness and fairness. The principle of balance, or the pursuit of the mean, provided the structure as well as the purpose of Aristotle's best possible constitution. Seeing the civic community in terms of the rich and the poor, the few and the many, oligarchs and democrats, Aristotle taught that the best constitution is one which brings about a balance between those opposing elements without denying to either participation in the government of the state. Thus Aristotle's ideal city will be governed by a constitution which ensures moderation through the predominance of a middle class (IV, 11, 12).

The ideal city for the Greeks was initially conceived as an alternative to tyranny; the city-state would represent, above all, the rule of the many and its reason for being would be the common good. During the debilitating aftermath of Athens' imperial adventure, social order, harmony, and stability became relatively more important as Plato developed a concept of the city which was essentially static and authoritarian in nature. Significantly, the philosophical stance from which Plato argued his scheme was a retreat into philosophical idealism, detached from the realm of day-to-day public life. For Pericles, Athens enabled individuals to transcend their private concerns and through involvement in the affairs of the city to form a community which would preserve human liberty and well-being. The purpose of the Platonic model was to ensure that men's base desires and passions, which were disruptive in effect, would be disciplined by reason, or a rational order, having harmony and transcendent unity as its essence. Aristotle's conception of the city revived the ideal of general participation in government as both the duty and privilege of citizenship. Moreover, by viewing human societies as analogous to the natural world, he introduced the value of diversity and complementary functions as necessary to the vitality of the city.

Platonic and Aristotelian concepts have proven so enduring in modern social and political thought, and hence so pervasive in modern perceptions of what the good city represents, that their contribution can be too easily taken for granted. They deserve mention here, however, for variously applied they formed a substantial portion of the conceptual foundations of the colonial American city as manifest in the creations of Boston, Philadelphia, Williamsburg, and Savannah.

Pre-eminent within the Platonic and Aristotelian contribution was the view that the city exists to foster the moral enhancement of human life. Henceforth, the city could be measured by its success or failure at promoting the moral education of the human personality. Secondly, good citizenship was defined not as a passive condition, as in an accident of residence, but as an active role incumbent upon all those who would share in the benefits of society. That role was participatory; it was necessary to city and citizen alike, for no personality could be complete without its public dimension as a politically and socially responsible person.

In Platonic and Aristotelian analysis the city became inherently a social and political form and only accidentally a place in time. Civic responsibility was thus essential to its vitality and survival. Moreover, through their stress on justice and harmony, Platonic and Aristotelian conceptions would place upon the city the burden of realizing a true common weal. The political mechanisms by which justice and harmony were to be achieved might vary according to time and place, as would the understanding of justice itself, but the imperative remained. Furthermore, the Greek ideal of balance, whether in the design of the best constitution for the commonwealth, or in the architectural design of a public edifice, or in the education of the public citizen, would survive to influence the aesthetic, as well as political configurations of the colonial American city.

The aesthetic ideal of harmony, mathematically described as first suggested by Pythagoras, would be mirrored architecturally at Williamsburg. Boston and New Haven were each conceived as instruments of an historic process of spiritual regeneration; Philadelphia at its inception was expected to play a similar role. To the extent that social and moral improvement could be distinguished from spiritual regeneration, each of these northern cities was originally intended to fulfill that purpose as well. And if religious motives were less pronounced in the conception of the latest of these colonial American cities to be founded, Savannah, that city was nonetheless regarded as the center of an effort on the part of the Georgia Trustees to recover a world of social harmony and economic integrity, aspirations which, as we shall see, were distinctly moral in tone. Finally, each of these cities was conceived in the hope that it would achieve social cohesion and harmony in contrast to that self-seeking individualism which was perceived as being as much an enemy to the ideal secular city as it was to the New Jerusalem.

Dependent upon the compact, self-sufficient urban settlement, the Greek conception of the city-state was no more suited to the cosmopolitan world of Alexander or Augustus than was its polity suited to the administrative and political demands of empire. The city had to be redefined to accommodate a universal humanity bound not by local loyalties but by laws universally acknowledged throughout the empire. This redefinition took place during the first century B.C. in imperial Rome.

The conceptualization of Rome as the city of the world, the home of humanity and the universal law-giver, would not have been possible without the application of the Stoics' ideas of universal humanity and natural law to the Greek inheritance of the city-state. This was the achievement of Cicero's *Commonwealth*. The development of the idea of Rome as the universal city occurred, however, only with great stress between the conservatives' nostalgia for the republican Rome of the patrician families and the more cosmopolitan, expansive ideal of empire.[22] The conservative view, complemented by the appearance of the pastoral style in poetry, was voiced by Livy, for whom a "real sense of community" could be founded only upon "respect for the family and love of the soil."[23] In Livy's *History* the city became the worthy object of our loyalty only as the result of a previous fidelity to family and soil, which was the essence of the patrician outlook. Rome's course of empire thus created misgivings within the minds of those who sought to preserve the integrity of the older, exclusive city of the patriciate. Her imperial expansion ought not be allowed to become brute conquest; rather, Roman imperium could be justified only by an extension of law to all, a cosmopolitan citizenship.

This conceptual transition, which Lidia Staroni Mazzolani has located in the years between Sulla and Augustus (79–27 B.C.), drew heavily upon Hellenistic sources and the example of Alexander. In turn, it provided the historical basis for the rise of the early Christian conception of the city as universal, eternal, and belonging to all humanity, an ideal which owed much of its development to Philo of Alexandria (c. 30 B.C.–A.D. 45). In Cicero's *Commonwealth* we learn from Philus that "our home is not a structure of four walls, but is this entire universe, which the gods have given us as a habitation and as a country, to be shared in common with them," (I, xii) and from Scipio that "the whole world [is governed] by [a single] soul" (I, xxxvi). Because, as the Stoics argued, nature and human nature, gods and men, all share in common the principle of reason, law is the governing element in nature and must, therefore, be the governing element in human society. "There is in fact a true law," argued Laelius, "namely, right reason—which is in accordance with nature, applies to all men, and is unchangeable and eternal . . . there will be one law, eternal and unchangeable, binding at all times upon all people; and there will be, as it were, one common master, and ruler of men, namely God, who is the author of this law, its interpreter, and its sponsor. The man who will not obey it will abandon his better self" (III, xxii).[24]

While the rise of empire, as George Sabine argued, may have rendered the city-state historically and theoretically obsolete,[25] the notion that man acquires his identity and fulfills "his better self" only in the city was not;

this conception remained from Thucydides to Cicero. What underwent a subtle but important change is the character and scope of that ideal for which the city exists. Civic virtue—from the speeches of Pericles to the arguments of Cicero's Laelius—evolved from the simple expression of patriotic loyalty and service to the exclusive and geographically compact *polis* to the higher purpose of the assurance of justice in Aristotle's program for the good state, and thence to the honoring of one's common humanity through adherance to a universal law of nature based on the universal principle of reason. The realization of civic virtue became only incidentally political. One's commitment must be to a supreme nature which is prior to political institutions. This may explain Cicero's willingness to contemplate in the *Commonwealth* the rule of a *Princips,* if circumstances should prove the *Senatus Populusque Romanus* incapable of achieving the more universal destiny for which the new city was now intended (VI, xii–xiii). What became far more important historically, however—the legitimatization of Rome as a universal city whose justice was a law of nature—could serve, as it did serve, as a justification not only for the rule of princes but for revolutions against them.

During the century of English colonization in North America the actual Roman empire had not only long since disintegrated, but Englishmen regarded themselves as engaged in a momentous spiritual struggle against Rome as the seat of the Antichrist. Nonetheless they were legatees of the philosophical justification for the imperial city—that all mankind is bound together by a natural law accessible by universal reason. Sustained throughout the Middle Ages and the Renaissance by the survival of stoicism within Christian theology, the principle which the Roman publicists used to give legitimacy to empire could itself be turned against empire. And that principle ultimately did serve the American colonists both as one of their key intellectual weapons against the supposed tyrannies of their English prince and as the foundation of their new republican order.

✸

The American colonies were settled at a time when the vast majority of Europeans still lived in a rural setting and a rural economy. Nevertheless the process of urbanization which had first begun in antiquity revived in the later Middle Ages and was taking place about them in England. The growing importance of merchants, financiers, and specialized trades with nonfeudal values, the increased chartering of towns during the twelfth and thirteenth centuries by kings and princes seeking more revenues, and the expansion of the seaborne trade in what J. H. Parry called the "age of reconnaissance" all contributed to the revival of urban life. As a result of that gradual commercial evolution of the twelfth century which had begun to transform a manorial economy into an economy of freehold land and liquid capital, the city of this world became a place of trade corporately governed by guilds of merchants and artisans. The early medieval identity of the city as an administrative unit—first of the empire and then of ecclesiastical seats—did not disappear entirely, but episcopal authority alone would not, after the twelfth century, sustain the life of the modern European city. [26]

The late medieval city as commercial center bore within it the seeds of new values which, once institutionalized, would bear the fruit of altered political and social expectations having momentous consequences for the concept of the secular city itself. Chief among these was that personal liberty and status no longer depended upon privilege or one's inherited place on the land. Merchants and tradesmen required personal liberty to pursue their callings and this they achieved for themselves by membership in the commercial, corporate community which they created out of the towns where they gathered for both convenience and protection. Secondly, the commercial town insisted upon and won jurisdiction over itself. It became a body corporate and politic. Thirdly, residence in the city meant freedom from seigneurial fiscal obligations on the one hand and the acceptance of the obligation, through a rationalized system of taxation, to support the defenses and services of the city itself. The new identity of the city which resulted from these transformations, which were sought less by principle than by necessity and were won with the growing economic power of the merchant middle class over the countryside, was that the city was an autonomous, self-governing legal body whose membership enjoyed personal liberty dependent only upon their fulfilling the obligations of citizenship. [27]

Accompanying the emergence of modern cities—modern in the sense that they no longer served simply as imperial outposts or centers of episcopal administration but had acquired an independent legal and economic identity—was an evolving articulate consciousness of the special characteristics produced by the urban ambiance, or of urbanity. The abstract conceptions of the city which the seventeenth century received from both Christian and pagan antiquity were joined with an elaboration of the secular city as a place having a distinctive setting, producing a unique cultural style.

The urbane style first appeared in the cities of the Hellenistic world and the meaning of urbanity has since remained fundamentally unchanged. Cosmopolitanism and worldliness characterized the society of the new professional classes created by the vast bureaucratic structures of the empire and the needs of its far-flung trade. As would be true centuries

later during the Renaissance, these classes beautified their cities—
Alexandria, Athens, Rhodes, and Pergamum—with buildings, sculpture,
and fountains and patronized the arts and scholarship. A shift of emphasis
in the perception of the city is evident in Greek descriptions of Athens
from the fifth century to the third century B.C. Thucydides, in the
Funeral Oration of Pericles, described Athens in terms of political and
cultural activity, rather than architecture or topography. Heraclides, in
his third century travelogue, would show a greater interest in the city's
public buildings and in her role as a theater for artistic and intellectual
diversions and amusements for the tourist. While the later emphasis
might be expected from the writer as traveler, the altered condition of the
city—Athens' decline from political pre-eminence—nonetheless suggested a change in perception of the role the city is expected to play. [28]

Stoicism and Epicureanism contributed the attitudes of world-weari-
ness eased by philosophical individualism and reserve on the one hand,
and materialism, on the other, with which urban life has been therever
after associated. The urbane type portrayed in the New Comedy was a
member of the Hellenistic middle classes, living in the cities and supported by the income from lands worked by tenant farmers. He was
refined and polished in bearing, gracious in manner, and elegant but
moderate in speech. Throughout the ancient world, when public discourse was still dominated by the spoken word, speech was the essential
characteristic by which the urbane man could be distinguished from the
"rustic." This new man was also expected to possess a sense of humanity,
a quality which Plato had insisted upon in his portrait of Socrates, and has
never wholly disappeared from the makeup of the urbane man, or complete gentleman. [29]

The term *urbanitas* was used during the early Roman empire to
describe the sophistication and refinement of the city-dweller. In contrast
the country-dweller was portrayed as dull and ignorant, his boorishness
explained by the fact that rural life is hard and coarse. During the
Augustan Age urbanity became more than the distinguishing mark of the
refined Roman; it represented characteristics belonging to the city-
dweller generally. The view of just what these characteristics were
varied. For Horace, urbanity was more an attribute of character than of
manner. Moderation, loyalty in friendship, nobility, and goodness of soul
can render a man urbane even though "his hair is cut in rather rustic
fashion" or "his toga drags the ground." For Ovid, however, urbanity was
largely a matter of self-conscious cultivation of the social arts of conversation, music, and dance.

At the same time, the Roman view of the country underwent elaboration and the contrast with life in the city more finely drawn. The
classically educated Englishman could recall from memory Livy's portrait

of Cincinnatus, "wiping the grimy sweat from his hands and face" as he left his "little three-acre farm" to join his countrymen in defense of Rome against the Sabines. No longer merely the habitat of rustics and foreigners, who were identical for much of Roman history, the country became for Horace (68–8 B.C.) a place of rest and quiet where one could escape the noise and bustle of the city. Whereas the country of Theocritus was a place of work, of "the herding of goats, sheep and cattle," producing those rural virtues of prudence and industry, the *Eclogues* of Virgil (70–19 B.C.) introduced a pastoral landscape which appealed against "the disturbance of war and civil war and the political chaos of cities." What was evoked in the countryside of Juvenal (60?–140 A.D.) was "not the rural economy, past or present, but a purchased freehold house in the country, or a 'charming coastal retreat.' " City and country were both necessary to urbanity—the one to stimulate and refine, the other to refresh and restore human capacities. What might appear later as a veneration of country life was often merely the literary assertion of the "dichotomic life" which had become a commonplace for urbane Romans by the end of the first century. [30]

The Italian Renaissance, experiencing both the rebirth of urban life and the recovery of antiquity, articulated an enthusiasm for civic life which was largely secular in orientation. The individualism of the period, illuminated by Jacob Burckhardt, was not an individualism of ascetic withdrawal, but of social involvement. The personality, exercised in the life of the city, became the paramount dynamic in civilization. And it was personalities—men like Petrarch, Leo Battista Alberti, Pope Aeneas Silvius, Leonardo da Vinci, and Lorenzo the Magnificent—who gave definition to urbanity by being themselves participants in the creation of a revitalized urban culture. Refinement as an objective of the civic culture of the Renaissance can be discerned as the governing ideal of that period's various modes of cultural expression. Leonardo Bruni, in the *Laudatio Florentinae Urbis* (1402?), extended the Renaissance vision of the city beyond the perimeters of the ancient *polis* by likening the city to a work of art: her magnificence enhanced the Florentine countryside while the organic interworking of her institutions, their "inner order, neatness, and workman-like construction," created the pleasing harmonies of a well-tuned harp. [31] Of no less importance was the influence of the ideal of refinement upon the newly developing programs for a lay education fostered by the commercial and political activity of the Italian communes.

Although lay education was necessitated by the demand for diplomatic and commercial skills, the true purpose of education for the Italian humanist went beyond the satisfaction of professional needs. At their broadest the educational ideals of the period always point toward "universal" men like Alberti, Leonardo, or Aeneas Silvius. The well-educated man is one who knows how to live well; he is a man of refined taste, manners, sensibility, and speech. He is eloquent and well-read—especially in the pages of Cicero's *De Oratore* and Quintillian's *Institutio Oratoris* whence, for the humanists, the models for rhetoric, letters, and civic virtue were derived. He is, in short, urbane. The great educators of the age, Vergerio, Vittorino da Feltre, and Guarino da Verona, devised a lay education which aimed at the development of the whole man in all of his capacities, physical, moral, and intellectual, an aim which would have been impossible without the aesthetic and intellectual stimuli of an urban milieu. Their program included not only the mastery of the Latin and Greek writers and early church fathers, but also physical exercise and an awareness of the powers of the personality. "To a vulgar temper gain are the sole aims of existence," wrote Vittorino, "to a lofty nature, moral work and fame."[32]

Worldiness moderated by a well-developed moral sense, individualism, sociability, refinement not only in taste and manners but in terms of man's higher moral, intellectual, and aesthetic capabilities, the liberation of the self not from the world but into this world, the striving for individual distinction or "fame" in the affairs of the city—these were the attributes of urbanity in the northern Renaissance and in Tudor and Stuart England as well.

The elaboration of perceptions of urban life to include a distinct social and cultural style of cultivation and refinement, and the contrasting perception of rusticity as peaceful retirement if not ignorant boorishness, would be reflected in the attitudes surrounding the conception of the city in early America. The American landscape offered the greater lure of rural retirement with its connotation of superior virtue to men like William Penn, while urbanity as a canon of self-cultivation endured to shape the public and private lives of seasonal denizens of colonial Williamsburg like William Byrd II.

The combination of secularism, humane studies, and a cosmopolitan awareness aroused by oceanic travel during the Renaissance resulted in a revived interest in the city as a cultural and aesthetic theater. Signaling the renewed view of civic life, earlier suggested by Heraclides, was the appearance of Giovanni Botero's *Treatise Concerning the Causes of the Magnificence and Greatness of Cities* (Rome, 1588). According to Botero whether or not a city becomes great has little to do with the nature of its internal government. Men are not drawn to cities only because life in the *polis* may be critical to their own concerns; rather, they go for "civile conversation," "profit," and "pleasure." Rome offered not only liberty, municipal franchises, and offices, but "continuall entertainment." The modern city as conceived by Botero, to use Lewis Mumford's distinction, is "magnetic" rather than "protective." Citing illustrations from history and geography Botero concluded that magnificent cities become so because of a combination of factors. People might collect in cities for their common safety, but security does not make a *great* city. In fact, the remoteness of a secure place, such as "mountains & craggy places, or small and little Ilands [sic]," may deprive a city of that "commoditie of the scite, the fertility of the soyle, the easinesse of conduct" necessary "to make a cittee great and famous." If a city is to become magnificent there must be wealth or profit—religion, for example, "causeth much commerce"—for "the habitacions of men, enforst at first by meere necessity, are not mayntayned long, if profit and commodity go not companions with it."[33]

Cities aspiring to magnificence should also provide "learned Schooles" for "there be two meanes for men of wit and courage to rise . . . to some degree of honor and reputation in the world, the one by armes, the other by bookes."[34] Men will also be drawn to cities which "have royall audience, Senators, Parliaments or other sorts and kindes of courts of justice." The truly great cities are seats of "supreme Authority and power: For, that draweth dependency with it, And dependency, concourse, & concourse Greatnes." If a city is to remain great it must preserve "Justice, Peace and Plenty." In addition to all these things the great city will provide "delight and pleasure that eyther the Scite of the place, or the art of man doth minister and yield unto them." Nature can beautify a city with fresh breezes and water, pleasing vistas, and cool woods with ample game. But to the art of man

> belongeth the strayte and fayre streets of a cittye, the magnificent & gorgious buildings therein . . . the theaters, Porches, Circles, Races for running hourses, Fountaines, Images, Pictures, and such other excellent and wonderful things, as delight and feede the eyes of the people with an admiration and wonder at them.[35]

The far-reaching achievement of the Renaissance conceptualization of the city was to free it from the narrow confines of the ancient *polis* on the one hand, and on the other, from the distant and extraordinary realms of universal empire or medieval eschatology. Both ideal city and citizen were in their highest forms the creations of man, manifesting not only the moral but the intellectual and aesthetic refinements of civilization.

As the Renaissance moved north it generated a whole new genre of literature designed, like Castiglione's *The Courtier*, to serve as guides for the creation of the refined or well-constructed self. The spread of "courtesy books" was concurrent with the gradual urbanization of the English gentry as they gravitated to cities like London and Liverpool in search of greater economic opportunity. The genre is in itself a product of social changes inherent in urbanization, or the shifts in status made possible by wealth and talent, for it is addressed to those for whom the aristocratic mode must be contrived. The question of what exactly was a gentleman bedeviled many sixteenth-century writers because so many were posing as one. Thus ensued elaborate discussions distinguishing gentility from nobility, and nobility "native" from nobility "dative." Ultimately the problem resolved itself with the realization that what mattered most was that those who claimed gentility conduct themselves in a manner worthy of that attribution.[36] Englishmen could be assured by Henry Peacham, in his *Complete Gentleman* (1622), that while "the exercise of merchandise hath been . . . accounted base and much derogating from nobility," a gentleman could now be in the trades. "The honest merchant" must be included "among the number of benefactors to his country

> while he exposeth as well his life as goods to the hazard of infinite dangers, sometimes for medicinal drugs and preservatives of our lives in extremity and sickness; another for our food and clothing in times of scarcity and wants . . . or lastly for those *sensus et animi oblectamenta*, which the Almighty Providence hath purposely for our solace and recreation . . . created, as apes, parrots, peacocks, canary, and all singing birds.[37]

This was an important concession to the city as well as to social change.

English writers differed from Continental and Italian authors of guides to gentlemanly conduct by placing greater stress on actual service to the state, as contrasted with personal perfection at court, and the relatively greater degree of moral earnestness and piety they expected of the true gentleman. Sir Thomas Elyot's *The Boke Named the Governour* (1531), for example, had combined the medieval and antique noble figures of knight and orator into the lawyer who serves his state in some official capacity.[38] Toward the seventeenth century, English courtesy books tended to emphasize stoic religiosity, distinguishing between the good and the bad gentleman, as the state of his soul became more important than his position.[39] "Next to the fear of God," frequent prayer and the study of "tractates of piety" alone did Peacham place the importance of "good learning." Good learning for him involved a knowledge of Greek and Latin, a mastery of eloquence, and the study of history, cosmography, geometry, painting and drawing, antiquities, music, and poetry—"to sweeten your severer studies."[40] Of the complete gentleman let it still be said that moderation was his virtue, liberal his education, piety his religion, and honorable and graceful his conduct.

Since Henry Peachman also offered counsel on the life of London, let us see what sort of a place he thought that city to be:

> our most populous places are cities, and among us London . . . the city whither all sorts reside, noble and simple, rich and poor, young and old, from all places and countries, either for pleasure (and let me add besides, to save the charge of housekeeping in the country) or for profit, as lawyers to the terms, countrymen and women to Smithfield and the markets; or for necessity, as poor young men and maids to seek services and places; servingmen, masters; and some others, all manner of employment.

The chief preoccupation of the visitor to London had better be for his "purse sake." Peacham's view of London is interesting for it reflects not only an awareness of the social instability of urban life but a dimension of the idea of the city which will grow in importance from his time forward as the effects of that instability became everywhere more apparent. His contrast of city life with country life—implicit in his notion that the virtuous and honest man comes *from* the country and goes *to* the city, where he had better tend "to his main business . . . with all expedition," is quite explicit in his assertion that to live "in a solitary and private place among a few . . . is the happiest life of all."[41] This point of view honors a tradition of contrasting city-country imagery which can be traced back to Greek and Latin literature. Honesty and innocence abide in the country, while the city breeds corruption or the violation of social and moral order. But Peacham himself conceded to the city an important characteristic: it *is* where the gentleman must go to do business, to see a play, to "play at ordinaries." He may have claimed that the solitary life was happy, but he also agreed with Socrates that "learning . . . [is] sooner attained unto by the ear in discourse and hearing than by the eye in continual reading."[42]

The code of the gentleman as defined during the Renaissance was closely identified with the life of the city. It was the merchant prince, not the rustic farmer, who, because of his close ties to an urban milieu, had access to the economic, intellectual, and aesthetic means by which one acquired cultivated and refined learning and tastes. As the Renaissance gentleman traveled to England the different political and religious circumstances in which he found himself measurably affected the conception of urbanity which was to become one of the Old World's contributions to the cultural processes of the new. Civic virtue as developed and refined in the Italian commune had to be exercised in the English nation, whose fortunes were entwined first with those of a glorious queen leading her people against the satanic forces of Rome, and then with the outcome of the internal struggles between Cavalier and Puritan, court and country. The urbane gentleman became progressively more pious and more sombre in his outlook. Denied by political and religious tumult a secure assurance of "fame" in the city, he might, as did Sir Walter Ralegh, despair of public wisdom: "the common people are evill Judges of honest things, and whole Wisedom (saith Ecclesiastes) is to be despised."[43] While Ralegh, writing from the Tower, had particular reason to feel betrayed, the pious and dutiful gentleman of Tudor and Stuart England was even more liable to cynicism in the urban world of post-Restoration London.

The exemplary city for the eighteenth century was London. The city on the Thames served as the model of an urbane society and culture not only for the French, who found English civilization far more "enlightened" than their own, but for the American colonies which could offer for comparison only Philadelphia. London's contribution to the concept of urbanity was a diverse vitality and culture which was the outgrowth of the very forces which characterized her growth from the sixteenth to the eighteenth centuries. The urbanity of the eighteenth century is best captured in the juxtaposition of Gainsborough's portrait, *The Honorable Mrs. Graham*, with *The Countess's Dressing Room* from Hogarth's *Marriage a la Mode*. On the one side is the intelligent reserve and confident refinement of the prosperous English bourgeoise; on the other, a lively satirical portrait, barely confined to the canvas, of the ludicrous pretentions of the *beau monde*. Both scenes belong to the urbanity of the eighteenth century, making it truly a culture of the modern city. Every face of all sorts of mankind is suddenly in continuous view, revealing what it must.

The arrival of new men to society and the heightened sense of class they occasion, is hardly a recent phenomenon. Whether immigrating from the country, or ascending from lower orders and occupations, their assimilation into society has tended to be accompanied by a reinvigorated sense of class distinctions. The new men of the early modern period were pre-eminently creatures of capital whose struggle for culture and refinement produced the entertainments, theaters, parks, clubs, coffeehouses, and private residential neighborhoods for which eighteenth-century London is known.[44] Because they were ever susceptible to that vulgarity which, mused Voltaire, would produce a charlatan for every arriviste,[45] greater care was taken by the genteel to clarify how they were to be distinguished. A preoccupation with social distinctions can, however, destroy the necessary openness of a true urban milieu. Urbane refinement pushed to its extremes becomes a static attribute, one which accompanies the triumph of snobbery everywhere, as is illustrated in the letters the fourth Earl of Chesterfield wrote to his son over a period of thirty years beginning in 1737. An intimate of Alexander Pope's, an avid auditor of Addison and Steele, acquainted in Paris with Montesquieu and Fontaniele, both admired and despised for his wit, Chesterfield became the epitome of the "constructed character."[46]

"The graces; the graces! remember the graces!" admonished the father. And what were the graces? "Brilliance," "joy," and "bloom," or what constitutes "good breeding." True refinement involves speech, movement, and conversation; "an ungraceful manner of speaking, awkward motions, and a disagreeable address, are great clogs to the ablest man of business." The "Manniers Nobles . . . are only to be acquired in the very best companies" which are found among "people of considerable birth, rank, and character"—but not in the *beau monde*, or at court, where lurk "splendor and dissipation."[47] A morning devoted to study and an evening devoted to "the pleasures of good company" is the formula by which the urbane gentleman becomes both learned and knowledgeable in the ways of the secular city. Finally, neither the learned, who are innocent of the world, nor lawyers with their casuistry can teach the "undisputed rule of morality and justice" which can be learned through "right reason" and "common sense:" "do as you would be done by."[48] Try as he might to instruct his son in the ways of aristocratic gentility Chesterfield's prescription yields the character of the bourgeois. Private status, not public duty; a common-sense morality rather than religious piety; learning to enhance one's sociability more than one's character and soul—these were the distinctions which were blurred on the streets of eighteenth-century London.

There were those of the eighteenth century who demurred at the magnetism and cultural dominance of the city. In France the *Encyclopédie* instructed that the city promotes great social and material inequalities and impoverishes the countryside, a view drawn from the physiocratic conservatism of some of its contributors who, like François Quesnay, described the city "as a parasite that threatens to impoverish and depopulate the nation if it is allowed to grow unchecked."[49] Much of the gentry opposition in England to the Age of Walpole—an age of finance capital and grasping individualism centered in the city—was informed by a nostalgia for a purer age when a patrician and hierarchical social order was the basis of politics. This opposition, which crystallized around Henry St. John, Viscount Bolingbroke, was highly articulate, including Jonathan Swift, Lord Chesterfield, John Gay, and that most consummate of all Augustan wits—Alexander Pope. It was to Bolingbroke that Pope dedicated the *Essay on Man*, which invoked the stoic vision of nature as an hierarchical and harmonious cosmic order, an order which, as Pope's life bore witness, could be best appreciated in the retirement of the countryside. While, as in the *Dunciad*, Pope satirized the indifferent and seemingly corrupt life of London, his attitude was in fact ambivalent.

Like the Roman poets, whose pastoral imagery provided much of the vocabulary of the later Augustan poet, what Pope lamented was not the city as such—for where else could one share one's sophisticated wit and the literary fruits of rural seclusion?—but the corrupting ambition which threatened to undermine the true purpose of the city—the advancement of civilization.[50] The more virtuous way of life for many eighteenth-century Englishmen and Americans became the life of a modest country seat wherein one could practice prudence and honest industry while contemplating through intimate association the pure harmonies of nature.

The nature of disenchantment is best understood by an appreciation of those expectations left unfulfilled. To many thoughtful and articulate Englishmen of the eighteenth century, whose vision of the ideal society had been formed out of the literature of that earlier Augustan Age, two things disturbed them most about the modern city. The first was the intrusion of the new men—enriched and emboldened in finance and commerce—upon the stable and hierarchical social order of the gentry. The second was the hopeless poverty and dissipation of the city's underside. The horrors which would find their way into William Blake's "London" challenged not only sensibility, but intellect, for they represented a severence in that chain of mutual dependencies and obligations by which alone the conception of nature and society as harmonious unities could be justified. What remained was not a forsaken view of the city as the center of civilized society; the city still provided a theater of intellectual and aesthetic stimulation, sociability and involvement in affairs, while rural retirement was just that. The conception of the city in the eighteenth century was, rather, part of an ambivalent attitude toward the country and the city which fostered the "dichotomic life."

The most immediate urban experience shared by the founders of Boston, Philadelphia, Williamsburg, and Savannah had been London. Whether the London of the 1620's or of the 1720's, the city they knew, in varying degrees of intimacy, had begun to display those social and economic disparities which would render it suspect in the minds of moralists. Did its role as a cultural theater compensate for the fragmentation of traditional social ties, the seeming deterioration of the economic probity of an agrarian world, and the corrupting ambition of court and commerce apparently fostered there? John Winthrop, William Penn, and John Percival evidently had begun to doubt that it did. As they turned to the task of founding cities in the New World they imposed upon their undertakings the same ambivalence toward the city that was at last fully articulated in the writing of Augustan England.

At the moment of its physical inception the city is the result of a decision about the use and arrangement of space. The most primitive town plan, or the rise of a town without a plan, has something to say about the way in which a town or city was conceived by its first inhabitants. Urban design can be the outgrowth of thousands of private decisions about the use of the land or a visual representation of cultural identity arrived at by deliberate planning and architectural execution. The people who created North America's first cities had access to several traditions of urban design, each making revealing statements about the societies which created and employed them. The two most fundamental of these traditions were the orthogonal plan, commonly known as "grid," and the radial plan. The third tradition was less a product of conscious design—although it became so in the nineteenth century. The irregular plan, commonly associated with medieval cities, grew out of the casual alignment of village lanes along natural topographical contours or irregular property boundaries which had been held and recognized for generations. Town-planning theory had always recognized the desireability of winding streets for defense, but these considerations were generally outweighed by others when opportunity enabled a city to be laid out anew.

The oldest of these traditions, we now have reason to believe, was the radial system of spatial division first practiced in seventh-century B.C. Greece. The focus of this system of spatial arrangement was the visitor to the site at the most common station of entry. Lines of horizontal perspective radiated from the level of his eyes into a field of vision divided into ten parts. The purpose of this system was to provide the visitor with a scene in which all buildings were seen in their entirety. Further, buildings were situated, according to size, in such a way as to harmonize with the natural features of the landscape.[51] While such a system may be subject to various interpretations, its principal characteristic, the creation of an harmonious visual setting expressly for the pleasure of the individual pedestrian observer, seems especially appropriate to the ideal city of ancient Greece. The absence of evident utilitarian or strategic considerations would distinguish this ancient approach toward urban design from both the grid plan and later uses of radial planning which, largely because of their magnification of scale, were considerably more ambitious both aesthetically and strategically.

The grid plan, in contrast, is the product of a utilitarian and strategic attitude toward urban design. It was Aristotle who first noted the convenience of the grid (*Politics*, VII, 11), first devised by Hippodamus for the rebuilding of Miletus in 479 B.C. While there is evidence that "Hippodamean" cities were laid out during the Greek colonization of the seventh and sixth centuries B.C., it was the perfection of the plan into a uniform and regular system, especially in its emphasis on monumental squares and harmonious effects, which Hippodamean planning came to symbolize. Roughly at the center of the Hippodamean city lay the *agora*, an open place where religious, civic, business, and social activity could occur amid the general concourse of citizens. The acropolis, originally a fortress stronghold and seat of the king, was gradually displaced in importance by the Prytaneion, or common hearth, which functioned like the French *hôtel-de-Ville* and symbolized the emergence of the city-state as a democratic conception.[52]

The orthogonal plan was further developed by the Romans both in theory and in the practice of castrametation. For Rome and Greece alike, colonization provided the opportunity and the need for the orderly division of land, a task which was executed by a surveyor who, with his *groma* set at the four points of the compass, divided the land into squares and rectangles emanating from a central crossroads.[53] The great theorist of Roman town-planning was the architect and engineer, Vitruvius. His *De Architectura Libri Decem*, dedicated to Augustus, later served as a manual for Renaissance architects, such as Bramante, Palladio, and Alberti, and Spanish town-planning in the New World.[54] A well-designed city, according to Vitruvius, was located in a healthy, elevated setting, its corners facing the four winds, surrounded by fertile lands and readily accessible by land and by water. The aesthetic principles of its design were determined by strategic, climactic, and geographic considerations, while monumentalism was implied by Vitruvius' suggestion that "temples, the sites for those of the gods under whose particular protection the state is thought to rest . . . should be on the very highest point commanding a view of the greater part of the city." Vitruvius' stress on architectural harmony and symmetry derived from mathematically determined proportions, moreover, would be echoed in the town plan as well as the architecture of colonial Williamsburg.[55]

The great exception to the relative absence of planning in the medieval secular city were the *bastides*, or new towns, first built by Louis IX, one of the best surviving examples of which is undoubtedly Aigues-Mortes begun in 1241. Since the primary function of the *bastide* was to serve as a frontier outpost it was necessarily compact and enclosed by walls. Most were laid out in the form of a grid, for convenient division of buildings plots, and provided open spaces for market and church. The *bastide* thus perpetuated the principles of Roman castrametation, although neither the literature of that art nor Vitruvius' *De Architectura Libri Decem* were known until the fifteenth century.

The orthogonal plan was especially suited to empire. Not only could it be laid out quickly with relatively crude instruments but it facilitated the strategic movement necessary to the efficient transport of goods and the military control of surrounding territory. This, in part, explains its hardy survival, especially on the American frontier. The English surveyor of the late seventeenth century, who may have learned his art from a military manual and practiced it in the course of colonization, was likely to employ some variant of a rectilinear plan. Thomas Holme, who had served in Ireland, did so at Philadelphia in 1683, as did Colonel James Edward Oglethorpe and Colonel William Bull when they laid out Savannah in 1733. The continued appeal of the rectilinear system of urban planning was due to the fact that the basic layout of streets could be retained through an indefinite expansion, even while adjusting for topographical variations. The ease with which it could be surveyed made it eminently suitable to a society preoccupied less with the aesthetic expression of a communal vision than with the private ownership and speculative exchange of landed property.

The visual representation of the ideal city in the Middle Ages, during which towns with their winding streets were most often an extension of the *burg*, was largely the work of iconography. The iconographical representation of the celestial city, carefully described in the Revelation of St. John, symbolized the church. Typically, Jerusalem was rendered as a cube or circle, signifying universality, in a cloister enclosure with twelve gates, ornamented with precious stones and inhabited by the twelve Apostles, angels, and, set in the center square, a figure of the lamb.[56] Scripture provided literal as well as iconographical suggestions for those who strove, like the Puritans who emigrated to New England, to establish a New Jerusalem in the wilderness. The celestial city described in Revelation was largely a recapitulation of Hebrew encampments described in Numbers and Ezekiel. The plans of the Hebrew cities were themselves dictated by divine ordinance and a typological reading of scripture may have warranted the imitation of their essential features at New Haven. There, as laid out in 1638, one could find the square enclosing nine squares of equal sides typifying the pictoral representation of the encampments of the twelve tribes of Israel common to late sixteenth-and early seventeenth-century biblical commentaries.

The Renaissance, a period of transition in so many ways, witnessed a sophisticated revival of interest in the architectural treatment of the city. Botero's "strayte and fayre streets of a cittye" were elaborated upon in Leo Battista Alberti's *De Re Aedificatoria* (1472?). This Florentine humanist, wrote one of his early biographers, sought to restore the art of architecture "to its ancient purity . . . order and proportion; insomuch that he was universally called the Florentine Vitruvius."[57] The *Ten Books on Architecture*, however, was more than a gloss on Vitruvius. Like the pioneering work of history, Niccolo Machiavelli's *History of Florence* (1525), Alberti's treatise mirrors the tumultuous nature of his city's political history. Alberti's planned city would be delineated by concentric circles—the "round" city being the most "capacious"—and each circle would be a fortified wall. The inner circular wall "should be built so strong . . . and raised so high . . . that it may overlook all the private houses."[58]

Alberti's concern with internal dischord is again reflected in his introduction of social segregation and functional sectioning in urban design. His interior circle, for example, serves not only as a fortification but as a means of separating "the richer sort" from the "Cooks, Victuallers and other such Trades; and all the scoundrel Rabble belonging to Terence's Parasite."[59] "Others are for having every District of the City so laid out," complained Alberti, "that each Part might be supplied at Hand with every thing that it could have occasion for" and are thus willing to countenance "the meanest Trades in the Neighborhood of the most honourable Citizens. But," he advised, "Convenience is one thing, and Dignity another."[60]

The streets of a "noble and powerful" city should be "strait and broad" because they will then convey "an Air of Greatness and Majesty." Streets which wind "like the Course of a River" are better for smaller towns in which they provide security in the event of an enemy assault. The city must also offer "a large Number of Edifices well distributed, and disposed in their proper Places" so as to give it "a great Air of Magnificence." All "Streets, Squares and publick Edifices" must be "laid out and contrived beautifully and conveniently, according to their several Uses; for without Order, there can be nothing Handsome, Convenient or Pleasing."[61]

The significance of Alberti's *Ten Books on Architecture* for the history of urban design is that his architectural treatment of the city reflected a heightened consciousness of its inherent social circumstances and its power as a seat of not only political but cultural authority. The concern for appropriate "dignity" and "magnificence" in the appearance of the secular city signaled a view of the city unprecedented in the modern era. Two centuries later in Virginia, plans for the building of Williamsburg would reflect an identical concern for an architectual setting "suitable for the reception of a considerable number and concourse of people."[62]

Leo Battista Alberti was not, of course, the only Renaissance figure to propose a model of urban design. Leonardo had sketched a plan of Florence transformed into a *città ideale* by a harsh straightening of the Arno River to bisect symmetrically and orthogonally realigned streets of the city. The painter and fortress engineer Francesco di Giorgio suggested a similar plan. More familiar to students of the iconography of urban planning is the centrally oriented polygonal plan with radiating streets for a *città ideale* devised by the Florentine Filarete (Antonio di Pietro Averlino); it is possible that Filarete's scheme was suggested to him by Alberti's treatise.

None of these urban plans left a traceable imprint on the laying out of Boston, Philadelphia, Williamsburg, or Savannah. Their legacy was the more general one of a concern for the formal modeling of open spaces into complementary geometric forms which characterized the architectural attitudes of their designers and culminated in the flamboyant display of baroque planning in the redesign of Rome during the pontificate of Sixtus V.[63] The Renaissance architect's sensitivity to vista was a translation into open space of the painter's enthusiasm for perspective. His proclivity toward radial avenues, whether incorporated into an orthogonal or circular plan, and often connecting civic or religious monuments, was another manifestation of Giovanni Bottero's understanding of civic grandeur. These elements—perspective and monumentality in the treatment of principal arteries—rather than a single identifiable urban plan, were the enduring contribution of the Renaissance to modern urban design. They were reflected in plans submitted for the rebuilding of London after the Great Fire of 1666, once again in the remote colonial capitol city of Williamsburg, and in Pierre L'Enfant's design of 1791 for the new federal city in the District of Columbia.

❧

Conceptions serve not only to identify real and abstract things but to schematize experience and provide the means and ends of human activity. The first American frontier was settled by a people whose world lay between the city and the country. While their material well-being depended upon the soil and seas, their spiritual well-being was conceived of in the terms of the Two Cities of Augustine and John Foxe. Toward the end of the seventeenth century the imaginative force of the Two Cities of Christian eschatology loosened its hold on the colonial mind, to be replaced by alternative conceptions informed no less than before by European experience and tradition. The pagan authors of antiquity had erected the models of the city first as democratic commonwealth and then as the center of a world empire. The legacy of those cities, a legacy confirmed in the re-emerging cities of the late Middle Ages, was of the city as a body corporate and politic. Common adherence to universal laws of nature as the source of legitimacy for the imperial city added a momentous principle to the political vocabulary of the mature colonies. From the Renaissance the founders of America's first cities inherited an elaborated view of the city as a seat of power and cultural authority. This power could be manifest in the intellectual and aesthetic vitality of the city, mirrored in the architectural elegance of its visual dimensions and in the special

30

character of its inhabitants. Civilization came to be embodied in the urbane man and woman.

The reality of the secular city as it was experienced by late seventeenth- and early eighteenth-century Englishmen evoked still another tradition. Sensitive to the social and moral disparities posed by the urban world of commerce and nostalgic for the more simple and stable ways of the countryside, they summoned from antiquity and memory the language of a pastoral world of innocent pleasures and virtuous industry in the embrace of nature. As the city continued to pose disturbing moral ambiguities—the concentration of poverty amid concentrated wealth, the corruption of political authority—the city itself came to be viewed ambiguously. The availability of land and, more importantly, the opportunity for private ownership and self-enrichment in the land, enabled colonial Americans to persist in the "dichotomic life." Their expectations of society remained informed by inherited ideas of the city as the source of civilization, while their expectations of themselves depended upon their ability to possess and exploit a rural wilderness. The outcome of their divided aspirations is the history of the American city.

2

The Two Cities
of Massachusetts Bay

🙟

The Puritan hegira into New England of the 1630's involved a transplanting of expectations and dissappointments, visions and realities whose roots were first formed in the soil and seasons of English and Continental history. For the men and women who survived the voyage of the *Arbella* and her sister ships the emergence of the modern city in America was neither necessary nor inevitable. As their small struggling settlements crept outward from Massachusetts Bay they sought to create and preserve centralized, homogeneous communities. And John Winthrop had expressed the hope that he and his company might become "as a Citty upon a Hill." But beyond the desire for social cohesion, and beyond the metaphorical suggestion that their lives should be exemplary in the love of God, the original Puritan image of the city as reality and symbol lay embedded in the shared memory and imagination which formed the larger body of their religious and social perceptions and yearnings.

That memory was of a world in which the city, and especially London, first appeared as an aberration. Their world, so they believed, was part of a cosmos still apprehended in largely medieval terms of theocentricity and hierarchical balance. Correspondingly, their society was predominantly rural, rightly governed, so they imagined, by the principles of personal rank and status, and mutual dependencies and obligations. It was these principles, like the analogous planes of the cosmos, which preserved human society from anarchy and gave it order and coherence. Suffusing the whole was the providential purpose of God—the punishment of the wicked, the salvation of the regenerate, and the ultimate triumph of Christ enthroned over the New Jerusalem.

That was the world as they imagined it. But recent memory taught that the world of manors and deferential villagers, if not the medieval cosmos itself, and the fulfillment of divine providence in the history of the English nation was not as securely with them as the glorious days of Elizabeth had seemed to promise. Everywhere corruption threatened, but nowhere more than at London. Thence spread out, like the insidious maneuverings of the devil himself, the lure of mammon unrestrained by concern with moral probity; there, it seemed, flourished a Court resolved to subvert the appointed destiny of a reformed nation as the seat of the New Jerusalem; there the honest toil of the husbandman or the social authority of the patriarchal householder counted for nothing.

Against this memory prevailed the "Citty" of Winthrop's imagining, the city as symbol of the primitive church of an earlier time when men harkened to the voice of God in the Holy Scripture in all their earthly undertakings. Not one, but two cities served as leitmotifs of the Puritan enterprise in the making of an early American society. The one was the city of mammon, a city of strangers, a city without God. The other was the "Citty upon a Hill," exemplar to all of God's chosen people. Both of these cities were mirrored in the Puritan errand. If Boston failed to fulfill Winthrop's "medieval dream"; if "as the second decade gave way to the third" Boston revealed itself dominated less by men "singly and collectively devoted to God" and rather more by "individualism and materialism" and "a clear distinction between the sacral and secular affairs of men,"[1] Winthrop's dream nonetheless had its momentary embodiment. That would be the work of one who forsook the company of Massachusetts Bay for a more rigid, if no more durable, pursuit of the dream elsewhere. There emerged from Massachusetts Bay yet another attempt to make a reality of the image of the city that inspired John Winthrop. For that attempt we will turn to John Davenport's New Haven.

❧

The Puritan experience began—as does all religious experience—with chaos, the formless void, the infinite darkness of a universe without God. It was the first wonder of God that he "moved upon the waters" and filled the universe with an infinite fullness of creatures and things from the angels about his throne down to the lichen under the footfall of man and beast and to the merest stone upon which it grows. Because all things were of God nothing was unknown to him and hence all things could be explained of him. Not only did God give the universe substance, he gave it order, an order which was intelligible to man, an order principled on harmony. Here Christian doctrine drew heavily on Pythagorean and Aristotelian foundations, for it was the Pythagorean cosmos of concentric and harmoniously revolving spheres which, through Boethius, formed the basis of the medieval world-view, no where in literature better illustrated than in Dante's "Paradiso." As in heaven, so also on earth; all things and creatures exist in an hierarchically ordered world, fulfilling their divinely appointed particular destinies in a sweet sympathy of corresponding dependencies and responsibilities. Finally, state and society had been ordered upon the same principle of hierarchy, the body politic being a microcosm of the cosmos. Each part has its special destiny and purpose while being, at the same time, subordinate to another.

The theocentric and hierarchical cosmos, with its corresponding planes of being and exact correspondences of detail, remained an essential part of the Elizabethan imagination, as is amply evident not only in the writings of Shakespeare but of Sir John Elyot and Richard Hooker.[2] While the educated Elizabethan was probably aware of the new Copernican astronomy, it is possible to overestimate the "revolutionary" impact of the Copernican system which could be regarded, as it probably was, as "just the old Ptolemaic pattern of the skies with one or two of the wheels interchanged and one or two of them taken out."[3] What mattered, to those whose principal business was not mathematics or geometry but the relationship of man to God, was less the precise calculation of the movements of the heavenly spheres than the lessons to be drawn from the fact of their orderly movement. And in this Copernicus served as well as Ptolemy.[4]

The "Elizabethan world-view" survived into the seventeenth century, not withstanding new pronouncements of astronomy, anatomy, and Thomas Hobbes, surely because it provided the comfort of order and stability and, for the layman especially, it assured that the world above and about was coherent and harmoniously governed. When that world-order began to disintegrate the challenge to its verity could come as much from the social and economic dislocations of later Elizabethan society as from any technical dislocation in the firmament. The men and women who founded the colony of Massachusetts Bay were Puritans who had come to maturity in the waning days of the glorious Age of Elizabeth. John Winthrop was born in the year of the Armada while Thomas Hooker, Richard Saltonstall, Francis Higginson, John Cotton, Peter Bulkeley, Nathaniel Ward, and Thomas Dudley were all born before 1588. The world they aspired to re-create in the wilderness was shaped by their Elizabethan outlook as well as by their Puritan convictions.[5]

The persistence of a medieval view of the world as composed of hierarchies and mutual dependencies, which satisfied a fundamental human desire for coherence in nature and society, is suggested by the appeal among Puritans of old and New England of Ramist logic.[6] Logic was as necessary as theology to the Puritan intellect for logical analysis was essential to the understanding. But a logic based on axioms rather than syllogisms, and on concrete things rather than innate essences, which is what Peter Ramus propounded in reaction against peripatetic philosophy, was attractive in its directness and simplicity. Moreover, the Ramist system placed all statements in a schematic structure composed, symmetrically and hierarchically, of dichotomies, beginning with invention/judgment and proceeding through increasingly elaborate sets of affirmative and negative contraries and relations. Above all, the system had the virtue of affirming the perceived structure of the universe. The medieval world-view was thus extended among Puritans (although not exclusively among them) into a system of logic which could be applied to the explication not only of scripture, but of human relationships. As God was to man, so also were kings to subjects, parents to children, husbands to wives, and masters to servants. John Winthrop regularly likened the commonwealth to the family, wherein "the woman's own choice makes . . . a man her husband; yet being so chosen, he is her lord, and she is subject to him." Similarly, Thomas Hooker could defend congregational polity by pointing out that there can be no pastor without the people, just as there is no shepherd without a flock. Or John Cotton could attempt to refute democracy by arguing that as people are relatives to governors, the people can not at the same time be the governors.[7]

Early New England history abounds in affirmations of the hierarchical society described by the twelfth-century Englishman, John of Salisbury. For William Bradford, John Winthrop had been "a crowne" to Boston, while Winthrop and John Cotton had been the "ornaments" of New England's first years.[8] Among the general instructions which the Massachusetts Bay Company sent John Endecott in 1629 was the advice that planters who were not adventurers in the common stock and those who had received land by virtue of indentured service should, "by way of acknowledgment to such from whom they receive these lands, become liable to the performance of some service, certain days in the year, and by that service they and their posterity after them to hold and inherit these lands."[9] Inherent in Endecott's proposal was the traditional feudal principle that land should be held in exchange for service, and title to land thus becoming personal, is heritable through families. No less feudal in origin was the rationale for the General Court's attempts in the first two decades to impose sumptuary legislation on the colony. In this and in other ways the founders of Massachusetts Bay expressed a desire to perpetuate an hierarchical society ordered by status or rank.

Within a few years after the colony was first settled the apparent proliferation of "new and immodest fashions" provoked the General Court into a prohibition of the purchase or making of "slashed clothes" or garments adorned with lace, "silver, gold, silk, or thread," or the wearing of "gold or silver girdles, hat-bands, belts, ruffs, beaver hats . . . under penalty of forfeiture." While this sumptuary law was repealed in 1644, it was replaced with a law in 1651 attempting to confine more elegant apparel to men and women whose estate was valued at £200 or more, or, "to persons of greater Estates or more liberal Education." The Court, having recorded "its utter detestation and dislike that men or women of mean condition should take upon them the garb of Gentlemen," further exempted from its restriction magistrates and public officers and their families, "settled" military officers and soldiers, and "any other whose education and employments have been above the ordinary degree.[10] John Winthrop explained the exclusion of Maine from the Confederation of New England, formed in 1643, by the fact that the inhabitants of Sir Ferdinando Gorge's province "ran a different course from us both in their ministry and civil administratio; . . . they had lately made Acomenticus (a poor village)," sniffed Winthrop, "a corporation, and had made a taylor their mayor"—in addition to selecting a contentious and unchurched person for their minister.[11] When Robert Greville, Lord Brooke, William Fiennes, Viscount Say and Sele (both of whom had lent much of their influence and fortune to the launching of the Massachusetts Bay enterprise), "and other Persons of quality" proposed in 1635 that "as conditions of their removing to New England" there be established two ranks of citizens—freeholders and gentlemen, the latter to enjoy hereditary and personal rule in the upper chamber of the colonial assembly—John Cotton's objections were not to the notion that civil society should be organized by rank. Cotton was pleased to assure their lordships that "monarchy, and aristocracy . . . are both of them clearly approoved, and directed in scripture." Moreover, they would be happy to know that the General Court had already established a "standing councell" for life (which it had by the date of Cotton's reply, the distinguished members being Winthrop and Thomas Dudley). But the establishment of a hereditary aristocracy based on estate would violate the over-riding principle that none be admitted to the affairs of the commonwealth but church members.[12]

The founders of Massachusetts Bay who felt it necessary to stress the justification in nature and in scripture of the ranking in society of unequal men and the right rule of better men over lesser men were reasserting not only a medieval cosmic order but a feudal social order.[13] Moreover, it was by its very nature a rural order. Only in a world of rural parishes and townships and the nucleated settlements of manor and village could individual status and accomplishment, and its attendant ranking, be recognized; only in such a world could one assume a familiarity of persons and constancy in status. In contrast, the stability and orderliness of feudal rural society must necessarily be undermined by the intrusion of urban society, which brings with it anonymity, social and economic dislocation, and invisible wealth in the form of liquid capital and entrepreneurial skill. The fluidity and diversity of urban life can be a powerful force toward egalitarianism, if only by the default of the judgment of persons. The feudal outlook that formed the social sensibilities of the founders of Massachusetts Bay did not, in itself, necessitate a hostility toward the secular city. But combined with a nostalgic resistance to a commercial economy, with the "country ideology" developed in the struggled against the alleged ecclesiastical and constitutional usurpations of the Stuart monarchy, and with the eschatalogical vision of the New Jerusalem so fundamental to the Puritan enterprise, that view could and did foster an ambivalent attitude toward the city among the founders of the Massachusetts Bay colony.

The intrusion of the city into the rural landscape posed a challenge not only to the traditional cosmology and social outlook inherited by the Puritans from their Elizabethan origins but to economic values which placed the pursuit of riches in the service of religious and community well-being. Puritanism explicitly disavowed asceticism; one's soul could not be tested in combat with the devil's inexhaustible temptations by seeking refuge from worldly cares. "He which would have suer peace and ioye in Christianitye," wrote John Winthrop in 1616, "must not ayme at a condition retyred from the world and free from temptations, but to knowe that the life which is most exercised with tryalls and temptations is the sweetest, and will prove the safeste. For such tryalls as fall within compasse of our callinges, it is better to *arme and withstande them* then to avoide and shunne them."[14] The doctrine of the calling and the militancy of Puritanism's spiritual quest assured that economic striving would not be sinful *so long as* the self remained subservient to the needs of a community dependent upon limited goods and, above all, to the perfection of piety. Economic gain found its only justification in the furtherance of social and moral betterment.[15]

A world without labor had been left behind with the expulsion from Eden and neither technology nor capital manipulation had yet succeeded in undermining the conviction that industrious labor was in itself righteous. The doctrine of just price assumed a world of limited goods in which hoarding, or charging a price for goods or credit in excess of cost, constituted a sin against one's neighbor. Commerce required some degree of profit-making, but profits must be just. What a "just" profit was was a matter to be resolved by the conscience of the community practiced through official regulation, as Robert Keayne discovered when he was reprimanded in 1639 by both the General Court of Massachusetts Bay and the church for charging excessive prices for imported goods.[16] The merchant was not pursuing an ignoble calling so long as he pursued it not as an anonymous, self-seeking individual but within a closely ordered framework of social responsibility.[17]

Just as the judgment of persons necessary to the orderly ranking of rural society would become more difficult in a fluid and hetergeneous urban milieu, so also did the complexity of economic activity within the city defy attempts to attach social and moral values to the methods chosen in the pursuit of worldly gain. Most threatening were commerce and retailing, for both activities seemed to profit from the labor of others. Calculation and the accumulation of capital, more than visible industry and frugality, seemed the hallmarks of the successful urban merchant. The perceived moral threat of the city inherent in Puritan economic values can best be appreciated when contrasted to the awareness of the interdependency of capitalism and urban life that had emerged toward the close of the Elizabethan era.

John Stow's *Survey of London* (1598) suggests an appreciative grasp of the necessity of profit in the provision of goods and credit to urban—and by extension, national—prosperity. "The multitude . . . of this populous Citie," wrote Stow, "consist of three parts, Marchantes, Handicrafts men, and Labourers." That "the estate of Marchandise" is "necessarie and seruiceable . . . to this realm" is demonstrated by

> the inestimable commodities that grow thereby: for who knoweth not that we have extreame neede of many thinges, whereof forraine Countries have great store, and that wee may spare many thinges whereof they have neede . . . . we be both fed, clad, and otherwise with forraine commodities and delightes, as plentifull as with our domesticall: which thing commeth to passe by the meane of Marchandise onely.

Stow defended retail trade which, he argued, "is but a handmaide to marchandise, dispersing by peacemeale, that which the marchant bringeth in grosse." Nor are wealthy merchants to be despised. The "rich Marchantes" who flourish in London are the sort "which . . . onely is tollerable: for beggarlie Marchantes to byte too neare, and will do more harme then good to the Realm."

> truely Marchants and retaylars doe not altogether . . . profit themselves only, for the prince and the realme both are enriched by their riches: the realm winneth treasure, if their trade be so moderated by authority . . . & they besides beare a good fleece, which the prince may sheare when shee seeth good.[18]

Stow's understanding of the role of trade and retailing in the expansion of available goods and wealth was not unique for its time. Giovanni Botero's treatise on the causes of greatness in cities, published in Rome a decade before Stow's *Survey* appeared, also stressed the importance of commercial vitality to urban and national greatness.

It was not only the secularization of economic life that the New England Puritans were resisting in their attempt to affirm traditional moral values in the pursuit of gain, but the onset of the moral and economic disorder represented by urban commercial life. "We might reioyce greatly in our owne private good," Winthrop wrote his brother-in-law Thomas Fones in 1622, "if the sence of the present evill tymes, and the feare of worse did not give occasion of sorrowe." By 1629 his own circumstances had begun to decline. The income from his Groton estate failed to keep him out of debt or to provide an adequate patrimony for his sons and he had lost his position in London at the Court of Wards.[19] "Where is now the glory and greatness of the tymes passed? even of yesterdaye?" he lamented in his parting letter to his friend, Sir William Spring; "Queen Eliza [beth], king James, &c . . . . Happy he who could gett their favour: Now they are in the dust . . . . onely the good which that Queene did for the Churche hath stamped an eternally sunlustre vpon her name. . . . If we look at persons of Inferiour qualitye, how many have their been, who have adventured (if not sould) their souls, to rayse those houses, which are now possessed by strangers?"

Despair of traditional, social, moral, and economic continuity is no less pronounced in the lines of John Winthrop's "General Considerations for the Plantation in New-England," written in the summer of 1629. "The land grows weary of her inhabitants," begins Winthrop's third "consideration," "so that men, which is the most precious of all creatures, is here more vile and base than the earth they tread upon; so as children, neighbours and friends, especially the poor, are counted the greatest burdens, which, if things were right, would be the chiefest earthly blessings."

> Fourthly, we are grown to that excess and intemperance in all excess of riot, as no mean estate almost will suffice [a man] to keep sail with his equals; and he that fails in it, must live in scorn and contempt. Hence it comes to pass, that all arts and trades are carried in that deceitful manner and unrighteous course, as it is almost impossible for a good, upright man to maintain his charge, and live comfortably in any of them.[20]

When William Bradford reflected in 1647 on the Pilgrims' first flight into Holland, he contrasted the "plain country life and the innocent trade of husbandry" to which they had been accustomed with the "many goodly and fortified cities" of the "low-countries," where "they heard a strange and uncouth language, and beheld the different manners and customs of the people, with their strange fashions and attires . . . it seemed they were come into a new world." But "the fair and beautiful cities, flowing with abundance of all sorts of wealth and riches," were also heavily overpopulated and it fell to few with unsophisticated skills to share in those riches. As in the England which, for Winthrop, had grown weary of her inhabitants, the Low Countries offered no place in an economic scheme for pious and industrious husbandmen and craftsmen in Bradford's company; "the grim and grisly face of poverty" came upon them "like an armed man . . . from whom they could not fly." Only by attempting to re-create "their plain country villages" in the wilderness could the Pilgrims—and the Puritans—hope to forestall the economic chaos which hovered over them in England and the Low Countries.[21] Thus the towns of Massachusetts Bay, following the lead of the General Court, commonly pursued measures designed to impose order and mutual responsibility upon the economic activities of their inhabitants. They ordered regulated weekly markets, enacted wage and price controls to moderate the effects of inflation which plagued the colony almost from the start, and granted monopoly privileges in exchange for the carrying out of public-works projects or vital trading activities.

Stow's perception that profit-making in the trading of goods generated wealth which ultimately enriched the total society was not shared by men like the Reverend John White of Dorchester, a leading promoter of Puritan emigration. White expressed in 1636 the more ancient and moralistic view that such activities constituted self-aggrandizement at the expense of others. When he proposed that a group of his associates "lay their purses together" to provide Massachusetts Bay with "needfull provisions," White argued that none should object to such a scheme but "some few that desire to engross commoditys, to sell them at a deerer rate, & soe to take away from others the benefite of a good markett . . . an olde mischeife which hath proved a mothe to many Stats." White's proposal was accompanied by a warning against permitting the growth of retail trades in the colony. His words of caution reflected the rural assumption that retail tradesmen in themselves are not productive and therefore "live by the sweat of other mens brows." "Superfluity of shopkeepers, inholders, &c. are great burthens to any place," instructed White. As an example, "we in this town where I liue . . . are of my knowledg at charge 1000 Li per annum in maintaining several familys in that condition, which we might well spare for better employments, wherein their labours might produce something for the common good, which is not furthered by such as drawe only one from another."[22]

The failure to appreciate the role of "such as drawe only one from another" in increasing the wealth of the state was symptomatic of the resistance to the commercial economy of the city which was derived from the Puritan's understanding of a just economic order. The inclination to contrast "the innocent trade of husbandry" and the "sweat of . . . mens brows" with urban commercial life reflected an agrarian conception of economic probity. The labor which Puritans assumed as virtuous and socially useful was the rural labor of the farmer or of the craftsman, persons whose necessity to the public good, and hence whose moral legitimacy in their callings, were clearly demonstrable. By extension, the economic life of the countryside was morally viable for it provided food and necessities in a world of limited goods, whereas the economic life of the city, which generated only luxuries and the self-aggrandizement of some persons at the expense of others, was not.

The leaders of the Massachusetts Bay enterprise were not, of course, themselves mere husbandmen or craftsmen. Had they been, they would have probably welcomed changes which freed them from rural toil and hardship. The dramatic increase in population that occurred in England between 1500 and 1660, while accompanied by an increase in agricultural output, nonetheless bore down heavily on the "tens of thousands" of small landholders who suffered from enclosure, encroachments on common lands by big landlords, and inflation. The dispossessed formed a large portion of the laborers and vagrants who contributed to London's rapid growth during the same period.[23] The rural landscape that appealed to the Puritan of the 1620's appealed because it was a landscape of manor houses and deferential villagers, which, like the medieval cosmos and its corresponding feudal society based on hierarchies of status and mutual responsibility, seemed to assure an order and harmony rooted in antiquity.

The rise of urban society presented a negative reference to the nostalgic strain in the Puritan outlook, for the city represented the dissolution of the rural social and economic order which gave the gentry its status and purpose. The city, and especially London, represented as well a political challenge to the moral authority of the countryside. It was at the convergence of the religious opposition of Puritan to Anglican with the political opposition of country gentry to the Stuart court, that Puritanism coalesced into the powerful movement that brought down the monarchy. The emigrating Puritans who settled the Massachusetts Bay colony shared with their brethren who remained behind a common ideology as well as a common religious conviction. That ideology was the ideology of the opposition, a group advocating principles which began to be labeled in the 1620's as the "Country."

❦

An accurate understanding of the aspirations which motivated the Massachusetts Bay undertaking and shaped the vision of country and city as it relates to the initial political and social design of the colony requires recognition of the material as well as spiritual sources of the Puritan re-

41

bellion. The English revolution was not solely the result of social and economic class conflict. The basic cleavage between the Stuart court, its retainers, the Anglo-Catholics, and the parliamentary opposition, was a cleavage *within* the dominating or ruling class of a society, most of whose members accepted a social structure based upon status.[24] The opposition drew its support from London merchants as well as gentry from the counties, from the towns as well as the countryside. Its program— representative rule in parliament, the binding of royal government by ancient laws and liberties, and the disestablishment of ecclesiastical rule over religious conscience—was the product of a mentality which contained three fundamental sets of convictions: Puritanism, the sanctity of the common law with its supposed guarantees of private property and persons and dictum of the balanced constitution, and the Country ideology.

What distinguishes the founders of Massachusetts Bay from the Puritans who remained to lead the parliamentary opposition was not primarily ideological. Rather, circumstance indicated, and greater emphasis on a typological reading of scripture allowed, if not required, the transfer of the Puritan struggle into the wilderness. This difference is reflected in the poignant exchange between William Fiennes, first Viscount Say and Sele and John Winthrop, when Winthrop reproached Lord Say in 1640 for encouraging remaining English Puritans intent upon emigration to seek out the more hospitable climate of the West Indies. In Lord Say's reply to Winthrop he asked him

> wheather this be not a taking of Godes name in vayne, to misaply
> Scriptures . . . by assuming (for that must be granted you) that
> thear is the like cal from God for your goinge to that part of America
> and fixing thear, that thear was for the Israelites goinge to the land of
> promise and fixinge thear; the like grownde for your stayinge in that
> place & others cominge theather to you, that thear was for Ne-
> hemiah's buildinge the walls of Jerusalem; and for you to plant thear,
> and noe whear else, is as much a worke of God as his building
> Jerusalem in that place and noe whear else . . . Is this to be offered
> unto men of judgment? . . . I will grant that God is with you, that
> you are glorious churches, that he sent you theather in handfulls,
> vntill you wear soe augmented: will it att all be concluded from
> thence that you are bounde to stay thear . . .? For the barrenes of
> the lande, and the coldnes of the ayre in the winter . . . your owne
> losses may be sufficient witnes of it.[25]

The isolation into which John Winthrop's and John Cotton's hermeneutics carried them and the Massachusetts Bay colony should not obscure the fact that initially the association between emigrating Puritans and the parliamentary opposition to the monarchy was very close. As of 1630 the English Puritans shared the same values in questions of secular polity and the same ideological convictions of the emerging Country party. Unless a group of prospective colonists could obtain a special charter of incorporation from the Crown it depended for legal sanction upon patents received from existing incorporated trading companies, the Virginia Company of London, the Council for New England, or the London and Bristol Company.

The various colonizing companies that received patents in the 1620's and 1630's—including the Virginia, Saybrook, Providence, and Massachusetts Bay companies—all depended upon the influence of prominent Puritan lay figures who also happened to be active leaders of the parliamentary opposition. Men like Theophilus Fiennes-Clinton, fourth Earl of Lincoln, John Pym, William Fiennes, the first Viscount Say and Sele, Fulke Greville, the first Lord Brooke, Robert Rich, the second Earl of Warwick, and his brother, Sir Nathaniel Rich formed the nucleus around which both Puritan colonizing schemes and the Country party in Parliament took form. John Humphrey, who actively solicited aid and ministers for the Winthrop expedition in England, readily acknowledged the colony's indebtedness to these Puritan parliamentary leaders when he wrote Isaac Johnson at Charlestown, "we are all much bound to my Lord Say for his cordial advice and true affections. As also to my Lord of Warwick, Sir Natha: Rich deserves much acknowledgment of his wise handling." John Davenport looked upon Lord Say and Sele as an "honourable and faithful" friend. In turn, the Country members in parliament and their supporters, who were bound by ties of friendship and family as well as of conviction, after the dissolution of Parliament in 1629 used the meetings of the colonizing companies for political discussion and thus transformed them into a "virtual interlocking directorate of oppositionists."[26] Thus developed an alliance of Puritan gentry, merchants, and clergy whose loyalties were not only religious and familial, but ideological.

Whether or not the English parliamentary Puritans of the 1620's were predominantly members of the gentry matters less in this instance than that the ideology they adopted in their opposition to the Court was a gentry ideology. The textile industry, which suffered most during the trade depression of the 1620's, united the interests of laborers, landowners, and cloth merchants in East Anglia, Yorkshire, and the west country. Economic circumstances, which served as a partial stimulous to opposition and emigration, cut across distinctions of rank and occupation in the same way that did the religious yearning for the experience of conversion and the practice of moral reform. Thus not class, but a sympathy of experience and values, constituted the basis of the country ideology. In turn, the country ideology was less a systematic explication of political principles than a set of shared values. These values were articulated as the antitheses of those which allegedly prevailed at the Court and among its retainers who, more than previously, had become established in London. "The Country," writes Lawrence Stone, "is firstly an ideal."

> It is that vision of rustic arcadia that goes back to the Roman classics and which fell on the highly receptive ears of the newly educated gentlemen of England who had studied Virgil's *Georgics* at Oxford or Cambridge. It was a vision of environmental superiority over the City: the Country was peaceful and clean, a place of grass and trees and birds, the City was ugly and dirty and noisy, a place of clattering carts and coaches, coal dust and smog, and piles of human excrement. It was also a vision of moral superiority over the Court; the Country was virtuous, the Court wicked; the Country was thrifty, the Court extravagant; the Country was honest, the Court corrupt; the Country was chaste and heterosexual, the Court promiscuous and homosexual; the Country was sober, the Court drunken; the Country was nationalist, the Court xenophile; the Country was healthy, the Court diseased; the Country was outspoken, the Court sycophantic; the Country was the defender of old ways and old liberties, the Court the promoter of administrative novelties and new tyrannical practices; the Country was solidly Protestant, even Puritan, the Court was deeply tainted by popish leanings.[27]

Initially the words "country" and "Country" were not synonymous; the earliest use of the latter term, dating from the fourteenth century, referred to "county" and only later, in the sixteenth century, did it come to represent that which was rural, "distant from cities and courts."[28] The application of the term to the opposition to the Stuart court did, in fact, come to reflect an actual idealization of the moral and environmental superiority of the rural over the urban landscape. Wherever one's location or whatever one's occupation, the system of values adopted by the adherents of the country opposition were inherently rural values.

One development without which the successful parliamentary revolt against the monarchy would have been impossible was the substantial increase in numbers of the landed classes between 1540 and 1640. The number of gentlemen establishing themselves in country seats tripled during the period, their increased domination of the countryside facilitated by the sales by the Crown of its vast lands in order to pay for foreign wars. The size and authority of local elites grew as a consequence, as did the House of Commons (from about three hundred to five hundred members) and, more importantly, the number of its gentry members (from about 50 to 75 percent). The deeply embedded notion that privilege, in an hierarchical world, must be accompanied by responsibility, required of the rising gentry that it justify its growing power in some way to replace the medieval relationship of military service to the king. This justification it found in the ideal of civic responsibility, with its patriarchal overtones at the local level, and the Puritan conception of the calling. The Country, then, became a place in which one exercised self-justifying responsibilities as patriarch of the manor and member of the county bench of justices. The moral and environmental superiority of the Country became associated with loyalty to the local community and its institutions. At the same time, increased gentry participation in parliament promoted an ideological attachment to the nation in parliament.[29] Thus the alleged usurpations of the Stuart monarchy challenged the extension of gentry authority and responsibility into the affairs of the realm.

The particular legacy which the "rise of the gentry" bequeathed to the founders of New England was an intense localism sustained by a convergence of political, social, and moral values which were both historically and experientially rural in nature. T. H. Breen reminds us that "the religious beliefs that the colonists carried with them to the New World cannot in themselves account for either the original form or subsequent development of specific institutions in Massachusetts." When Charles I came to the throne the vast majority of the English people lived in small agricultural communities. They had been accustomed to considerable control over their own lives, incorporated boroughs having the right to "elect a mayor and burgesses, enforce local ordinances, hold fairs, and determine the qualifications for freemanship." Many, also, exercised the right of ecclesiastical patronage. Their concerns and outlook were predominantly insular, traditional, and particularistic. The importance of the Stuart monarchy and the English church under Archbishop William Laud to these rural communities lay in their attempts to extend religious and economic control into the countryside. Charles' taxation policies, the Privy Council's assumption of local poor relief, and the Crown's efforts to recruit a national soldiery out of the local militia all represented serious incursions into the authority of the local gentry. The diversity and localized spirit of the New England town had been nurtured by the resentment felt in England toward the centralizing "innovations" of the monarch and the archbishop.[30]

Much of Puritanism's strength "derived from its attempt to revive the community of the parish as a reality." The parish served as the religious embodiment of localized English rural communities and it, like the village and the county, was everywhere threatened not only by the centralizing tendencies of the Stuart monarchy but the increasing individualism and atomization which began to characterize late sixteenth- and early seventeenth-century England. If the Puritans, victims of religious intoleration in England, strongly resisted religious toleration in New

England, it was not because they were hypocrites; rather, religious toleration "would not only subvert the episcopal hierarchy, but would also make discipline impossible, and so threaten the domination of the elect over the ungodly, of masters of families over their servants."[31] At stake was the survival of feudal communities whose social, economic and religious continuity inhered in the judgment of persons. The only world in which such a society was possible was a rural world innocent of the innovations and heterogeneity which necessarily come with urban life.

The desire to achieve a society of "visible saints" was thus only the most explicit of the yearnings which inspired the Puritan emigrants to Massachusetts Bay. Evident, also, in the planning of the New England town and in the regulations enacted for its right ordering in the first two decades is the equally formative desire to re-create a predominantly rural society. Parochialism and homogeneity, of course, were necessitated in part by Puritan congregationalism; but the continuance of these attributes served nonreligious purposes as well. The successful achievement of a society and polity secure in those attributes promised internal cohesion and stability. Such a society also, however, necessarily embodied values which would resist the diversity and social and moral dislocations of the city.

The manner in which a society uses and apportions the land is central to the character of its urbanization. Land was the principal resource of the Massachusetts Bay Company. Order, homogeneity, and the re-creation of a predominantly rural society were the evident principles which guided its distribution of that resource. Initially the method of land distribution adopted by the Massachusetts Bay Company was similar to that used by the Virginia Company in Virginia, that is, land was apportioned on the basis of shares. In its meeting of May 19, 1629, the Massachusetts Bay Company resolved that "each adventurer paying £50" should receive two hundred acres of land. In addition, "those going over paying for themselves and being adventurers in the common stock, shall have 50 acres per person in the family," while "those not adventurers shall have 50 acres for the master of the family and what further the Governor and Council think necessary and available; for servants, 50 acres per servant to the master to dispose of as he wishes."[32] It was statutorially possible for anyone who had made a large initial investment in the Company to acquire a substantial private estate, and indeed several of the founders did receive individual grants which could have constituted the manor, or "country seat," they enjoyed or might have sought in England. John

Winthrop, who was one of the five "planters" who contributed to the recapitalization of the Massachusetts Bay Company when it faced bankruptcy in 1629 (the other four were Richard Saltonstall, Isaac Johnson, Thomas Dudley, and John Revell), received in all grants of more than 2,600 acres. John Haynes, who served as governor in 1635, was allocated 1,000 acres. Increase Nowell, elected Assistant in 1629, received a 2,000-acre grant. To the estate of Isaac Johnson was granted 3,200 acres, while Lieutenant-Governor Richard Saltonstall received the same amount. Thomas Leverett, who served as an elder in the First Church of Boston, was awarded by the General Court in 1629 a "tract of land between the Muscongus and Penobscot rivers and extending ten leagues inland" jointly with a John Beauchamp. While grants such as Leverett's were rare, the Company nonetheless awarded in the first decade roughly sixty grants of land to private individuals extending from fifty acres to fifteen hundred acres and averaging around three hundred acres. [33]

The basis was thus laid for a landed gentry in New England. And indeed, as early as 1636 there is evidence of stratification between a "gentry" and a "generalty." While the larger private grants made by the company in the early years were small by comparison with those received by numerous planters in the southern colonies, they were nonetheless considerably larger than those belonging to the mere yeomen of the English countryside. "In the end," writes Darrett B. Rutman, the roughly thirty families which constituted "Boston's gentry . . . had received almost one-half of the land granted by the town. . . . Tenantry and the use of stewards . . . familiar from the English manorial tradition" became "common features of the Massachusetts landscape." [34]

The land surrounding Massachusetts Bay was not regarded commercially as a source of revenue for the Company, which generally abandoned the practice of collecting quitrents. Its value, in addition to the obvious one of nurturing the planters, lay in its perceived ability to provide security, stability, and status for men who, like Winthrop and unlike the initial subscribers of 1629, were not primarily engaged in trade. Even those in New England who made their fortunes in trade turned to the land, following the example of generations of London businessmen who hoped thereby to acquire the status of the country gentleman. What set the New England land system apart from that of the other English colonies in North America was the requirement, established by an order of the Massachusetts Bay Company on May 19, 1629, that all allottments should be made within the bounds of a town, while residency remained, until the end of the century, a requirement of town proprietorship. The Plymouth and Dorchester companies similarly required settlement in towns. [35] The selection of a town site and the laying out of the town usually preceded the general distribution of lands. Only rumors of "French preparations against us" and fear "lest the winter should surprise us before we had builded our houses," explained Deputy Governor Thomas Dudley to the Countess of Lincoln, forced Winthrop's expedition to "plant dispersedly" before they could agree upon a "place fit to build a town upon."[36] The historical circumstance of colonization in unsettled land presented the founders of Massachusetts Bay with the rare opportunity to impose their own particular social design upon the emergent settlements of the region. The New England town was conceived as a place fundamentally rural, limited in size and density of population, and shaped by its polity into a homogeneous and orthodox community.

The New England township was a creature of the General Court. It was designed as an agricultural settlement containing homelots centered in the nucleated village and surrounded by apportionments in arable and meadow lands, and common fields. The plan of the town typically adhered to either of two patterns known in England: the rectilinear plan (i.e., Plymouth, Cambridge, New Haven, Hartford, and Fairfield, Connecticut) and the linear plan (i.e., Salem, Springfield, Providence, and Greenfield). The former tended to be the result of deliberate planning while the latter was the result of organic growth, determined largely by topography and natural property boundaries.[37] Other than a handful of maps and invaluable reconstructions executed by John W. Reps, the sole surviving documentary evidence we have of the formal principles which may have dictated the laying out of the township is an "Essay on the Laying Out of Towns, &c." probably written around 1635. The one specific example cited in the essay is "New Towne" (Cambridge). Since Thomas Graves, employed by the Massachusetts Bay Company in 1629 as engineer and surveyor, is the probable author of the Cambridge plan, which is, in turn, a rough gridiron (Figure 1), and since the "Essay" recommends a gridiron plan, it is probable that Graves was the writer of the essay. Moreover, the essay was written "in answering your desier for a little improvement [?] of my single pore tallent," a request which was most likely to have been made of Graves.[38]

Graves' suggested standard plan, if indeed the "Essay" was written by Graves, is predicated upon a township composed almost entirely of farm households. Indeed, the governing principle of the plan is the convenience of the township's farmers, "for they are ye tressells of ye tables of all ye kings of ye earth." The suggested configuration of the town is a square of six miles to the side, at the center of which should be located "ye meetinghouse" and the "howses orderly placed about." The town center, or "ye neerest circumference," should be a square three miles to the side; thus no house need be more than 2500 paces from the central meeting house so that all might enjoy "compfortable communion." The inner circumference should contain the farmlots. These, advised Graves, should average forty acres in size, for ten farmers can cultivate ten farms of forty acres each more efficiently, he argued, than one can cultivate, with servants, a farm of four hundred acres. The outlying area between the "neerest circumference" and the town bounds would be available for further division "in such maner as euery man may haue his due proportion . . . according vnto his present or apparent future occasion of imployment; & soe ye meane ones not be neglected" (Figure 2).

One can extrapolate from Graves' recommendations several features borne out by later practice. To begin with, the township was a rural unit with a small village center. When possible the village was located in the middle of the arable lands, while the division of those lands into farmlots of roughly forty acres would have meant a population of 144 farm households.[39] Graves' recommendations also favored individual ownership and enclosure as offering incentives to industrious and judicious cultivation. The design of the town necessarily limited the density of population. As new inhabitants came the towns themselves did not expand but, rather, new towns were created. Sudbury, Wethersfield, Hartford, and Windsor were such towns, resulting from the "hiving off" of groups of members from older towns.

One can appreciate the character of the township desired by Massachusetts Bay's first founders by considering not only what it was, but what it was not. It was not designed to accommodate a nonfarming population nor was it designed for a population which could not gather in a single assembly to discuss town affairs. Finally, its aesthetic, while orderly in its geometric configuration, was, as Anthony Garvan has suggested, "Counter Baroque." Absent is a striving for civic grandeur expressed in aesthetic terms. In its initial design, then, the New England town could be distinguished from the city in size or population, and was in fact an attempt to fix in time an intimate and rural world which could not readily be transformed into an urban landscape.

While the town plans of early Massachusetts Bay avoided the monumentality which would appear at Versailles or in the urban design efforts following the Great Fire of 1666, one can detect nonetheless an effort to articulate a simple town aesthetic. The few surviving descriptions we have of the first towns established in the colony cite certain features which, if they reflect the actual appearance of certain towns, suggest also what their observers thought worthy of comment. The author of "New Englands Plantation" (1630), "a reverend Divine now there resident," wrote that the settlers of Salem strove to "have a faire Towne" which would be the result of their building houses. The attributes which John Josselyn assigned to Dorchester and Charlestown were those of pleasant siting and "orderly" streets "beautified with Orchards and Gardens." William Wood's description of New England towns in 1634 focusses principally on their fertile lands, supplies of wood and fish, adequate harbors and pleasant situations. Yet he found Roxberry "a fair and handsome Country-Towne" because, its inhabitants "being all very rich," have "faire houses" and "fruitful gardens." Charlestown especially was "one of the neatest and best compacted Townes in New England, having many faire structures, with many handsome contrived streets." "Orderly," "strait," and "comly" streets, "comly" and "faire" houses, and orchards and gardens likewise characterized the aesthetic projection of Edward Johnson's New England towns. In contrast, Watertown, her settlers having scattered themselves among "the pleasant Springs, and small Rivulets" which ran "like veines throughout her Body," failed to show anything "delightful to the eye in any place."[40] Orderliness, both as it may have actually existed and as it was perceived, thus seems to have been the governing aesthetic principle of the early New England town. Orderliness was to have been achieved in the layout of the streets, in compactness of settlement, and in the intermingling of nature within the town through gardens and orchards, themselves the result of an imposed order on otherwise wild and unruly nature. An aesthetic of order would, however, entail a limited tolerance to the eye of the visual diversity, surprise, and accident one associates with a highly developed urban setting.

※

The system of land distribution and town–planning followed in Massachusetts Bay was only one of the means by which the colony's first settlers sought to recover the traditional world of rural England. Internal regulations also reflect a desire to sustain rural homogeneity and stability. Vital to this purpose was the perpetuation of the chief institution of rural life, the household. The continuity of the family served both religious and social purposes in the early decades of New England. The nuclear family was not only an emotional and economic unit which ensured propagation and embraced supportively all of life's stages. Perceived as a system of hierarchical, interdependent and deferential relationships, it served as well as a model for both church and society. As husband was to wife, parents to children, and masters to servants, so also were pastors and magistrates to the people. Moreover the family assumed vital social functions—it was an economic enterprise, a school, a vocational institute, a church in embryo, a disciplinary institution, and it provided nurture for the young and the aged and the orphaned.[41] The Puritan household, or family, was the primary unit of social cohesion.

Puritan typology provided a biblical sanction for the family in that God had been a father of families and among the Puritans of both old and New

England the household was the primary source of religous instruction. In his lonely journey toward religious justification John Winthrop found some comfort and assurance in the role of spiritual patriarch to his household at Groton. "Havinge been longe wearied with discontent for want of suche imployment as I could find comfort and peace in," he wrote in 1616,

> I founde at last that the conscionable and constant teachinge of my familye was a speciall businesse, wherein I might please God, and greatly further their and mine owne salvation, which might be as sufficient incouragement to my studye and labour therein as if I were to teache a publick Congregation; for as to the pleasing of God it was all one . . . so . . . I purpose by Gods assistance, to take it as a chiefe part of my callinge.

The identity of family with church and commonwealth was later made explicit by Winthrop in his defense of an order of the General Court of May 1637, which ruled that "none should be received to inhabite within this Jurisdiction but such as should be allowed by some of the Magistrates." The premise of Winthrop's defense of the order, made in response to the Antinomian crisis, was "that the care of safety and welfare was the original cause or occasion of common weales and of many familyes subjecting themselves to rulers and laws; for no man hath lawfull power over another, but by birth or consent. . . . A family is a little common wealth, and a common wealth is a greate family. Now as a family," he argued, "is not bound to entertaine all comers, . . . no more is a common wealth."[42] Homogeneity and cohesion—these were the evident watchwords of the early New England town. The General Court's disputed order of 1637, laws requiring that sojourners be taken in by families or bonded in service to responsible employers, the regulation of alienation by the General Court or town proprietors, and frequent exhortations to avoid conflict and preserve harmony, were all expressions of a general longing for stability, intimacy and continuity.[43]

Throughout the first two decades the General Court struggled to preserve its authority over the colony against the challenges to its discretionary prerogatives posed by the growth in number of neighboring towns and the desire for codification of the colony's laws. When, in 1643, expansion led the General Court to divide the plantation into four counties, the Court reserved to itself the right to appoint the magistrates of the local county courts. It was reluctant, moreover, to publish a "body of laws" which the "people had long desired" thinking "their condition very unsafe, while so much power rested in the discretion of the magistrates." Although the Court adopted in 1641 the *Body of Laws* drawn up by Nathaniel Ward, it did not see fit to publish the first edition until 1649.

The "two great reasons . . . which caused most of the magistrates and some of the elders not to be very forward in this matter," explained John Winthrop, were the "want of sufficient experience of the nature and disposition of the people . . . which made them conceive, that such laws would be fitted for us, which should arise pro re nata upon occasion" and that a body of laws "would professedly transgress the limits of our charter, which provide, we shall make no laws repugnant to the laws of England . . . But to raise up laws by practice and custom had been no transgression." Winthrop's second objection was patently contrived, for customary colonial laws were far more likely to violate "the laws of England" than codified laws which could be readily inspected—by "the people" of Massachusetts Bay no less than Crown officials. In truth, the General Court was attempting to perpetuate the same supremacy of the medieval conception of customary common law as the product of the discretionary rule of county courts that Sir Edward Coke had invoked in his opposition to Stuart assertions of royal prerogative. That this was its motive was indicated in 1647 when it ordered the legal writings of the reactionary English jurist "to the end that we may have the better light for making and proceeding about laws."[44]

The outstanding instrument of cohesion in Massachusetts Bay, however, was the insistence upon religious orthodoxy. The leaders of the colony took for granted that the perpetuation of New England's churches and the internal stability and intimacy of her townships were closely related problems. Families and churches were thus the posts and rails which both confined and protected these "Flocks of Sheep in a howling Wilderness." John Cotton declared that "the free Inhabitants of the Countrey" constituted "All the househoulders of every Town" while as early as 1631 church membership became a condition for freemanship, or enfranchisement.[45] "We have great Ordnance," wrote the author of "New-Englands Plantation" in 1630, "But that which is our greatest comfort, and meanes of defence above all other, is, that we have here the true Religion and holy Ordinances of Almightie God taught amongst us . . . and if God be with us, who can be against us?"[46]

As the internal unity of the New England township began to disintegrate the blame was attributed as much to the intrusion of "unsound doctrine" as to the lust for land. As "the people of [Plymouth] Plantation began to grow in their outward estates, by reason of the flowing of many people into the country, especially into the Bay of the Massachusetts," wrote William Bradford of the year 1632, and

> as their stocks increased and the increase vendible, there was no longer any holding them together, but now they must of necessity go to their great lots. They could not otherwise keep their cattle. . . .
> By which means they were scattered all over the Bay quickly and the town in which they lived compactly till now was left very thin and in a

short time almost desolate. And if this had been all, it had been less, though too much; but the church must also be divided. . . . And this I fear will be the ruin of New England.

When it seemed that ruin was imminent, that he saw "some great change at hand," Bradford bemoaned the "whimsey errors" which "have now got such a head, / And under notion of conscience, do spread / . . . Another cause of our declining here, / Is a mixt multitude; *as doth appear* . . . And of these, many grew loose and profane . . . whereas the Lord doth sow his good seed, / The enemy, he brings in tares and weed."[47] Edward Johnson, writing in 1652–1653, reminded his readers that the "Dutch come out of your hods-podge, the great mingle-mangle of Religion . . . hath caused the Churches of Christ to increase so little" with them; "the Churches of Christ have not thrived under the tolerating Government of Holland." Those who would "be a people to His prayse" should "purge out all the sowre Leven of unsound Doctrine."[48]

William Bradford and Edward Johnson wrote from the perspective of Puritan orthodoxy, although they differed on the point of separatism. They did not differ, however, in their conception of the foundation of the strength of the New England enterprise from John Josselyn, who, as a Royalist, viewed New England through a prism less pure. Describing New England in 1646, he noted that "the Government both Civil and Ecclesiastical is in the hands of the thorow-pac'd Independents and rigid Presbyterians." Nonetheless "the chiefest objects of discipline, true Religion, and morality, they want, some are of a Linsie-woolsie disposition . . . all like Aetheopieans white in the teeth only . . . they are . . . great Syndics, or censors, or controllers of other mens manners, and savagely factious amongst themselves."[49]

Bradford's belief that the disintegration of the churches was furthered by the tendency of settlers to disperse to larger, more isolated, homesteads may have resulted from his association of a thriving church with the parish and the intimacy of a cohesive rural village. The real encroachments upon doctrinal and social uniformity came, however, less from the geographic than the cultural perimeters of the New England town. Josselyn's observation of the "Linsie-woolsie disposition" of some New Englanders was incorporated in his satirical comments on the "covetous and proud" character of the colony's "grose Goddons, or great masters" and "Merchants." Such men were to be found not among the struggling farmers of Massachusetts Bay but at its social, political, and economic center. It was in the growing awareness of the importance of Boston as a nascent city that the sense of disintegration became most acute.

Boston, alone among the towns founded by the Massachusetts Bay Company or its grantees, was not intended primarily as an agricultural settlement. The lack of forest and meadow land on the Shawmut peninsula, explained William Wood, had to be endured because the town site was "fittest for such as can Trade into England" it being "the chiefe place for shipping and Merchandize." The settlement of the Shawmut peninsula took place gradually during the summer and autumn of 1630, encouraged no doubt by the protections of a peninsula and the presence there, if not of firewood, of water, a harbor, fertile soil—but most of all, of Isaac Johnson and other leaders of the colony, including, finally, Winthrop himself.[50]

The topography of the peninsula largely determined the configuration of the original town, which was located on a small plain between the Trimountain and the harbor. As in every other English and New England town public activity was centered at the crossing of the two main streets, Great Street (now State Street) and High Street (now Washington Street), which led respectively to the harbor and along the neck of the peninsula. This center and its immediate vicinity soon became the location of the town's market, the Town House built in 1657, the First Church of Boston, and the homes of Reverend John Wilson and Governor John Winthrop.[51] Maps prepared by Samuel C. Clough on the basis of data from the *Book of Possessions* (1643) reveal the clustering of construction along the waterfront, around the town center, and along the road leading to the neck, a pattern which only confirmed the importance to the young town of its merchant community and the town's political role. Boston's strongest aesthetic feature must have been the extension of Great Street into the long wharf which provided complementary vistas of the harbor with its ships and the town center (Figure 3), adorned in 1657 by the Town House built in part with a penitential bequest from merchant Robert Keayne. A reflection of the importance of commerce to the town's life is the reappearance in Boston of Cornhill Street, familiar to merchants who had hustled through the Cheapside section of London where ongoing family and trading connections helped to foster the mercantile life of the colonial capital. Cornhill Street rapidly became the principal thoroughfare of Boston and "the list of property owners on Cornhill between Milk and Dock streets during the first decade reads like the roster of expatriated tradesmen and shopkeepers of the old business district."[52]

The town's role as the center of colonial government joined that of its importance as "the chiefe place for shipping and Merchandize" to ensure Boston's vitality. "This Towne although it be neither the greatest, nor the richest, yet it is the most noted and frequented, being the Center of the Plantations where the monthly Courts are kept. Here likewise dwells the Governour," observed William Wood.[53] By the end of the second decade, Boston had acquired all the attributes of a growing urban center. There emerged the foreign trade activity and colonial retail trades and the industries—shipbuilding and outfitting—that increase with such activity (Figure 4). Most important from a cultural perspective was that not only did her share of the colony's population reach one-fifth, but only about forty of "the hundreds" who entered the town from 1642 to 1650 acquired any legal affiliation with the town. Boston was acquiring an anonymous and floating population of "sojourners," while fewer of her legal inhabitants could be identified with the farm household that had been the basis of the rural township. By 1649 there were as many in Boston who owned no property as those who did, and not one half of the town's families owned "more than a house and garden on the peninsula."[54]

Boston was on the way to becoming a city, a place foreign economically and socially to the countryside.[55] The relative density and anonymity of her population and the predominance of non-agricultural pursuits had begun to transform her into the moral and environmental opposite of the country, a transformation that was perceived with mixed feelings by contemporaries. Boston's merchants failed, in the seventeenth century, to acquire a political and social position commensurate with their economic influence. Rarely was a merchant elected to the Court of Assistants and no merchant achieved the position of governor or deputy-governor. The trading activities of Boston's merchants rested on economic rationales which defied the moral control of the colony's leaders. Their efforts to assert that control by creating a public retail monopoly bound to a 15 percent profit, or by subjecting all ships' inventories to inspection by the governor, failed in the face of merchant defiance. The merchants also appeared to favor religious heterodoxy, as when they supported the "dissenters" during the Antinomian crisis of 1636–1637. The Puritan oligarchy undoubtedly perceived a relationship between the threat to their moral authority posed by the merchant community and that posed by the town's growing population of anonymous artisans and tradesmen, for the General Court persistently denied requests from the inhabitants of Boston for incorporation made in 1650, 1651, 1659, 1662, and 1677, nor was the town ever incorporated under the colonial charter.[56]

At the same time Boston's flourishing condition did not go unnoticed and even her most pious chroniclers could not resist contrasting her "stately buildings" with the "Desart Wilderness." Edward Johnson marveled that Boston, "the which of a poor country village, in twice [sic] seven years is become like unto a small city . . . the Center Towne and Metropolis of this Wildernesse worke," whose virtues were nothing if not worldly: "the buildings [are] beautiful and large, some fairely set forth with Brick, Tile, Stone and Slate, and orderly placed with comly streets, whose continuall inlargement presages some sumptuous City." Where once were "hideous Thickets . . . such, that Wolfes and Beares nurst up their young" are now "streets . . . full of Girles and Boys sporting up and downe, with a continued concourse of people. . . . This Town is the very Mart of the Land." Cotton Mather looked upon Boston as "The Metropolis of the whole English America."[57]

John Josselyn, who was not so pious and delighted in ridiculing the censoriousness of Boston's inhabitants, conceded that Boston had grown from the mere "village" he had visited in 1638 to "the greatest town" in New England. Josselyn's description is not only an account of the town in 1663 but contains, in its relation of Boston's attributes, a virtual anatomy of a seventeenth–century urban place comparable to London in character, if not in size. To begin with, Boston was "rich and populous, much frequented by strangers." Its houses were "close together on each side the streets as in London . . . furnished with many fair shops," and "handsomely contrived" of "Brick, Stone [and] Lime. Many and large" were her streets,

> paved with pebble stone, and the South-side adorned with Gardens and Orchards. On the North-west and North-east two constant Fairs are kept for daily Traffick thereonto. On the South there is a small but pleasant Common where the Gallants a little before Sunset walk with the Marmalet-Madams, as we do in Morefields, &c."

A chief source of the town's prosperity, the harbor, "is filled with Ships and other Vessels for most part of the year."[58]

However impressive the growth and prosperity of Boston might seem, the "small city" soon began to reflect those characteristics against which the country posited its own moral and environmental superiority. The devil might do his handiwork anywhere, of course, but the city seemed especially vulnerable to his temptations. The moral and spiritual responsibility placed upon Boston was especially great because she had been envisioned as a "Citty upon a Hill," the beacon for New England's special errand into the wilderness. Samuel Sewall, whose *Diary* affords a valuable glimpse into the private sensibilities of one amiable Boston resident, confessed to having had "a very unusual Dream" in which "our Saviour in the dayes of his Flesh when upon Earth, came to Boston and abode here sometimes," an event which caused Sewall to reflect "how much more Boston had to say than Rome boasting of Peter's being there." Sewall's experience occurred during the autumn of New England's errand and thus as he awoke he realized the "chronological absurdity" of what he had dreamed.[59] But it was nonetheless fitting that had Christ chosen to come to New England, he would have come to Boston.

In a lengthy poem lamenting the moral and spiritual decline of New England William Bradford celebrated the abundance of God's mercies in the early years as the arriving multitudes were furnished with fruitful fields and gardens and, above all, a pious and learned ministry. Among those blessings was the town of Boston which Bradford likened to a great tree whose roots spread throughout New England as "all trade and commerce fell in her way." But then covetousness and greed overtook New England's plantations, exposing them to the wrath of God. In a second poem Bradford was more precise. Boston, "a great and wealthy town," is overcome by "drunkenness" and "excesse" and her people forget that they were once "poore." At first "all things were free and nothing sold," but now "sordid gaine" has led to the oppression of "the weake and poore. The trade is all in your own hand, / Take heed ye doe not wrong the land," Bradford warned, "Lest he that hath lift you on high . . . throw you downe from your high state, / And make you low and desolate."[60] The greatness of Boston had been compromised by the fact that it was no longer the pious town of the founders and seemed, to Bradford, to have suffered the loss of a simpler rural world in which God provided for those who lived industriously, charitably, and righteously with their neighbors.

More than a decade after Sewall's dream, Cotton Mather exhorted Bostonians not to forget their city's providential role. The town had survived famine, fire, the French, and the smallpox, but only because God had treated their city as he had "one of the Chief Towns in the Land of Israel" which he had saved from "the Irresistible Fury and Approach . . . of Destroyers, by an Immediate Hand of Heaven upon them." The people of Boston must do as Samuel did, who in gratitude to the Lord erected a stone which he called Ebenezer. They must make of their town a monument to Christ's mercy. They will have erected such a monument when they resist sinfulness, lest Boston become another Sodom; as they honor their ministers, who have been so many "Candlesticks in the Town;" and when they recover the piety of the early days and practice as well "extraordinary Equity & Charity." Cotton Mather must have believed such an exhortation was necessary, and in the conclusion of his sermon he explained why. Boston had begun to abound not only with "fortune tellers, bawdy houses, drinking houses and ale-houses," but "idleness . . . increases in the Town exceedingly . . . Beggars, do shamefully grow upon us, and such Beggars too, as our Lord Jesus Christ Himself hath Expressly forbidden us to countenance." Mortality has carried away "the old Race of our First Planters" and "the Power of Godliness is grievously decay'd among us."[61] The moral and religious antipathy toward the city that had first appeared in the countryside of the English Puritans had, with Cotton Mather's jeremiad, been transferred to Boston. The "Citty upon a Hill" could become, in sacred time, the City of God. Or it could remain the earthly city. It could not be both.

The idea of the city and of the country, the values associated with those discrete environments, and their manifestation in the design of the New England township were, as we have seen, the consequence of a yearning to secure a fixed, orderly, homogeneous, and cohesive arrangement of geographic and social space that was shared by emigrating English Puritans. Location in space, however, represents only one dimension of that human need to control chaos which was expressed, metaphorically, in the opening lines of Genesis. Everyman yearns also to know his location in time, and it is that longing which sustains myths and philosophies of history. An essential religious impulse of the Reformation lay in the willingness of thousands of men and women to reject the comfort of miracle, mystery and authority embodied in the Roman church. They sought, figuratively as well as literally, salvation in the wilderness. But in so doing they relinquished not only the spiritual comfort of the Roman church but also much of Christian history. "Where was your church before Luther?" Catholic might ask Protestant.[62] And so the creative energies of Protestantism, and Puritanism, were directed toward the restoration of the primitive church and the rewriting of the Christian experience in past, present, and future time.

In their effort to establish a Protestant eschatology, the English reformers had turned to Eusibius, Bishop of Caesaria, Augustine, and John Foxe. From the work of these patristic authors and Protestant martyrology they fashioned for themselves a past and a future in which the eschatological struggle between Christ and Antichrist was joined with the history of the English nation. In answer to the question, "where was your church before Luther?" Puritan and Anglo-Catholic alike might have replied: our church has been there all along; it is the only true church, the primitive church of the apostles before the corruptions of the Roman prelacy, and it is this primordial church that, in the lives of the elect, continues the struggle for Christ against Antichrist which is the meaning of the history of the world.[63]

The apposition of sacred and profane history, inherent in Christology itself, was affirmed in the Augustinian view of free will which rendered man a no less active participant with divine providence in the shaping of the world's events, although the nature and outcome of those events had been divinely foreordained. What gave the Puritan view of history its special character was its application of the Augustinian conception of the contention of the Two Cities to the history of the English nation and the typological reading of the New Testament through which they found their historical identity in the re-enactment of the wanderings of the tribes of Israel, a necessary prelude to the fulfillment of the promise of the New Jerusalem. The martyrology of the Marian exiles, summarized in John Foxe's *Actes and Monuments of these Latter and Perilous Times* (1554) provided a historical role and purpose for those outcasts of English Romanism who gathered in Germany and Switzerland. The Geneva Bible (1560) which along with the *Actes and Monuments* was the most widely adopted document of the Puritan reformation,[64] served as a virtually inexhaustible sourcebook, with its abundant marginal commentaries, for the typological identification of the churches of the elect with the people of Israel.

The woodcuts which adorn the title pages of both of these works are as eloquent as any textual citation in suggesting their meaning to Puritan readers. The illustration on the title page of an early edition of the *Actes and Monuments* portrays God enthroned upon a globe surrounded by trumpeting angels (Figure 5). At his left side below this scene a handful of churlish fallen angels trumpet downward, as if in parody of the angelic firmament, upon a gathering of worshipping Roman Catholics whose priest appears to be raising the Host toward the devilish group above. Below this group a multitude fingers its beads while listening to another priest. Beneath the right hand of God are assembled other angels with upturned trumpets while below them a group of Protestant martyrs blow their upturned trumpets, oblivious to the flames consuming their robes. At the very bottom, opposite the Roman Catholic multitude, a Protestant pastor directs the attention of his flock to the Hebrew "Jahweh" emblazoned over their heads.

The illustration that introduces both the Old and New Testaments of the 1560 edition of the Geneva Bible portrays the Exodus (Figure 6). The Israelites are gathered with their tents at the shores of the Red Sea. Beyond them a Holy flame rises to the sky, beckoning them to cross into the sea while behind them, in the foreground of the woodcut, the Egyptians are in hot pursuit, riding a horse-drawn chariot and waving a flurry of spears. Close analysis of Puritan literature reveals that Protestant eschatology and the typological reading of Scripture were persistent and pervasive in England in the first half of the seventeenth century and extended to the end of the century in New England.[65] In the effort to locate Puritanism in sacred and secular time, Puritan thought focussed on the two images, both dymanic, which could be found in the pages of the *Actes and Monuments* and the Geneva Bible. One was the Augustinian vision of the Two Cities extended into the postscriptural struggle between Christ and Antichrist; the other was the typological image of the Hebrew nation. Both images had a profound bearing upon the perspective with which the founders of Massachusetts Bay beheld the city.

When Augustine set out to defend Christianity against the charge that the abandonment of pagan worship was the cause of the barbarian invasions he chose as the twin motifs of his philosophy of history the Two Cities—the City of God and the city of earth, into which the universe was divided and whose parallel history is the world's history.[66] Thus when John Winthrop, drawing upon the apostle Matthew, likened the Massachusetts Bay venture to a "Citty upon a Hill" his expression was no mere figure of speech; Winthrop's city was to be the earthly agency of that divine community whose members are "knitt together" in the love of God and Christ, as "the sinewes and other ligaments" knit together the "naturall body." Similarly, John Davenport described "particular churches" as "distinct and severall independant [sic] bodies, every one as a city compact within its self, without subordination under or dependance upon any other but Jesus Christ," and in so doing made the churches of Puritanism figurative representations of Augustine's City of God.[67]

The belief that "the beauty of the course of this world is achieved by the opposition of contraries," as "oppositions of contraries lend beauty to the language," one of the intellectual foundations of Augustinian and medieval thought (to be perpetuated in Ramist logic), was inherent in Augustine's opposition of the Two Cities.[68] Similarly, the histories of the two cities were contrary to one another, as were the realms of the sacred and the profane. Because the founders of New England were intent upon preserving the church so that "they might enjoy Christ and his Ordinances in their primitive purity" and "raise a Bulworke against the kingdome of Antichrist," there could be no admission of worldly purposes in their undertaking. Theology as well as actual experience led Thomas Dudley to declare that "any [who] come hither to plant for worldly ends . . . commits an error, of which he will soon repent him; but if for spiritual . . . he may 'find here what may well content him." If the Virginia plantations failed, replied John Winthrop to the objection that the mishaps of earlier plantations foretold only misfortune for New England, it was primarily because "their mayne end was Carnall and not Religious." "New England differs from other Foreign Plantations," asserted Increase Mather a generation later, in that "other Plantations were built upon Worldly Interests, New England upon that which is purely Religious." The "purely religious" purpose of the city being erected in Massachusetts Bay required of its founders that they, first of all, "carry the Gospell into those parts of the world, to helpe on the comminge of the fulnesse of the Gentiles;"[69] that they retain a clear separation of church and civil government lest the City of God be corrupted by the earthly city; and that the colony's sacred mission be preserved through the maintenance of religious orthodoxy.

Thus a yearning for homogeneity and stability converged with a perceived eschatological imperative in Massachusetts Bay's limitation of freemanship to church members, its intolerance of religious as well as social dissension, and in the assertion of ministerial authority over the emerging particularism of New England's churches, reflected in the Cambridge Platform of 1648.

By reverting to Augustine the Reformers had been able to locate themselves in past, present and future time as Christ's combatants against the Antichrist. They needed only to argue that the sixth of Augustine's seven great ages of world history was not the Christian millenium but the reign of Antichrist to justify their break with Rome. But the Puritans faced as well the problem of an historical justification for their departure from the Church of England, advanced by John Foxe as the national church under whose leadership the war against Antichrist would be won. Foxe's transformation of sacred history into national history was more plausible in the age of Elizabeth than it was during the early years of the Stuart monarchy. The English church, argued the Puritans, had violated the covenant of grace by subjecting the elect to the instruments of national government, or, put in Augustinian terms, by subordinating the City of God to the City of Man. Resistance could be thus justified, but emigrating Puritans were left in an anomalous position. If they were truly intent upon purifying the English church, how could they justify their alleged abandonment of the national covenant?

The Puritans of New England were ever sensitive to the charge of separatism, protesting at the start that they remained faithful communicants of the English church. As John Winthrop and his company were about to leave Yarmouth in 1630 they wrote a "humble request" to those they were about to leave behind to "consider us as your Brethren" and

> to take notice of the principals, and body of our company, as those who esteeme it our honour, to call the *Church of England*, from whence wee rise, our deare Mother, and cannot part from our native Country, where she specially resideth, without much sadnes of heart, and many teares in our eyes, ever acknowledging that such hope and part as wee have obtained in the common salvation, we have received in her bosome, and suckt it from her breasts.

Increase Mather would later insist that the New England planters "agree with all other Protestant Reformed Churches; and more especially with England, in Matters of Doctrine and in all Fundamentall Points of Faith; yet as to the Liturgy, Ceremonies, and Church Government by Bishops, they were, and are Non-Conformists."[70]

The distinction between Separatist and Non-Conformist may indeed have rested only on questions of ceremony and church polity. But the distinction had considerable strategic importance. The king of England was empowered to grant charters of incorporation with virtual self-government to colonial enterprises, but he had never been empowered to grant ecclesiastical independence to religious sects. Whether or not the founders of Massachusetts Bay actually considered themselves mere nonconforming branches of the English church, political prudence required them to declare themselves as such. In the same "humble request" for the continued favor of the English brethren of Massachusetts Bay John Winthrop was careful to relate the coming enterprise to the Roman colony of Philippi:

> You are not ignorant, that the Spirit of God stirred up the Apostle *Paul* to make continuall mention of the Church of *Philippi* (which was a Colonie from *Rome*) let the same Spirit, we beseech you, put you in mind, that are the Lords remembrancers, to pray for us without ceasing (who are a weake Colony from your selves).[71]

This reference to Philippi was shrewd, but it was not as the church of Philippi that Winthrop and his followers found their place in the course of world history. Their historical identification of themselves hereafter was not to a Roman colony but, typologically, to the people of Israel.

In spite of the many protests of fidelity that emanated from New England during the first decades, the numerous references to the Israelites, the destruction of Babylon, the restoration of Jerusalem under Nehemiah, and the prophetic coming of Zion which constituted the New England Puritans' appeal to providential history for self-justification all point to a rejection of the English church as the final instrument of Christ's victory over the Antichrist. Edward Johnson proclaimed as much when he portrayed New England's churches as "neither Nationall nor Provinciall" but "churches . . . such as were in Primitive Times (before Antichrists Kingdome prevailed) . . . built of such living stones as outwardly appeare Saints by calling." Just as it had been "necessary that there should be a Moses and Aaron, before the Lord would deliver his people and destroy Pharaoh," he explained, "so now it was needfull, that the Churches of Christ should first obtain their purity, and the Civill Government its power to defend them, before Antichrist come to his final ruine."[72]

Both Winthrop and John Cotton were ready to defend the unquestioned rule of "the better sort" against democratic stirrings by citing "the practice of Israel," for "it was the Lord's order among the Israelites to have all such businesses [i.e., the division of lands] committed to the elders."[73] It had been one thing for William Bradford, a Separatist, to liken the history of New England to the history of Israel. But it was quite another for John Winthrop to invoke "the God of Israell" and the memory of Moses in his "Modell of Christian Charity," or to appeal to the people of Massachusetts not to abandon the colony in search of betterment elsewhere for they are "come together into a Wilderness" and are as near to their neighbors "as the Israelites were to Moses."[74]

Were Winthrop and his company presuming to abrogate God's covenant with the English nation in announcing themselves the true church of the elect? By the third generation in New England the location of sacred history in the American wilderness became more insistent. The English nation had renounced the covenant itself in its abandonment of the Puritan quest for godly rule, and thus providential history seemed to confirm Cotton Mather's declaration that the wonders of the Christian religion had flown to the American strand.[75] Mather's grand scheme of New England history can be read, with Johnson's *Wonder-Working Providence,* as an attempt to transform the providential history of New England into sacred history. Each sought by such a transformation to legitimize New England in historical place and time.

As we have seen, the Puritan longing for a fixed location in geographic and social space resulted in a desire to preserve a rural landscape coupled with a suspicion of the city as a place of moral, economic, and social innovations and dislocations. Out of patristic and reformed traditions Puritan religious thought combined soteriology with Protestant eschatology in order to locate itself in that other dimension of the cosmos, past, present, and future time, or in providential and sacred history. The Puritan search for a usable past resulted in the selective concentration upon two images from Christian history by which they would identify and justify themselves to man and God. The first was Augustine's construct of the Two Cities. The second was the image of the tribes of Israel. Both of these images, like the image of the virtuous countryside, had negative implications for the way in which the founders of New England would anticipate and respond to the imminence of an urban landscape.

The attributes of Augustine's Two Cities were such that those who accepted his characterizations of them could look upon the secular city only with alarm. The city built by man was the city first built by Cain; its "sinews" and "ligaments," to use Winthrop's expression, were the sinews of self-love—of vanity and worldly ambition, of the lust to power. John Bunyan used similar imagery in his dream allegory, *The Pilgrim's Progress* (1678–1684), in which Christian, who departs from the City of Destruction in his journey to the Celestial City, must pass through the Town of Carnal-Policy and the town called Vanity Fair. There he and his companion Faith are thrown into prison and await judgment by a jury composed of "Mr. Blind-man, Mr. No-good, Mr. Malice, Mr. Love-lust, Mr. Live-loose, Mr. Heady, Mr. High-mind, Mr. Enmity, Mr. Lyar, Mr. Cruelty, Mr. Hate-light, and Mr. Implacable."[76]

The glory of the celestial city lay in its absolute opposition to the secular city. The sinews which bound together the body of the elect were the sinews of the love of God. Rejection of worldly aspirations was, as it were, a condition of citizenship. A place where "the Streets . . .were paved with Gold, and in them walked many men, with Crowns on their heads, palms in their hands, and golden Harps to sing praises withal"[77] could never, in its exotic remoteness, serve as a working image of the most ideal of earthly cities.

The image of Israel, however, unlike the Augustinian City of God, could serve as a source for an ideal city on earth because the wanderings of the Israelites culminated in the erection of a city in providential time. Moreover, the building of Zion was a work of man acceptable in the sight of God. "When Religious Statesmen frame and build by the level and plummet of his [God's] wisdom," wrote Nathaniel Ward, "then People may say as his Servants of old, Look upon Zion the City of our Solemnities; Your eyes shall see it a quiet Habitation, a Tabernacle that shall not be taken down; not one of the stakes thereof shall be removed, neither shall any of the cords thereof be broken, Isai. 33.20"[78] Because the cities the Israelites built were not, and could not be, the Heavenly City, they could serve as examples of the earthly habitations of God's chosen people.

The Geneva Bible contains three descriptions of cities designed according to divine ordinance, all of which bear certain similar characteristics. The design of the first two cities, cities of the Old Testament (Numbers 2:1–31 and 35:5; Ezekiel 42, 45, and 48) are confirmed in Revelation 21:16, which describes "the great citie, holie Jerusalem, descending out of heaven from God." The twenty-six woodcuts in the Geneva Bible—five maps, illustrations of the tribes of Israel at the shores of the Red Sea, Noah's Ark, Hebrew implements of worship, Hebrew priests, various tabernacles, the temple, the dwellings of the Hebrew kings, and the throne of Solomon (I, II Kings)—include illustrations of the temple and city of the prophet Ezekiel's vision. Unlike the New Jerusalem of Revelation which, with its foundations of precious stones and streets of gold, was the singular creation of God, the cities of the Hebrews were works which could be imitated by the elect.

The biblical cities, although varying considerably in their dimensions, had certain features in common. First, all were square. Second, the prophetic city of Ezekiel incorporated the encampments of the twelve tribes of Israel, placed in contiguous groups of three along each of the city's four sides which were oriented toward north, south, east, and west. This pattern was repeated in the New Jerusalem of Revelation whose four sides were broken by three of the twelve gates entering the city. Third, the city proper was located at the center of the "suburbs" and, also measured in a square, thus formed with its suburbs two concentric squares. Finally, with the possible exception of the city in Ezekiel, the biblical cities were measured symmetrically around two central axes. While the city "for the whole house of Israel" pictured at the end of Ezekiel was located to the east of the "Sanctuarie," along the eastern "border" of the "land of promes," its interior arrangement was rectilinear, extending symmetrically from the road joining the gate at the center of the eastern wall with the temple. The woodcut accompanying Ezekiel's vision in the Geneva Bible was, however, only one of several sixteenth- and seventeenth-century attempts to reconstruct pictorially the encampments of the tribes of Israel and Old Jerusalem. The reconstructions of Ezekiel's vision prepared by Sebastian Catalion in 1551 and Villalpandus in 1604 differ from that appearing in the Geneva Bible in that they portray nine squares of equal sides arranged circumferentially around a center square containing the temple sanctuary. A comparison with the text suggests that Castalion's and Villalpandus's reconstructions were more accurate than that which appeared in the Geneva Bible woodcut. [79]

Granting that the orthogonal plan has had historical appeal as an urban form because of the relative ease with which it can be surveyed, [80] and that the well-known Roman art of castrametation could have served as a precedent for axial, rectilinear planning, it is still probable that the standard for the square New England township plan was derived principally from biblical sources. The presence of alternative plans in New England, in which lots and streets were laid out according to natural boundaries or in an otherwise irregular fashion, indicates that instances of rectilinear or square planning were the result of deliberate selection. Moreover, the normative use made of Old Testament precedents in New England political and social policy suggests that models of an ideal city were most likely sought from biblical sources as well. For example, the restricted land alienation common to the original land policy of the New England townships, while explicable in social terms, was also sanctioned in scripture: "And thei shal not sel of it, neither change it, nor abalienate the first fruites of the land: for it is holy vnto the Lord" (Ezekiel 48:14).

If we turn again to the "Essay on the Laying Out of Towns," probably written in 1635 by Thomas Graves, the official surveyor of the Massachusetts Bay Company in New England, what comes to the fore as the distinguishing characteristic of his model plan is the scheme of two concentric squares, the center containing the meetinghouse and townhouse lots, and the outer square containing the farms. The most striking example, however, of the use of Old Testament precedent in the design of the New England town is found in the plan of New Haven.

New Haven was established in 1638 by a group of emigrating Puritans under the leadership of John Davenport and Theophilus Eaton; both had supported the Massachusetts Bay enterprise while in England and John Davenport had been an intimate of John Cotton's. Davenport, unlike Winthrop, was a clerical leader of a new plantation and both he and John Cotton viewed the move of Davenport's group to New Haven as an opportunity to establish a bible commonwealth in the purest possible form. Davenport was the most rigid of all the New England patriarchs in his insistence that the colony be governed only by the covenanted elect. It was Massachusetts Bay's compromising of that principle in the institution of the General Court which may, as well as the shortage of good harbors, have led Davenport to decide not to settle there. He later resisited union with Connecticut because that colony favored the Half-way Covenant and failed to limit political privileges to the elect. Once New Haven was successfully incorporated into Connecticut in 1661 Davenport felt no longer bound to the plantation he founded and, in 1666, accepted a call to the First Church of Boston, a move which resulted in the secession of the First Church's more liberal-minded communicants to form the Third, or Old South, Church at Charlestown in 1699.[81]

Davenport, who spoke of the Lord as "the Holy one of Israel," was not unlike the majority of the Puritan clergy in the breadth and depth of his learning. Only the threat of pennilessness would lead him to consider parting with his library, which contained "Ancient wrighters, or schoolemen, or moderne wrighters, or hystorians or expositors."[82] It is almost inconceivable, therefore, that he would have been unacquainted with contemporary biblical commentaries as well as the Renaissance architectural writings based on Vitruvius (and Vitruvius himself), both of which have been advanced as probable sources for New Haven's distinctive town plan. Certainly he knew the Geneva Bible as thoroughly as any Puritan. The plan of New Haven is remarkable not for its use of concentric squares for the external boundaries and the town center; as we have seen, such a plan was suggested by Thomas Graves in 1635. Rather, the New Haven plan uniquely incorporates the nine squares of equal dimensions, symmetrically placed within the larger square indicated in contemporary pictoral reconstructions of the Old Testament cities, (Figures 7–9). Furthermore, the dwelling lots were not clustered around the central square with garden and farm lots extending behind them, but were located at the edges of each of the peripheral squares, making of each a separate unit and thus recapitulating the apportionment of land according to tribes described in Numbers 2 and Ezekiel 48 (Figure 10).[83]

New Haven's plan is also distinctive for its siting. Anthony N. B. Garvan has argued that the siting of New Haven was derived from Vitruvius, whose elaborate instructions for the laying out of streets to intersect the prevailing winds in the first book of his *Ten Books on Architecture* were available not only in Latin but through John Shute's *First & Chief Groundes of Architecture* (1563).[84] The siting of New Haven, however, would have had a precedent more compatible with that of its internal layout had it been based not upon Vitruvius, but again upon Ezekiel's dream, wherein "the land of promes" is bounded on the south by waters that "go into one sea" and "runne into another sea," the water's edge being 1,000 cubits (or 1,500 feet, using an 18-inch cubit measure) from the house at the center of the city containing "the holy chambers of the Priests" (Ezekiel 47:1–8). New Haven, as laid out in 1638, is bounded on the south by the Quinnipiac River; the small tributary which bordered the southeastern side of the town was approximately ninety rods, or 1,485 feet from the center of the town.

Mirrored in the plan for New Haven was a conception of the city which approximated more closely than Boston itself John Winthrop's "Citty upon a Hill." And, indeed, had the settlers who arrived with Winthrop and Deputy-Governor Thomas Dudley been able to agree on a location for the colony's central town before the threat of winter forced them to "plant dispersedly" where expedient, Winthrop's town, like Davenport's, might have resembled the biblical city in appearance, as well as attempted social and political organization. In the early days of December 1630, Winthrop and Dudley had agreed to establish a central town at a place between Roxbury and Boston which they would call "Newtown." However, few could be persuaded to relocate there, and Winthrop himself had his dismantled house brought to Boston the following year.[85] The "Essay on the Laying Out of Towns," probably written by Thomas Graves at the request of the General Court, suggests that Newtown, the colony's first intended central town, had been laid out according to a definite plan, a plan that resembled New Haven's in its regularity. Had subsequent towns of the Massachusetts Bay colony been laid out according to Graves' guidelines they too would have followed the plan of concentric squares used at New Haven.

Thus Boston, which soon grew to dominate the political, social, and economic life of the colony, may have been at its inception an aberration on the New England landscape. As the town matured into a young city its character was the antithesis of that which its founders had hoped to see flourish in New England. Its commercial vitality augured ill for the future of that imagined "Citty upon a Hill." That image, which lay memorialized, instead, along the banks of the Quinnipiac River, had been reinforced by the memory of the religious, political, and moral controversies between Court and Country in the England of James I and Charles I.

The Puritan township in New England was designed to preserve the social homogeneity, order, stability, and religious uniformity remembered of the nucleated settlements of rural England. Its imaginary representation was the tribal city of Old Jerusalem, the habitation of God's chosen people, a providential manifestation in prophetic history of the transcendant New Jerusalem of postscriptural and posthistorical time. Social diversity, moral innovation, heterogeneity of persons and ideas, and material and aesthetic display, were all attributes of urban life alien to the Puritan men and women who first settled in the New England wilderness. Thus they could only behold the Boston of the 1640's, as they had looked upon the London of the 1620's, with a fear that reached to the very marrow of their belief.

If the success of Boston meant, ironically, the failure of the Puritan image of a "Citty upon a Hill," so too would the rise of Philadelphia a century later signal the defeat of another man's image of the city, William Penn's "greene country towne." The founder of Philadelphia had been far more at home in the London of Restoration England than Winthrop would have been, and he was far better schooled in the arts and pleasures of urban life. But the Quaker leader looked upon the opportunity to engage in a "holy experiment" in the New World as a providential chance to bring to life once again the same memory of a traditional rural, hierarchical and God-loving world that had been one of the dreams of the founders of Massachusetts Bay.

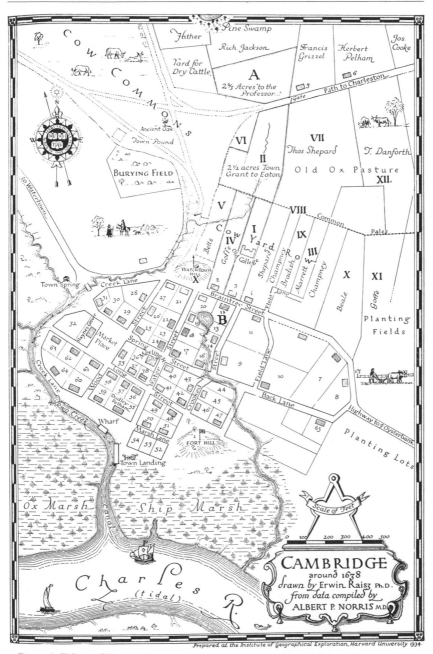

Figure 1. "Mapp of Cambridge around 1638," drawn by Dr. Raisz, from data compiled by Dr. Albert P. Norris. Reprinted from Samuel Eliot Morison, *The Founding of Harvard College* (1968). Courtesy Harvard University Press.

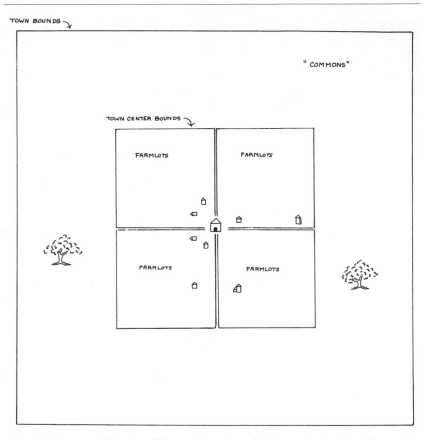

Figure 2. Conjectural drawing of Thomas Graves' standard town plan for Massachusetts Bay, ca. 1635. Prepared by the author.

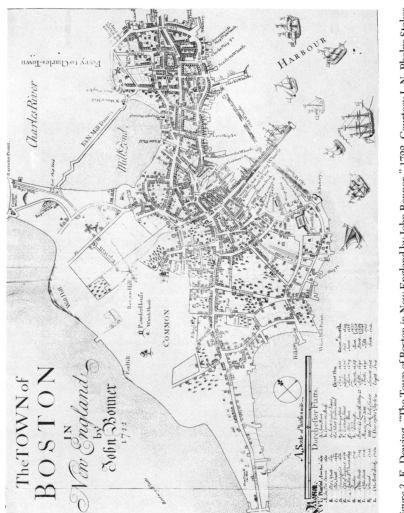

Figure 3. F. Dewing, "The Town of Boston in New England by John Bonner," 1722. Courtesy I. N. Phelps Stokes Collection, Prints Division, The New York Public Library, Astor, Lenox and Tilden Foundations.

Figure 4. "A North East View of the Great Town of Boston," attributed to William Burgis, 1723–1728. Courtesy Essex Institute, Salem, Massachusetts.

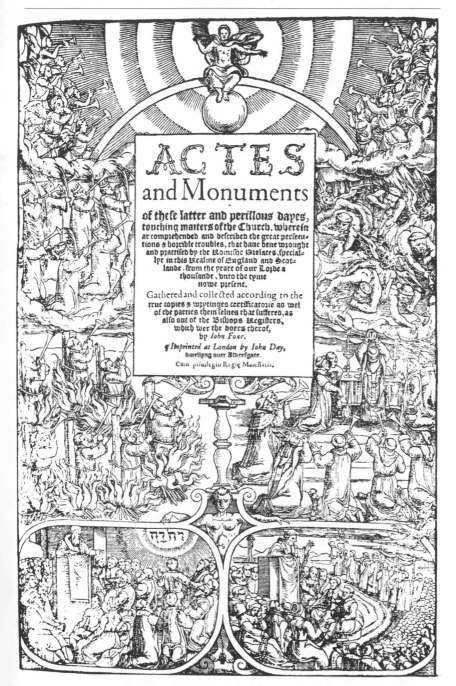

Figure 5. Title page of John Foxe, *Actes and Monuments of these Latter and Perilous Times,*
1563.

THE
NEWE TESTAMENT
OF OVR LORD
IESVS CHRIST,

Conferred diligently with the Greke, and beſt appro-
ued tranſlacions in diuers languages.

EXOD. XIIII, VER. XIII.

FEARE YE NOT, STAND STIL, AND BE-
holde the ſaluacion of the Lord, which he wil ſhewe to you this day.

THE LORD SHAL FIGHT FOR YOU:
therefore holde you your peace, Exod.14, vers.14.

AT GENEVA.

PRINTED BY ROVLAND HALL.

M. D. LX.

Figure 6. Title page, *The Geneva Bible,* 1650. Courtesy University of Wisconsin
Press.

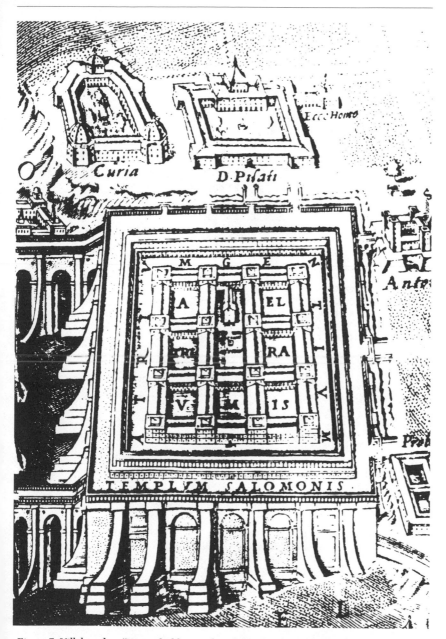

Figure 7. Villalpandus, "View of Old Jerusalem," detail, 1604. Originally published in *The Journal of the Society of Architectural Historians*, XXXIV (May 1975), 147–149; © copyright 1975, Society of Architectural Historians (USA).

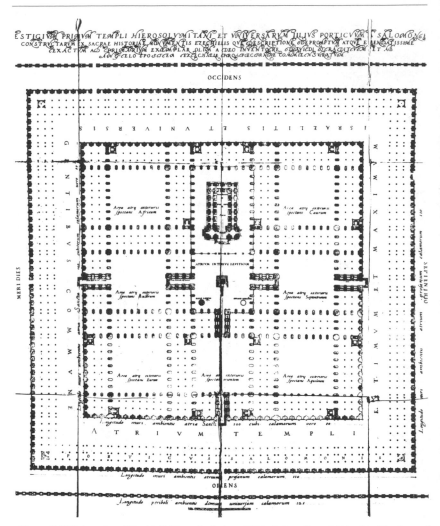

Figure 8. Villalpandus, "Ezekiel's Temple," plan, 1604. Originally published in *The Journal of the Society of Architectural Historians*, XXXIV (May 1975), 147–149; © copyright 1975, Society of Architectural Historians (USA).

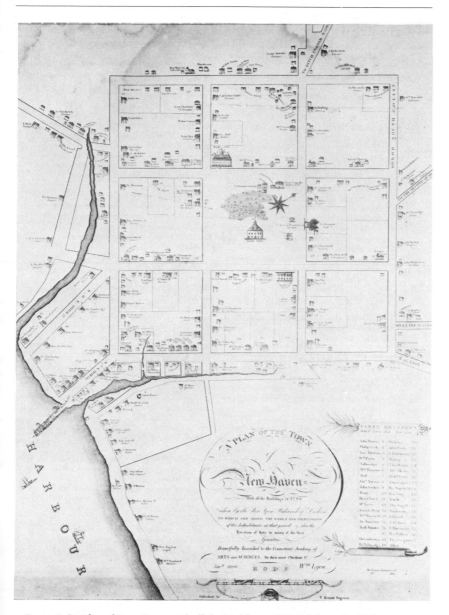

Figure 9. "A Plan of New Haven with all the buildings of 1748," drawn by William Lyon, published by T. Kensett, 1806. Courtesy New York Historical Society.

The porcions.　　　　Ezekiél.

b That Is, the portion of the grounde, w̄ they ſhal ſeparat & appoint to the Lord, which ſhalbe deuided in to thre paries for thePrieſts, for the prince & for the citie.

7 And by the border of Reubén, from the Eaſt quarter vnto the Weſt quarter, *a porcion* for Iudáh.

8 And by the border of Iudáh frō the Eaſt parte vnto the Weſt parte b ſhalbe the offring which thei ſhal offre of fiue & twentie thouſand *redes* broade, and of length as one of the *other* partes, from the Eaſt ſide vnto the Weſt ſide, and the Sanctuarie ſhal be in the middes of it.

9 The oblacion that ye ſhal offre vnto the Lord, ſhalbe of fiue and twentie thouſand long, and of ten thouſand the breadth.

10 And for them, *euen* for the Prieſts ſhal be this holy oblacion, toward the North fiue and twentie thouſand *long*, and towarde the Weſt, ten thouſand broade, & toward the Eaſt ten thouſand broade, and towarde the South fiue and twentie thouſand long, and the Sanctuarie of the Lord ſhal be in the middes thereof.

Chap. 44.15.

11 *It ſhalbe* for the Prieſts that are ſanctified of the ſonnes of* Zadók, which haue kept my charge, which went not aſtray whē the children of Iſraél went aſtray, as the Leuites went aſtraye.

12 Therefore *this* oblacion of the land that is offred, ſhalbe theirs, *as* a thig moſte holie by the border of the Leuites.

13 And ouer againſt ȳ border of the Prieſts the Leuites *ſhal haue* fiue and twētie thouſand long, & ten thouſand broade : all the length *ſhalbe* fiue and twētie thouſand, and the breadth ten thouſand.

14 And thei ſhal not ſel of it, nether change it, nor abalienate the firſt frutes of the land: for it is holy vnto the Lord.

15 And the fiue thouſand that are left in ȳ breadth ouer againſt the fiue and twentie thouſand, ſhalbe a prophane place for the citie, for houſing, & for ſuburbes, and the citie ſhalbe in the middes thereof.

c Meaning, ȳ it ſhulde be ſquare.

16 And theſe ſhalbe the meaſures thereof, ȳ North parte fiue hūdreth and foure thouſand, and the South parte c fiue hūdreth & foure thouſand, and of the Eaſt parte fiue hundreth and foure thouſand, & the Weſt parte fiue hundreth, and foure thouſand.

17 And the ſuburbes of the citie ſhalbe towarde the North two hundreth and fiftie & towarde the South two hundreth & fiftie, and towarde the Eaſt two hundreth & fiftie, and towarde the Weſt two hundreth and fiftie.

18 And ȳ reſidue in length ouer againſt ȳ oblaciō of the holy porcion ſhalbe ten thou ſand Eaſt warde, and ten thouſand Weſt warde: and it ſhalbe ouer againſt the oblacion of the holy porcion, & the encreaſe thereof ſhal be for ſode vnto them that ſerue in the citie.

19 And thei that ſerue in the citie, ſhalbe of all ȳ tribes of Iſraél that ſhal ſerue therein.

d Euerie way it ſhalbe fyue & twēty thouſand.

20 All the oblacion ſhalbe fiue and twenty thouſand w̄ d fiue & twentie thouſand : you ſhal offre this oblacion foureſquare for the Sanctuarie, & for the poſſeſſion of ȳ citie.

21 And the reſidue ſhalbe for the prince on the one ſide & on the other of the oblacion of the Sanctuarie, and of the poſſeſſion of the citie, ouer againſt the fiue and twentie thouſand of the oblacion towarde the Eaſt border, & Weſtward ouer againſt the fiue & twētie thouſand toward the Weſt border, ouer againſt ſhalbe for the porcion of the prince: this ſhalbe the hōlie oblacion, & the houſe of the Sanctuarie ſhalbe in the middes thereof.

e So that Iudáh was on ȳ North ſide of the Princes & Leuites portions, and Beniamin on the Southſide.

22 Moreouer, from the poſſeſſion of the Leuites, & from ȳ poſſeſſion of the citie, that which is in ȳ middes ſhalbe ȳ princes: betwene the border e of Iudáh, & betwene the border of Beniamín ſhalbe the princes.

23 And the reſt of the tribes ſhalbe thus: frō the Eaſt parte vnto the Weſt parte Beniamín ſhalbe a porcion.

24 And by the border of Beniamín, from the Eaſt ſide vnto the Weſt ſide Simeón *a porcion*.

25 And by the border of Simeón frō the Eaſt parte vnto ȳ Weſt parte Iſhakár *a porcion*.

26 And by ȳ border of Iſhakár frō the Eaſt ſide vnto the Weſt, Zebulún *a porcion*.

27 And by the border of Zebulún from the Eaſt part vnto ȳ Weſt parte, Gad a porciō.

f Which is he re taken for dumea.
g Which was Iericho the ci tie of palme- trees.
h Meanīg, Niſus ȳ runneth into ȳ ſea called mediterra neum.

28 And by the border of Gad at the South ſide, toward f Tcmáth, the border ſhalbe euen frō g Tamár *vnto* the waters of Meribáth *in* Kadéſh, & to the h riuer, *that runneth* into the mayne ſea.

29 This is the land, which ye ſhal diſtribute vnto the tribes of Iſraél for inheritance, and theſe are their porcions, ſaith the Lord God.

30 And theſe are ȳ boundes of the citie, on the North ſide fiue hundreth, & foure thou ſand meaſures.

31 And the gates of the citie ſhalbe after ȳ names of the tribes of Iſraél, the gates Northward, one gate of Reubén, one gate of Iudáh, & one gate of Leuí.

32 And at the Eaſt ſide fiue hundreth and foure thouſand, and thre gates, & one gate of Ioſéph, one gate of Beniamín, *and* one gate of Dan.

33 And at the South ſide, fiue hundreth and foure thouſand meaſures, and thre portes, one gate of Simeón, one gate of Iſhakár, *and* one gate of Zebulún.

34 At the Weſt ſide, fiue hundreth & foure thouſand, *with* their thre gates, one gate of Gad, one gate of Aſhér, *and* one gate of Naphtalí.

35 *It was* rounde about eightene thouſand *meaſures*, and the name of the citie frō that day ſhalbe, " The Lord is there.

" Ebr. Iehouáh Shammáh.

Figure 10. Ezekiel 48: 7–35, from *The Geneva Bible*, 1650. Courtesy University of Wisconsin Press.

3

William Penn's *"Greene Country Towne"*

✿

The precocious growth of Philadelphia from the last city founded in the seventeenth-century English colonies in North America to the largest city in the colonies by the middle of the eighteenth century was an amazement to some of her earliest inhabitants. Her first historian, Gabriel Thomas, waxed poetic over the city's nascent grandeur in 1698, commending her thousand "stately" houses ("of Brick, generally three Stories high, after the Mode in London"), the nobility and beauty of her aspect, her "Schools of Learning," and the plenitude of her trades, all of which would soon make the city on the Delaware "a fine Figure in the World . . . a most Celebrated Emporium." "If anyone were to see Philadelphia who had not been there [before]," observed another newcomer in 1700, "he would be astonished beyond measure [to learn] that is was founded less than twenty years ago."[1]

The cultural and economic ascendancy of Philadelphia in the first half of the eighteenth century, made possible primarily by her fortunate location, has been amply described, and the visual aspect of the city did indeed soon reflect the prosperity of the provincial trade and service center.[2] And yet the Philadelphia of 1750 was no more a fulfillment of William Penn's vision of his "greene country towne" than was contemporary Boston the fruition of John Winthrop's hopes for his "Citty upon a Hill." William Penn's design for Philadelphia did not in fact anticipate an urban place but rather the recovery of a world rapidly receding into the memories of many Englishmen as urbanization began to characterize the landscape of late seventeenth-century England. In his plan for the distribution and the use of the vast lands of his province generally Penn hoped to perpetuate a traditional rural society ordered and stabilized by a common adherence to the principles of individual proprietorship and a consensus in social hierarchy and common religious conviction.

✿

The son of Sir William Penn the Admiral must have cut a fine figure when he approached Charles II in 1680 with a proposal to rid the realm of dissident Quakers while paying off a debt to his father with a grant to himself of a large tract of land in North America.[3] Sir William has sought to make a true English gentleman out of his son by sending him to Chigwell to learn Greek and Latin, to Oxford, and then to Paris, whence he returned with "much of the vanity of the French garb, and affected manner of speech and gait." The young man, regarded as "modish" by his contemporaries, learned to fence and "jump" well enough to amaze the Indians. After a Continental tour he studied briefly at Lincoln's Inn and then was sent to manage his father's vast estate at Shangarry in Ireland. He was presented to the courts of Louis XIV and the czar and became a friend of Charles II, James II, and William III.[4]

Unfortunately from the elder Penn's point of view, the most careful upbringing in gentility could effect but the outer man in his son. The religious emotions which stirred within the boy of twelve did not pass with adolescence. While in Ireland Penn was exposed to the teachings of George Fox and conversion to Quakerism soon followed. Since Quakers refused to take the oath of supremacy required to declare their innocence when arrested for gathering in Non-Conformist assemblies, Penn found himself in prison in 1668, 1669, and again in 1671. Yet while the penalties of the Quaker way heightened Penn's sensitivity to religious toleration, his conversion was not the affront to his aristocratic upbringing that his father perceived.

Stoicism has always been present in Renaissance courtesy literature, as it has been in ancient views of urbanity, but in the early seventeenth century the ideal of a self-sustaining inner strength took on a new importance in the literature of gentlemanly conduct, fostered perhaps by the gradual spread of religious nonconformity. The state of his soul became as important to the gentleman as his prerogatives before men. As Richard Brathwaite instructed in the opening pages of *The English Gentleman* (1630), "the greatest signall and symbol of Gentry: is rather expressed by goodness of Person, than greatness of Place." Later seventeenth-century writers like Sir Matthew Hale would also stress, as Brathwaite had, the importance of useful activity. "Every man," advised Margaret Cavendish, Duchess of Newcastle (*The Worlds Olio*, 1655), "should like a Bee, bring Honey to the Hive, and not, like the effeminat [sic] Drone, suck out the sweet, and idely live upon the Heroick labour of others." The ideal of service to mankind was reaffirmed as a Christian duty rather than simply a justification for nobility in an hierarchical world order.[5]

The followers of George Fox shared with other Puritans a concern with first-hand religious experience and the rejection of ecclesiastical formalism and hierarchies. Professing a love for all men and refusing to recognize distinctions among men, the Quakers may have given added impetus to the leveling impulses which stirred throughout seventeenth-century England. But William Penn's conversion to Quakerism did not extend fully to its political or social implications. His view of society and his place in it remained that of a traditional gentleman landlord, and while he preached simplicity his tastes remained more suited to the courtier who remained loyal to James II after 1688 and whose proprietary was preserved against parliamentary assaults from 1701 to 1705 largely through Tory support.[6] While he despaired of the "sumptuous apparel, rich unguents, delicate washes, stately furniture, costly cookery . . . masques, music, plays, romances" of the world of Restoration England, he nonetheless rejected the notion that the recovery of the true Christianity of primitive times could be brought about by "a recluse life," for such was "unnatural," a "lazy, umprofitable self-denial, burdensome to others." Christ's cross was to be borne in this world.[7] This position, though sincerely arrived at, nonetheless also enabled him to maintain the social attitudes and associations to which he had been born. Thus was laid the foundation of that blend of reactionary religious radicalism and social conservatism which would characterize William Penn's aspirations for his proprietary colony, as well as his planning for the city of Philadelphia.

When Charles II granted Pennsylvania to Penn in 1681 he provided the gentle courtier with an opportunity to create the kind of world he believed would nourish the Quaker spirit and his own sense of civility. Young William Penn's own "new world" was essentialy nostalgic or conservative in conception. Dominated by a rural economy and a feudal, or hierarchical social order, Pennsylvania would have been a recapitulation of the vanishing English countryside had its founder's vision been fulfilled. It would have been free not only from religious oppression but from the corruptive influences of the emergent urban life of the period. Penn perceived that life dimly as one in which wealth through finance capitalism and the social dislocation of congested, transient and heterogenous urban populations fostered the deterioration of a virtuous and deferential rural society. This perception, manifest in his planning for Pennsylvania and Philadelphia, was the common thread binding his political and religious views with his aspirations as a promoter of a vast colonial enterprise.

As William Penn looked out upon the world he saw an hierarchically ordered creation of God. Just as God created the stars in the heavens in "their several degrees of Glory," so also on earth do we find "subordination and dependency" among the "Trees of the Wood, from the Cedar to the Bramble . . . among the Beasts, from the Lyon to the Cat; and among Mankind itself, from the King to the Scavenger . . . he has not

81

rang'd or dignified them upon the level."[8] Some are meant to be ruled;
the government of some men over others is divinely ordained, for
"Higher Ranks of Men are but the Trustees of Heaven for the Benefit of
less Mortals." In this, as in other aspects of Penn's thought, however,
contemporary experience attached itself to an old point of view; those
"higher ranks" of men are not kings, lords, and bishops, who claim their
divine appointment through inheritance, spiritual or material, but those
who have been "raised above Necessity or any Trouble to Live, that they
might have more Time and Ability to Care for Others." Inversely, some
are meant to be servants, and "a true servant is Diligent, Secret and
Respectful: More Tender of his Master's Honour and Interest, than of his
own Profit."[9] This hierarchical world should be governed by a modern
aristocracy of wealth and talent. William Penn was such a man, and he
looked upon Pennsylvania as "my country . . . God . . . has given it
me."[10]

A world of masters and servants, patriarchs like the Penns and their de-
pendents, was one which could not well endure the social dislocations of a
money economy. And the arena in which money made masters of those
who had been servants, or reduced to servility those who had been
masters on the land, was the city. There was little moderation in Penn's
discourse against "the Town" which became an important part of his rationale for colonization in his promotional tract of 1681, "Some Account of
the Province of Pennsylvania." After pointing out that the increase in
trade and shipping engendered by plantations results in a net gain in
wealth to the colonizing country, Penn asserted that the alleged decline
in the English population was due not to the magnetic pull of colonies,
but of towns, and especially of London. There is little moderation in this
Quaker discourse against "the Town" which nurtures the "Pride of the
Age" and lures unto itself noblemen and gentry who, in turn, bring with
them "country-People . . . addicted to . . . Gentlemens Service." De-
bilitated by the "soft and delicate Usage" of town life and "Effeminated by
a lazy and luxurious Living" the newcomer to town, often "resorting to
London," is soon rendered unfit to return to the "Labour of a Farming
Life." At the same time, because of the "excess and sloth of the Age," few
servants in a town household can afford to marry and raise families. The
young men "chose rather to vent their Lusts at an evil Ordinary," or become "Souldiers . . . Gamesters, or Highwaymen" while the women
"too frequently dress themselves for a bad market." Meanwhile, the
countryside is depopulated and its toils become all the more unremitting
"for want of hands," which further discourages the natural increase of
families and leads more country men to seek their livelihoods elsewhere.
Thus it is that "both the Stock of the Nation decays and the Issue is corrupted." It is against the background of this introduction, overcast as it is

by a long Juvenalian shadow, that one must read Penn's proposal to "Industrious Husbandmen and Day-Labourers," "Laborious Handicrafts," "Ingenious Spirits," "younger Brothers of small Inheritances" and "Men of universal Spirits," to settle his "good and fruitful Land."[11]

The first proprietor of Pennsylvania believed that cities augured ill for the physical, moral, and spiritual well-being of the people. "Let my children be husbandmen and housewifes," Penn wrote his wife on August 4, 1682; "tis industrious healthy, honest, and of good example like Abraham & the holy antients, who pleas'd god . . . this leads to consider the works of god and nature of things . . . and diverts the mind from being taken up with the vain arts and inventions of a luxurious world . . . I prefer [for them] a decent mansion of an hundred pounds per Annum. before ten thousand pounds in London. or such like place. in a way of trade."[12] William Penn shared the same antipathy toward the city that has surfaced periodically throughout Western literature, but became more pronounced at the close of the seventeenth century.[13]

Wheras the city seemed to represent in microcosm all the foibles of an artificial, man-made world, especially liable to human corruption, the country promised the recovery of innocence, sincerity, honor, and, because of its association with nature, access to the sublime truths of the universe—an aspiration especially sympathetic to the Quaker spirit. Penn wrote that he preferred the privacy and retirement of country life where one could contemplate "the Works of God" which are a constant reminder of His "Power, Wisdom and Goodness." In cities one sees "but the Works of Men" which are, "for the most part, his Pride, Folly and Excess." The country "makes a better Subject for our Contemplation" because God's works are "for use," whereas man's works are "chiefly, for Ostentation and Lust." The only righteous cause that should draw a man from the privacy of country life was public service, for though it be "servile and noisy," "the Publick must be served; and they that do it well, deserve publick Marks of Honour and Profit."[14]

The world that William Penn sought to re-create in Pennsylvania was a world into which the corruptive powers of the city should not reach. By the terms of his patent he became the proprietor of a vast feudal domain of approximately two thousand square miles. He held his land from the king "in free and common Socage by fealty only." He was empowered to erect manorial estates and courts, to establish whatever form of goverment he chose, and to subinfeudate to one degree.[15] The terms on which he offered land to prospective settlers in Pennsylvania suggest that he hoped that political and social authority in the province would rest in the hands of a substantial landed gentry. While rentiers would be confined to amounts "not exceeding Two hundred Acres" and servants would be allocated fifty acres of their masters' portions (and granted outright the same amount when their terms expired), purchasers were offered "shares" of 5,000 acres. The first fifty purchasers of 5,000-acre shares would, according to Penn's first draft of the "First Frame of Government" (1682), constitute the upper chamber of his proposed provincial legislature, which held the power of veto over all legislation and of the appointment of public officers. Seats in the upper chamber would devolve upon the heirs of the first fifty purchasers.[16]

While the people of Pennsylvania, promised its founder in 1681, would be secure in "the Rights and Freedoms of England (the best and largest in Europe)."[17] Penn's Charter from Charles II nonetheless reserved to the proprietor extensive powers. He retained the right to initiate and promulgate all laws as well as to the rents on all the lands, of which he was absolute proprietor except for the traditional reservation to the Crown of one-fifth of all gold and silver found within the bounds of the grant and two beaver skins annually. In addition Penn could appoint provincial judges and officials, regulate currency, levy taxes, and take whatever measures he chose to the benefit of the colony provided, of course, those measures did not conflict with the laws of England.[18] The "Frame of Government" which was hammered out of seventeen successive drafts in London during 1682 granted legislative, executive, and judicial power to the combined governor's council and upper house of the legislature. While the seventy-two members of the Provincial Council could be elected by the freemen of Pennsylvania—liberally defined in the "Laws Agreed Upon in England" of the same year as any Christian who had purchased one hundred acres of land "and cultivated ten acres thereof," servants released from indenture who held fifty acres of land, and "every inhabitant, artificer, or other resident . . . that pays scot and lot"[19]— common understanding would assure that "only men of considerable estate, demonstrably successful in their private affairs and proven leaders at the local level, could expect to reach the council."[20]

When Penn was confronted with the task of devising a structure for the government of Pennsylvania the formulae he chose were similar to those advocated by the Whig Republicans of the seventeenth century. Parallels between the 1676 "Frame of Government for New Jersey," possibly drawn up by Penn, the "First Frame of Pennsylvania," and the proposals in James Harrington's *Oceana*, suggest that Penn may have been strongly influenced by Harrington's views. Those similarities are the decimal division of the land (New Jersey), secret balloting, rotation of officials (Council members in Pennsylvania), and the separation of the functions of debate and result between two representative assemblies.[21] This later provision was Harrington's way of assuring that the interest of neither would prevail over the other, as he illustrated with his little fable of two girls, each of whom wanted the largest portion of a single cake and could resolve their dilemma, he advised, only by the one girl dividing the cake and the other having the first choice.[22]

Penn shared with Harrington the presumption of a continuing polity based upon an agrarian economy, but there is nothing to suggest that he was more than marginally concerned with the Whig theorist's interest in the ways that the greater dispersion in land ownership many be conducive to a more balanced distribution in the exercise of political power. The purpose of Harrington's Agrarian Law had been to break up large landed estates into units not having more than £ 2,000 annual income to prevent the amassing of an excess of power into the hands of a small landowning aristocracy. Rotation in office, the ballot, and mutual control between debating and approving assemblies were only the means for Harrington of assuring a republican polity devised through a redistribution of land. William Penn, however, undertook the settlement of Pennsylvania virtually as a feudal lord. It was Penn who created the freemen of Pennsylvania by selling them parcels of his grant. Had he been able to find purchasers for 10,000 acre units as he originally intended,[23] the freemen of Pennsylvania might have been mostly large landowners, the famed "liberal" constitution of Pennsylvania a document which essentially confirmed a landowning aristocracy in power, and the spirit and republican purpose of Harrington's *Oceana* wholly defeated. Penn's real attitude was perhaps best revealed when in 1686 he proposed that the Pennsylvania legislature repeal all existing laws, with the intention of later re-enactment, to avoid objections to them by the Lords of Trade when they came up for quinquennial review in 1687. If any members of the legislature should refuse, he advised Thomas Lloyd, then president of the Council, "lett them know how much they are in my power not I in theirs."[24]

In making an assessment of any constitutional document one must reflect not only upon how and by whom the laws are made, but to what purposes they can be made. While a society may be made just by the rule of law consented to by the people, it is inherently necessary that the law itself be just; constitutional processes and principles are a way of ensuring that statutory law can not become unjust, as, for example, the Federal Constitution's prohibition against "cruel and unusual punishments." A man may be unjustly condemned by the statutory consent of a majority of the "people"; the statute is not the less unjust for that. This was the reason for the struggle over the Bill of Rights in the opening hours of the American republic. Herein lay the crucial shadow of difference between

Penn's patriarchal and biblical view of law and the republicanism of the Whigs, who were as concerned with the uses of the law as with its origins. For Algernon Sidney and other seventeenth-century republicans rule by law was the necessary guarantee of the people's liberties, and for Sidney in particular, if those liberties were violated, the people had a right to rebel.[25]

For Penn rule by law was also the measure of a just polity, but the law was ultimately an instrument of Christian order and moral discipline, and thus the burden of interpretation would always belong to the law-giver and -maker. "Rulers are not a terror to good works," advised Penn, "but to Evil." "Lust prevailing upon duty," wrote the Quaker Puritan, man "made a lamentable breach upon . . . the law." Therefore, "such as would not live conformable to the holy law within, should fall under the reproof and correction, of the just law without, in a judicial administration." Government exists by "divine right . . . for two ends; first, to terrify evil-doers; secondly, to cherish those that do well; which gives government a life beyond corruption, and makes it as durable as the world."[26] Penn declared his indifference to actual constitutional forms in the text of the "First Frame" itself when he wrote:

> For particular frames and models . . . I will say nothing . . . the age is too nice and difficult for it; there being nothing the wits of men are more busy and divided upon . . . I choose to solve the controversy with this small distinction . . . any government is free to the people under it (whatever the frame) where the laws rule and the people are a party to those laws.

And yet a goverment of laws alone was not for Penn the final guarantee of a good and just society. Like John Milton and Sidney, Penn never abandoned the belief that some kind of an elite, or assembly of the better sort, was necessary:

> Lastly, when all is said, there is hardly one frame of government in the world so ill designed by its founders, that in good hands would not do well enough . . . though good laws do well, good men do better.

The social outlook of the manorial lord in Ireland and the Puritan hope of "Godly Rule" were united in Penn's own confusion of men of estate with men of Christian virtue.[27]

In the Body of Laws passed in an assembly at Chester in 1682 ("The Great Law") one hears, rather than the voices of English classical republicanism, the echoes of John Winthrop in William Penn's assertion that the purpose of the Laws is to "preserve true Christian and Civil Liberty, in opposition to all Unchristian, Licentious, and unjust practices."[28] The "Laws Agreed Upon in England" (1682), after declaring that the Provincial Council and General Assembly shall be elected by the freemen of the province,[29] had called for trial by a jury of twelve and grand jury indictment in capital cases, and ensured religious liberty to "all persons living in this province, who confess and acknowledge the one almighty and eternal God, to be the creator, upholder and ruler of the World." It then proceeded to list a frightful host of moral offenses and offenders who shall be "severely punished":

> scandalous and malicious reporters, backbiters, defamers and spreaders of false news . . . swearing, cursing, lying, prophane talking, drunkenness, drinking of healths, obscene words, incest, sodomy, rapes, whoredome, fornication, and other uncleanness (not to be repeated) . . . stage plays, cards, dice, may-games, masques, revels, bull-baitings, cock-fightings, bear baitings and the like, which excite the people to rudeness, cruelty, looseness and irreligion.

Strict moral and religious discipline, so essential to the purposes of the colony's founder that he would specify its particulars in the fundamental laws, was necessary because "careless and corrupt administration of justice draws the wrath of God upon magistrates, so the wildness and looseness of the people provoke the indignation of God against the country."[30]

Roughly one-half of the chapters of the "Great Law," which was all inclusive in its provisions for a provincial judicial system and its commercial regulations, was devoted to what we today would regard as moral or religious crimes—that is, offenses not against the person or property of other citizens but against Quaker mores and religious beliefs. Most of these offenses were the same as those listed in the "Laws Agreed" to in England but specified and their punishments indicated. Significantly the religious requirement for citizenship was also more detailed. There shall be no labor on the sabbath not simply so that "they may the better dispose themselves to worship God according to their common understandings," but in order that the people "may the better dispose themselves to read the Scriptures of truth at home, or frequent such meetings of religious worship abroad, as may best sute their respective understandings." Furthermore, "all officers and persons Commissionated and employed in the service of the goverment in this Province, and all Members and Deputies elected to serve in the Assembly thereof, and all that have a Right to elect such Deputies, shall be such as profess and declare they believe in Jesus Christ to be the son of God, the Saviour of the World."[31]

Not only was righteous conduct a significant preoccupation of the author of the first "Body of Laws of Pennsylvania," but there was great potential for the frustration of political discourse in its prohibition against "scandalous and malicious reporters, backbiters, defamers and spreaders of false news." Neither in the General Assembly (which could not debate measures presented to it) nor on the public by-ways, did the modern conviction that truth is best arrived at through the open interchange of views enjoy the sanction of law. The liberties which William Penn offered "his people" were those claimed by an oppressed religious minority and, like the Christian and civil liberties advocated by John Winthrop, the liberty only to be a good Christian.

✿

The agrarian world Penn envisioned for Pennsylvania would be bound into a localized social order through a network of rural settlements. While he was not indifferent to the necessity of tradesmen and craftsmen to a rural society he hoped that such persons could be scattered throughout villages and townships. Through an initial requirement that "every man shall be bound to plant or man so much of his share of Land as shall be set out and surveyed within three years after it is so set out and surveyed," he sought to avoid "Wilderness vacancies" and achieve, through his system of townships, "Society, Assistance, Busy Commerce, Instruction of Youth, Government of Peoples Manners, Conveniency of Religious Assembly, Encouragement of Mechanics" and "distinct and beaten Roads."[32] Each township, according to Penn's scheme, would be square in configuration and contain 5,000 acres composed of at least ten families holding parcels of five hundred acres each, "the regulation of the Country being a family to each five hundred acres."

A "village," for which five hundred acres were to be reserved, would be placed in the center of each township. Assuming a settlement of ten families, each village homestead would contain fifty acres regularly laid out contiguously in the form of a square. Each house would be placed at the edge of the village square, the houselots meeting at the center and adjacent to 450-acre farm lots "so that conveniency of Neighborhood is made agreeable with that of the Land." A second proposal would have placed the village house lots opposite one another along a road running through the center of the township with farm lots extending beyond.[33] One need look no further for the conceptual origin of Penn's own plan for Philadelphia than his scheme for township settlement, the principal difference between Penn's plan and the New England township being that no township lands in Pennsylvania were held in common.

One of the responsibilities reserved to the governor and the provincial council in Penn's "First Frame of Government" of 1682 was that it was

88

they who should "at all times settle and order the situation of cities, ports and towns in every county, modelling therin all public buildings, streets, and market places, and shall appoint all necessary roads and highways." The proprietary government was thus given the authority to implement the provision of the "Certain Conditions or Concessions" agreed to by William Penn and the first "adventurers and purchasers" of Pennsylvania in July 1681 that as soon as they had arrived in the province "a quantity of land or Ground plat shall be laid out for a large Town or City."[34] In September of that year Penn instructed his commissioners, William Crispin, John Bezar, and Nathanial Allen "to settle a great Towne" as soon as the first comers has been provided with food and shelter.[35] By the end of 1683 Surveyor-General Thomas Holme had completed the survey and laying out of the city and published a detailed description of the streets and allocation of city lots accompanied by a map or "portraiture" (Figure 11). Holme's map shows the familiar grid suspended between the banks of the Delaware and Schuylkill rivers substantially as it remained throughout the eighteenth century.[36] Because Penn in his "Instructions" specified that the streets of the city be "uniforme downe to the Water" and that "the Houses built be in a line," while Holme, in turn, wrote that the city portrayed in his "Short Advertisement" had been "so ordered by the Governor's Care," scholarly convention has regarded the Philadelphia city plan of 1683 as identical with William Penn's intentions.[37]

However, a close examination of Penn's "Concessions" and "Instructions," as a surveyor might have read them and without regard to the city plan which Holme ultimately prepared in 1683, suggests that the "city" conceived by the two men differed markedly. The city plan that Holme described in his "Short Advertisement" is a rectangle roughly two miles in length and one mile in breadth. It is intersected by two axial avenues, Broad Street and High Street, which meet in a central square on a slight elevation. The remaining twenty-seven streets—seven crossing the plan lengthwise and twenty crossing it from river front to river front, are arranged in a grid. In addition each quarter of the city plan contains a square of eight acres. Rectangular city lots, which were sized in direct proportion to the total quantity of land taken up by the first purchasers to whom they were first allocated, were arranged so that the narrower boundary faced the streets. The largest lots were placed on the Front and High streets while smaller lots were placed on the "Backward Streets." In its general configuration, Holme's plan is similar to Robert Newcourt's 1666 plan for the rebuilding of London. And yet, as we shall see below, there are significant conceptual differences between the two plans.

Holme, a Yorkshireman who had spent much of his life in Ireland, was also undoubtedly familiar with the grid plan used in the establishment of the Ulster towns of 1609–1613, especially Londonderry, by the London–

based Irish Society.[38] Although the smallest lots in Holme's plan were, at one-half acre, large enough "for House, Garden and small Orchard" according to Penn's order that Philadelphia be a "greene country towne, which will never be burnt,"[39] Holme's plan is inescapably urban in conception. The scale and contiguousness of the lots and their location, along with the streets, according generally to traffic patterns rather than topography, indicate a nucleated urban unit. Moreover, the spatial dimensions of the plan are determined by the needs of trade, on the one hand, and the centrality of government in the city's functional role, on the other. It is this later role, Philadelphia as a seat of government—represented in Holme's placement of a ten-acre square at the center of the city for the location of "Meeting House, Assembly or State House, Market House, School House and Several other Buildings for public concerns"[40]—that might designate Philadelphia as a city. However, the extant evidence suggests that the "city" Penn conceived and which was suggested to and agreed upon with the First Purchasers, bears little resemblance to the final outcome.

The nature of the city that William Penn intended to be created at Philadelphia is best revealed by his expectations as of the year in which he promised the great town as a bonus to Pennsylvania's First Purchasers. The importance he gave to the location of Philadelphia—that it be placed where the Delaware River "is most navigable, high, dry, and healthy . . . where most ships may best ride, of deepest draught of water, if possible to Load, or unload at ye Bank or Key side"[41]—indicates that Philadelphia was to serve primarily as a market outlet for Pennsylvania's rural economy. However, lest Philadelphia become another London, the same gentry which governed the countryside would also rule in the town. In the "Certain Conditions or Concessions" Penn promised that lots in Philadelphia would be reserved to the First Purchasers who would acquire them at the ratio of ten acres for every five hundred acres purchased.[42]

Although William Penn later sold land in units smaller than five thousand acres—the mode average size of parcels sold by 1700 was only five hundred acres—he had originally hoped that each share sold would be in the amount of five thousand acres. Thus, had his initial expectation been fulfilled, Philadelphia would have consisted of one hundred vast "town" lots of one hundred acres each.[43] Even if we grant that Penn was prepared to sell Pennsylvania land in parcels considerably less than five thousand acres, 44 percent of those who had bought land from him by 1682 acquired at least five hundred acres each [44] and were thus entitled, according to the "Certain Conditions and Concessions" of 1681, to ten-acre lots in Philadelphia. Had Penn's first draft of his "Frame of Government" gone into effect, the same First Purchasers who controlled the provincial legislature through the upper house could also have been the exclusive propietors of Pennsylvania's capital city. This interpretation of the "conditions" proposed in "Some Account of the Province of Pennsylvania" and of the "Certain Conditions and Concessions," both drawn up in 1681, is borne out by Penn's instructions to his commissioners of 1681 for the laying out of Philadelphia. "The proportion in the said Towne," ordered the Proprietor, "is to be . . . every share of five Thousand Acres shall have an hundred Acres of Land, out of y^t ten Thousand Acres" which was intended as "the bounds and extent of the Libertyes of the said Towne." If, however, "more than one be concerned in the share, as it may easily fall out," the commissioners were to divide the town portion as the purchasers wished. [45]

The configuration of Philadelphia prescribed in Penn's instructions further indicates that the proprietor did not envision the appearance of a city either in population density or predominant nonagricultural activity. Rather than draw country people away from the virtuous and industrious cultivation of the soil as did London, Philadelphia would be but an extension of the countryside. "Be sure to Settle the figure of the Towne so as y^t the streets hereafter may be uniforme downe to the Water form the Country bounds," wrote Penn, "each share to have fifty Poles [825' or 251 m] upon ye Front to ye River, and ye rest Backward."[46] Had Thomas Holme carried out Penn's instructions and had Penn succeeded in selling one hundred shares of 5,000 acres each initially, Philadelphia's streets would have run parallel down to the water; they might have been 825 feet apart and bound by town lots one mile in length (825' × 1 mile = 100 acres). There would not have been the rectangularly laid cross-streets which result from Holme's grid plan. Rather, Philadelphia would have consisted of a row of one hundred strip lots of a hundred acres each, the whole 15.63 miles in length along the Delaware River and one mile back from the river, or 10,000 acres. Finally, each house was to be set "in ye middle of its platt as to the breadth way of it, that so there may be ground on each side, for Gardens or Orchards or fields [sic], y^t it may be a greene country towne. . . ."[47]

The residential squares which appear in Holme's plan were not a part of Penn's instructions—not envisioning a densely built urban place residential squares would have been a superfluity—nor, indeed, did the proprietor anticipate a large central square. The center of the city that Penn envisioned lay not at a high point between the Delaware and Schuylkill rivers but "in the middle of the Key" on the Delaware. "Market and State houses" would be built there, much as they had been located in Boston, and flanked on either side by a line of houses running lengthwise a quarter of a mile from the water's edge. What Penn did expect to see at the center of Philadelphia, that is, in the middle of the strips of town lots running down to the Delaware River, was a three hundred–acre estate belonging to himself in the center of which would be the "scituation" of his own house (Figure 12).[48] The "great Town or City" that William Penn planned thus did not resemble Londonderry or Richard Newcourt's 1666 plan for the rebuilding of London so much as it resembled the traditional strip pattern of the New England village such as one finds at Providence, Rhode Island (1638) where "long, narrow home lots" ran down to the waterfront and "farm fields in the customary New England pattern were allotted beyond the village home lot boundaries."[49]

It has been suggested, on the strength of the second provision in the "Certain Conditions," (viz. "that the land in the Town be laid out together after the proportion of ten thousand acres of the whole country, that is two hundred acres, if the place will bear it") that Penn did in fact conceive of two distinct areas as laid out by Holme—"a greene country towne" consisting of 10,000 acres and a smaller town, or commercial center, of two-hundred acres.[50] However, there is no corroborating reference in Penn's own writings to a separate commercial center of two hundred acres. In the same document in which this provision appears Penn promised ten-acre lots in his "first great Town or City" to every purchaser of five hundred acres. Had Penn intended that Philadelphia be but two hundred acres the entire city would have been quickly taken up by the first twenty purchasers of five hundred acres. Moreover the three hundred–acre seat he instructed his commissioners to reserve for him in the center of the city would have been larger than the city itself. On the other hand, if Penn had intended his "greene country towne" to include the area encompassing the Liberty Lands from the start, he would have violated his own chief requirement for the location of the city—that it front on the Delaware where it was "most navigable, high, dry, and healthy." The Liberty Lands, as they appear on an early map by Holme (c. 1687) barely front on the Delaware at all, and then only to the north of the city where high banks discouraged the erection of wharves.

A further indication that Penn expected that lots *within* Philadelphia (not including the Liberty Lands) might be as much as one-hundred acres in size and would run the entire length of the town back from the river can be found in his letter to the Free Society of Traders of August 16, 1683. "Your Provincial Settlements both within and without the Town," Penn wrote, "for Situation and Soil, are without exception: Your City-Lot is an whole Street, and one side of a Street, from River to River, containing near one hundred Acres . . . which is besides your Four Hundred Acres in the City-Liberties, part of your Twenty Thousand Acres in the Country.[51]

A more likely explanation of the second provision of the "Certain Conditions" is that Penn was here merely indicating the proportion of town to country lands generally, since the ratio of two hundred acres is 2 percent of ten thousand acres, the same percentage specified throughout Penn's proposals and instructions regarding the laying out of Philadelphia. A good indication of the sort of city the First Purchasers thought they had agreed to with William Penn in 1681 can be gotten from their reaction to his maneuvers to adjust his land policy to Thomas Holme's plan.

The quarrels which ensued upon the proprietor's apportionment of Philadelphia lots in 1682 suggest that the First Purchasers took the provisions of the "Certain Conditions" and "Instructions" to the proprietary commissioners of 1681 to mean what they said. It was their understanding, they argued, that a town of 10,000 acres had been reserved to them exclusively as an unencumbered bonus for their land purchases. These early purchasers thus objected to Penn's later position that land in the city was granted gratuitously by the proprietary, a point he adhered to to explain critical discrepencies in the understood terms of land tenure in the city. Not only was it discovered in 1684 that city lots would be subject to an additional quitrent, but Penn insisted that land tenure in Philadelphia was "as of our manor of Springettesberry" (Penn's manor in the northern Liberties), with its uncertain conditions and privileges, rather than the more conventional term of freehold tenure, "as of Windsor." Moreover, the failure of the proprietor to issue the city a charter before 1701 was interpreted as a further sign that he did not intend to honor the conditions of purchase in the "Certain Conditions and Concessions" of 1681.[52]

Although Penn looked for much of his early support for the Pennsylvania undertaking to Quaker merchants,[53] the proprietor himself was not a merchant and was suspicious of the kind of society produced by mercantile capitalism. His own economic values were those of a man whose fortune depended on the land, as is suggested by the criterion he offered as a measure of the growing prosperity of Philadelphia: "the Improvement of the place is best measur'd by the advance of value upon every man's lot . . . the worst Lot in the Town, without any Improvement upon it, is worth four times more than it was when it was lay'd out, and the best forty." Even absent owners ("though it seems unequal") could enjoy the "advantage" or rising real estate values in Philadelphia.[54] It is probable that Penn never envisioned for Philadelphia a more complicated economic function than the city in fact had until about 1750; that is, as a port for the export of provisions produced by the rich Pennsylvania hinterland and for the importation of manufactured goods trans-shipped through the colonial ports of Boston and New York. Confined to a community of "small traders" until the middle of the eighteenth century,

Penn's great town need not herself become a large center of capital and manufactures with all the social and moral dangers that implied to her founder. [55]

❦

Geographic reality conspired with human nature to frustrate the proprietor's designs for Philadelphia. William Penn's commissioners soon discovered that much of the land between New Castle, Delaware and the confluence of the Schuylkill and Delaware rivers, or at Upland where Penn had wished the town located, either belonged to other owners reluctant to give it up or did not satisfy the proprietor's requirement that the town be located on a "high, dry, and healthy" site. As a result Holme laid out the town on a 1,200-acre site where it lies today. Why he followed the grid plan which appeared in the "Short Advertisement" can only be conjectured. However, it was clear that the site of 1682 would not accommondate the 10,000-acre expanse, with town lots 825 feet in breadth and one mile in depth, which Penn had originally anticipated. Penn himself offered an explanation for the changed configuration of the town when he wrote in his "Further Account" of 1685 that "tho this Town seemed at first contrived for the Purchasers of the first hundred shares . . . . yet few going, and that their absence might not Check the Improvement of the Place, and Strangers that flockt to us be thereby Excluded, I added that half of the Town, which lies on the Skulkill, that we might have Room for present and after Commers, that were not of that number."[56]

When Penn arrived in Pennsylvania on October 27, 1682, one of the first problems he confronted was that of accommodating the radically constricted town plan drawn up by Holme to the expectations of those First Purchasers who might be looking forward to settlement on their ten- to one hundred-acre city lots. This he accomplished by designating a 10,000-acre tract along the northern boundary of the town as "Liberty Lands" in which the First Purchasers might have the full portion of town lands they claimed (Figure 13). Second, the commissioners had apportioned city lots by lottery (as, in fact, Penn proposed they do in his "Certain Conditions")[57] the previous month. However, those English and Irish investors to whom Penn had sold several 5,000-acre shares, instead of to original First Purchasers who had rescinded their offers, had not been represented in the September drawing of lots. The distribution of city lots would have to be by a system that would allow for later purchasers as well as renters who leased land from the proprietor out of the one-tenth proportion of Philadelphia which, as with every 100,000 acres in the province, was legally reserved to him.[58] In keeping with his initial principle of land distribution Penn apportioned city lots in Philadelphia first according to the size of each adventurer's investment. Purchasers of 10,000 acres received the largest waterfront properties on the Delaware (with 204 feet frontage) in addition to a waterfront lot on the Schuylkill River and four interior lots, each "a city block in length and 102' in breadth." Smaller investors received proportionally smaller waterfront lots on the Delaware and one interior lot. All purchasers received any unallocated town land yet due them in the Liberty Lands.[59]

Size of investment, however, was not the sole criterion Penn finally used in the apportionment of lots in Philadelphia. Penn had expected the Delaware shore to be the principal center of activity in his town and so he tended to place colonists who actually emigrated to Pennsylvania on the Delaware side while he gave to nonemigrating colonists lots on the Schuylkill side of the town (Figures 14, 15). Moreover, since not everyone could be placed on the Delaware River front their removal elsewhere was sweetened by Penn's promise to place the public market-place at the north end of the waterfront, "where the high banks of the river made wharfing difficult," and to establish his own seat, "Fair-Mount," on the Schuylkill side of the city.[60]

Penn was forced to compromise his initial conception when he had to satisfy after-purchasers of smaller shares and renters by extending their holdings toward the Schuylkill side of the city. Furthermore, the establishment of "fee simple" ownership and the revocation of the proprietor's power of escheat after 1701 opened the way not only to further dispersion in the occupation of city lots but to alienation of lots for speculative purposes as well. These changes—the decentralization of city lots and their use for speculative purposes—were rather facilitated than discouraged by Holme's grid plan, a plan which has always lent itself to such uses because of the ease with which regularly presurveyed lots can be located.

The frustration of Penn's original conception of Philadelphia was symptomatic of what would occur with his broader scheme of orderly and regular land settlement throughout the province. The agricultural villages he hoped to see failed to materialize, excepting Newtown (Chester County) and Wrightstown (Bucks County). Individual farms were settled in a dispersed, indiscriminate fashion and tended to be neither regular in configuration nor located near central roads.

The failure of the proprietor to control the acquisition and occupation pattern of the land as he had hoped was due to several reasons. The proprietary land office was ineffective in controlling the pattern of settlement after 1701 and surveyors and officials alike conceded to settlers' demands that their lots be laid out according to optimum geographic conditions rather than a preconceived plan. Penn's correspondence with his secretary, James Logan, betrays a constant preoccupation with a near desperate and losing battle to recover "quit-rents . . . fines, forfeitures, escheats, deodants and strays." Finally, Penn's practice of selling rather than granting much of the land and the gradual establishment of *de facto* pre-emption rights marked the triumph of rural individualism over feudal organization.[61]

The question remains of the nature of the conceptual change involved in the adoption of Thomas Holme's plan for the city of Philadelphia over William Penn's. The architectural historian expresses a common reaction to the grid system of Philadelphia's plan of 1683 when he calls it "conservative" and "monotonous."[62] One would be doing Thomas Holme an injustice, however, to allow the explanation for his plan of the city to rest with the fact that the surveyor can lay out a rectilinear plan more expeditiously than any other. Not only does Holme's plan contain four parks placed each in a quadrant and a large central square, but the grid plan itself rarely appears in history wholly spontaneously. Movement toward and from the center of the city is equally facilitated in a radial plan, while with the grid land parcels are divided not only without reference to the character of the land, but are not readily adaptable to variations in topography. (Holme's center square, however, does lie on a slight elevation in the land between the Delaware and Schuylkill rivers.) Militarily, a city with an irregular street plan is easier to defend from within than is the grid which allows ready access to all its parts from the exterior, and is thus more suggestive of attemped control from without. Moreover, the uniform placement of buildings which is virtually dictated by such a scheme, and which Penn in fact intended, does not permit the individual builder to take the best advantage of the site.

Thomas Holme's use of the grid at Philadelphia reflected not only the practical knowledge of the surveyor but an historical context of expanding trade and empire. In this the surveyor's expectations were more contemporaneous than those of the province's proprietor. Land could be readily surveyed with simple instruments and equitably distributed. Because the grid allowed for the most regular and compact use of land spaces it lent itself readily to the identification and sale of town lots. Finally, because it maximized the flow of traffic about the city and throughout it from the exterior the grid plan was eminently suited for both trade and government.

Holme's Philadelphia plan may thus have been a more appropriate diagrammatic expression of the range of concerns which underlay the Pennsylvania enterprise: colonization, profit throught the sale of land, local
trade, and political and moral control.

Holme's plan of 1683 acquired its distinctive character from the five
squares it contained. The presence of these squares has suggested that
Holme was following a precedent established either in Londonderry or
with Richard Newcourt's plan for the rebuilding of London after the
Great Fire of 1666 (Figure 16). Similarities between the 1683 plan for
Philadelphia and Newcourt's plan may, however, be illusory. Newcourt's
was an ingenious scheme for fragmenting the larger city into fifty-five
geometrically uniform smaller units, each serving as its own parish, or
self-contained religious and social neighborhood. Each of these smaller
units contained its own square which was heightened to the eye and for
movement, in true baroque spirit, by the entry of streets into the parish
square at the center of each side. Thus traffic was designed to enter into
and through these many smaller neighborhood parish units rather than to
by-pass them, as would have been characteristic of the conventional
square within a grid. The parishes of Newcourt's plan, while laid out in a
uniform geometric pattern, imply a far more concentrated and
heterogeneous neighborhood life within the larger urban environment
than is indicated by Holme's grid.[63]

The chief similarity between the Holme and Newcourt plans lies in the
pattern of the five squares. Holme himself explained that in the case of
the four smaller squares located in each quadrant of the city he was attempting to replicate London's Moor Fields.[64] However, the Moor Fields
were legally restricted for use as playing fields while Philadelphia's
squares, in view of "their small extent, the use of the term square as opposed to fields and the allocation of surrounding property all suggest the
intimacy of the residential squares of Bloomsbury, the pleasures of which
were reserved for tenants of the square's owner."[65] Street traffic entered
and left Holme's squares not at the center of their sides but at their
corners so as to by-pass the square rather than interfere in whatever tranquility or activity its bordering residents might intend for it.

The most plausible model for Holme's plans was the model of a
seventeenth-century English military encampment used by Thomas
Phillips in his plan for the building of Londonderry in 1609. This plan,
characterized by an enclosed grid in which two central axial avenues
intersected into a large central square reserved at first for the mustering
and parading of troops and later used for civic purposes, had become a
cartographical symbol for the city by the end of the seventeenth
century.[66] Thomas Holme, like William Penn, had been an English land-

lord in Ireland. It is likely that the model of town-planning with which he was most familiar was one which was readily available at Londonderry, planned to serve the military and social needs of colonization, viz., a readily accessible gathering place in a foreign territory.

The principal difference brought about by Thomas Holme's revision of William Penn's own original plan for Philadelphia was a change from a vast rural township to a relatively urban scheme allowing for a relatively more densely populated nucleated settlement. This change is signified not only in Holme's application of the grid but by the surveyor's shift of the principal focus of the city from the waterfront to the geometric and geographic center of the plan. In other respects, however, Holme's conception was not at great variance with Penn's. Both plans are dominated by the distribution of land among private owners. Penn's strip lots were intended for individual proprietors. Lands withheld from sale were withheld for the Penn proprietary, not for the community. Similarly, Holme's plan is markedly lacking in truly accessible public spaces with the single exception of the center square. Comparison with Richard Newcourt's plan suggest what Holme might have done to ensure an intermingling of public with private activity; instead the four squares in each of Philadelphia's quadrants became residential squares closed off, by traffic patterns and the placement of dwelling lots, from the general life of the city.

For both Penn and Holme Philadelphia was conceived as the private preserve of her wealthier proprietors. In its first moments, the city could be distinguished diagrammatically by the "privatism" by which the first century of her life has been characterized. With her first incorporation in 1701, writes Sam Bass Warner, Jr., the municipal government of Philadelphia continued to be "a club of wealthy merchants" and "the town was hardly governed at all." The principal responsibilities of the corporation even into the late eighteenth century were "the management of markets and holding of the Recorder's Court," and until the Provincial Assembly in 1712 initiated a committee system "most streets went unpaved, the public wharves little repaired. There were no public schools, no public water, and at best thin charity."[67]

Absent also is evidence that either Penn or Holme thought of the city as a distinctive aesthetic statement. Urban design was in the service of utility and private property in land, not the delight and pleasure in site and ambiance which would create the fine baroque colonial towns of Annapolis and Williamsburg. Whether or not the lack of this aspect in the design of Philadelphia can be attributed to the Quaker distrust of worldly pleasure and Penn's association of corruption with the city can only be speculated upon. It is probable that a vision of community which stresses homogeneity and consensualism is unlikely to result in a conception of the city which ventures architectural or cultural innovation. William Penn's idea of the city, an idea only partially altered in Thomas Holme's plan, was a strictly limited one—limited to a stable and orderly rural township enlarged by the vast new possibilities of extended private land ownership on a virgin continent.

If the age was "too nice and difficult" for William Penn to attempt to draw more than the simplest distinctions between "particular frames" of government, he was no more precise in his use of "town" and "city." And yet Penn's plan for the settlement of townships in his province suggests that he did distinguish the town from the city, and that the town meant for him what it had meant for the early settlers of New England: "not . . only a nucleated urban-type settlement but instead the entire community of village lots and farm fields."[68] Penn did not, like Gabriel Thomas, refer to London as a model which Philadelphia might someday equal or surpass, but as a place which threatened to undermine the social and moral order of the English countryside.

William Penn's plans for the use and allocation of the vast lands of his grant from Charles II were designed to secure a predominantly rural society governed by men sympathetic both in matters of the spirit and in their acceptance of the rule of the "better sort." His political convictions, "republican" only in their fidelity to constitutionalism, were informed no less than his designs for Pennsylvania and Philadelphia, by a desire to perpetuate a righteous, hierarchical, and consensual world. Just as there were various perspectives from which the English classical republicans arrived at their convictions, it is probable that Penn, like his ally Algernon Sidney, was inspired by a "nostalgia for the medieval world in which master and man, landlord and tenant, formed a Gothic balance."[69] This was the world William Penn sought to recapture in Pennsylvania.

The countryside in which Penn hoped to see his nostalgic vision fulfilled would have been interwoven with villages and townships which—like Philadelphia—would have served as instruments of social stability and homogeneity. The country he longed to remain in rather than return to London in 1701 promised most of all tranquility,[70] and the life he cherished there was not only one of intimacy with nature but, as his cash books and inventories reveal, of the ease and dominion of a prosperous aristocratic landlord. Penn himself was not loath to enjoy the "Marks of Honour and Profit" to which he believed public service entitled him. An indifferent farmer, his chief care at Pennsbury was for his gardens, for which he employed several gardeners.[71] Penn's country was one in which benign and bounteous nature was in liege with an hierarchical and spiritual order. Philadelphia combined and, he hoped, would animate that vision to which Francis Daniel Pastorious gave poetic expression:

> The Young city round whose virgin zone
> The rivers like two mighty arms are thrown
> Marked by the smoke of evening fires alone,
>
> Lay in the distance, lovely even then,
> With its fair women and its stately men
> Gracing the forest court of William Penn, [72]

It was given to few men during the seventeenth century to perceive that the energies released by the concentration of wealth and talent in the city might bring about a new era not ignoble in character and purpose; and it was not William Penn's aspiration to facilitate the dawning of that new age. The opportunity presented by Pennsylvania was for Penn an opportunity to extend the country, with all its imagined and real political, social, and moral qualities of virtuous industry and righteous tranquility. In spite of his care, his vision never fully materialized because it was not shared with equal conviction by those upon whom ultimately fell the burden of carrying out his enterprise. The farmers and tradesmen who settled in Pennsylvania in the first half of the eighteenth century were less ready than he to countenance an eternal world of deference and well-ordered rural towns and villages. Rule by a Quaker elite promised little but frustration to those who had less to gain from stability than from the unstable process of individual self-betterment. The best planning could not cleanse the soul of material ambition.

A growing, wealthy Anglican population began to countervail against the Quaker penchant for earnest simplicity and distrust of more urbane entertainments, while political competition between both groups forced them to draw the working-class and German-speaking elements into politics, thus democratizing the political life of the city by the eve of the Revolution. Eventual democratization had been anticipated as early as 1683 when the "Second Frame of Government" denied the proprietor his triple vote in the Provincial Council and the Assembly usurped the right not only to deliberate upon but to initiate legislation, rather than to meet merely for the purpose of approval or disapproval, as had been the intention of the First Frame.

The importance of an accurate understanding of William Penn's plan for his "greene country towne" is that it enables us to appreciate the nostalgic character of the founder's vision and the extent to which it inspired his own ambitious and costly effort in the English colonization of North America. The Penn proprietary was originally designed to recover a rural world of hierarchical social and political relationships, protected from the imminent dislocations of urban life by the perpetuation of private wealth in land and the imposition of moral and religious uniformity through the preservation of "true Christian and Civil Liberty, in opposition to all Unchristian, Licentious, and unjust practices." That Penn could design a place so governed by rural values and call it a "city" also tells us something about the conceptual origins of the American city. The predominance of the value of individual proprietorship in land, "privatism," and the suspicion of a heterogeneous urban milieu reflected in the initial planning of Philadelphia continued to undermine the creative vitality of many modern American urban communities. If civic irresponsibility has denied American cities the full enjoyment of their potential as culture bearing institutions the cause may lie deeply rooted in the very ambiguity of their origins.

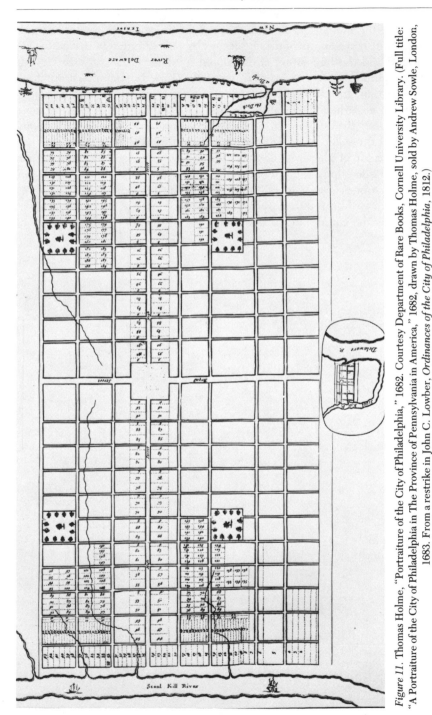

Figure 11. Thomas Holme, "Portraiture of the City of Philadelphia," 1682. Courtesy Department of Rare Books, Cornell University Library. (Full title: "A Portraiture of the City of Philadelphia in The Province of Pennsylvania in America," 1682, drawn by Thomas Holme, sold by Andrew Sowle, London, 1683. From a restrike in John C. Lowber, *Ordinances of the City of Philadelphia*, 1812.)

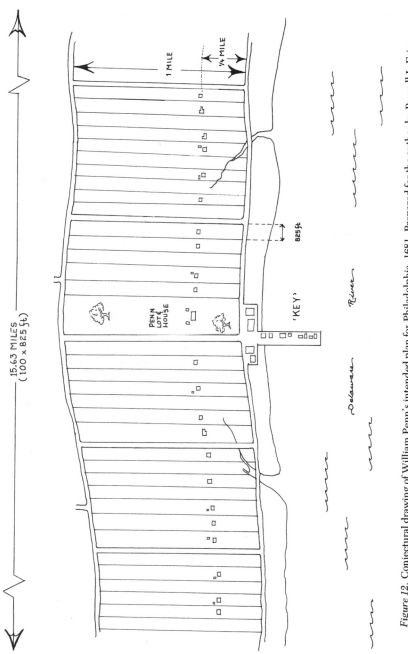

Figure 12. Conjectural drawing of William Penn's intended plan for Philadelphia, 1681. Prepared for the author by Russell I. Fries.

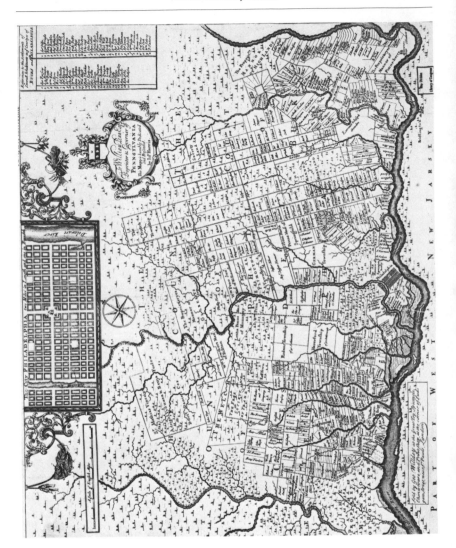

Figure 13. "A Mapp of Ye Improved Part of Pensilvania in America," plan of Philadelphia, Pennsylvania, and vicinity with an inset plan of Philadelphia, drawn by Thomas Holme, published by Ino. Harris, ca. 1720. Courtesy Library of Congress, Geography and Maps Division. (Full title: Holme, Thomas. "A mapp of ye improved part of Pensilvania in America, divided into countyes, townships and lotts." London; sold by Geo. Willdey, [1715?; another copy marked 1720?] Dedication signed: Ino. Harris. Scale ca. 1: 170,000. Inset of city of Philadelphia. Black and white.)

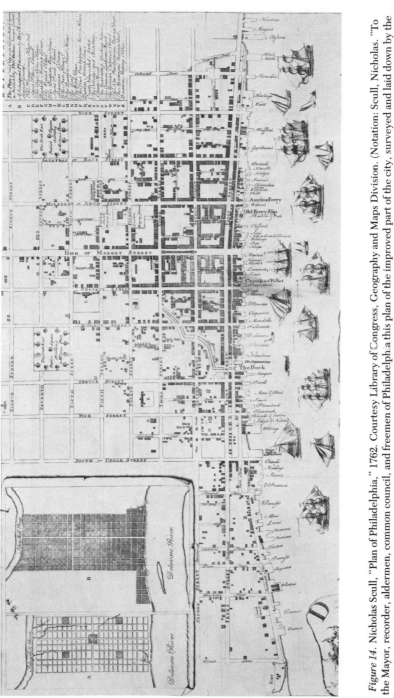

Figure 14. Nicholas Scull, "Plan of Philadelphia," 1762. Courtesy Library of Congress, Geography and Maps Division. (Notation: Scull, Nicholas. "To the Mayor, recorder, aldermen, common council, and freemen of Philadelph a this plan of the improved part of the city, surveyed and laid down by the late Nicholas Scull, Esqr., Surveyor General of the Province of Pennsylvania, is humbly inscrib'd by the editors." Philadelphia: sold by the editors, Matthew Clarkson and Mary Biddle, 1762.)

Figure 15. J. Carwitham, "An East Perspective View of the City of Philadelphia," 1731. Courtesy I. N. Phelps Stokes Collection, Prints Division, The New York Public Library, Astor, Lenox and Tilden Foundations.

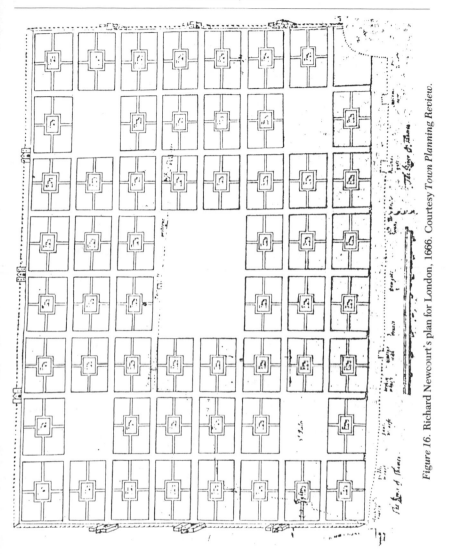

Figure 16. Richard Newcourt's plan for London, 1666. Courtesy Town Planning Review.

4

The Curious Case of Williamsburg

❦

The founding of Boston and Philadelphia occurred simultaneously with the initial settling of the colonies for which those towns became the capital cities by the end of the eighteenth century. Yet, as we have seen, in both instances those cities developed as they did in spite of, rather than because of, their founders' expectations. Those expectations had been for the recovery of a traditional rural society in which the new towns on the Charles and Delaware rivers would serve only limited roles as regional trading centers and loci of moral and political authority in the midst of an agrarian landscape. What those towns should not become was other Londons, places of economic dislocation, social disintegration, and religious and moral corruption. So long as rural communalism prevailed over private ambition, so long as uniformity of belief could be secured in combination with deference to the "better sort," John Winthrop's and William Penn's constricted visions for their country towns might have been realized. But as the sinews of consensualism and deference loosened under the strain of the drive for individual self-betterment that characterized later generations, the towns they conceived could but mirror the disintegration of their original purposes.

To the south, Virginia, the oldest English colony in North America, was the last seventeenth-century colony to attempt to establish a city. As it did so, the colony that would stand apart from its northern neighbors in the persistence of its agrarian economy declared itself prepared to incorporate the very kind of place Winthrop and Penn had so feared—not another modest country town, but a "city." From the start, Williamburg was intended to serve as a theater of culture and politics, a "commodious place, suitable for the reception of a considerable number and concourse of people." Her residents and visitors, less distrustful than Puritan and Quaker of worldly delights, would practice there the cultivation of urbanity that has characterized the aspirations of those planters who created her.[1]

So it would seem that the Act of the Virginia assembly of 1699 which called for the creation of that capital city stands as a curious anomaly in the urban history of colonial America. Or was Williamsburg such an anomaly after all? Was the city conceived in 1699, whose very architectural aspects would be prescribed in subsequent legislation, if not merely another "greene country towne," nevertheless also not another London in miniature? Would the idea of the city reflected in the creation of Williamsburg become one of those peculiarities, like the advocacy of liberty in a land of slavery, that would leave its indelible mark on the face of American society?

❧

The Englishmen who settled Virginia in the seventeenth century had largely overcome their fear of that "vague, rich jungle of repellent or terrifying things, animals, plants, and men" which was the New World as pictured by sixteenth-century explorers. They might marvel over the exotic fecundity of the wilderness, urging the faint of heart back home to come and take advantage of the

> excellent temper, and pure aire, fertility of soile, of hils that sheltered off the North-west windes, and blasts, vallies of grapes, rich mines, and millions of Elkes, Stags, Deer, Turkeys, Fowl, Fish, Cotton, rare fruits, Timber, and faire plains, and clear fields.[2]

King William directed his governor in Virginia to procure for him "mocking birds . . . Baltimore birds, black birds with red upon their Wings; and any other sorts of small birds that are curious for their colour, or singing; partridges, pheasants, wild Turkeys, and any other such sort of Fowl . . . fishing-Hawks, or any other sort of Hawks, bald Eagles, & all sorts of eagles."[3] But that did not mean that man's proper habitation was the jungle, however well-tamed. Rather, the wealth of the wilderness was to be gleaned and taken away to enrich a life elsewhere. The ambivalent American attitude toward Nature, that she be at once honored and conquered, is deeply rooted in the Englishman's first responses to the New World.[4] Providence might restore Paradise to man, but man had not been restored to Paradise; the destiny of labor and law would go on unrelieved.

The disturbing prospect of disorder and chaos, the disintegration of society, alarmed some seventeenth-century Virginians who beheld the scattered and isolated pattern of settlement in a seemingly unbounded land. In Ireland, where the English had had their only previous experience in colonization and rationalized that because the Gaelic population was barbaric, subjugation was a Christian duty, they became convinced that cohabitation in a central town "engendereth civility, policy, acquaintance, consultation, and a firm and sure seat." As the London Company undertook its Virginia venture, it believed that the creation of "if not hansome Townes, yet compact and orderly villages" was "the most proper, and successful maner of proceedings in new Plantacons, besides those of the former ages [presumably the Romans], the example of the Spaniards in the West Indies, doth fully instance."[5] In 1662 one anxious parson wrote the bishop of London asking him "to acquaint the King with the necessity of promoting the building of Towns in each County of Virginia." Because of "their dispersed manner of planting themselves" the settlers had failed to build churches and conduct regular worship. Thus "their Families disordered, their Children untaught, the publick Worship and Service of the Great God they own, neglected," the settlers were not only likely to succumb to irreligion themselves, but could hardly be expected to provide a good example "for the heathen." The gospel would be better promoted among them if they could live in "the Cities and Towns with the Christians" where they might be so impressed by "their Meeknesse, Humility, Charity . . . Righteousnesse" that conversion would follow as day does the night. The concerned cleric closed his appeal with a poetic explication of the town as a symbol of cultural authority and the perpetuation of civilization which, we may suppose, he assumed the good bishop would rightly understand. "His Lordship" should

> contemplate the poor Church (whose plants now grow wilde in that Wildernesse) become like a garden enclosed, like a Vineyard fenced, and watch'd like a flock of Sheep with their Lambes safely folded by night, and fed by day; all of which are the promised fruites of well ordered Towns, under Religious Pastours and Magistrates.[6]

The shepherds of the Anglican church were not the only Englishmen concerned for the prospects of civilization in the colonies should settlement be allowed to take place at random. In so far as military preoccupations affected the origins of colonial institutions within England's expanding empire, Virginia's military governors from Captain John Smith to Colonel Alexander Spotswood would regard compact, garrisoned towns as vital military nodes "of English conquest and colonization in America."[7] Royal instructions to British governors in North America from the beginning of the eighteenth century until the Revolution reveal a constant desire on the part of the Crown to bridle the lust for land and its attendant land speculation in favor of an ordered course of settlement. Repeated instructions throughout the first half of the century forbade, as did the order to "Prevent Exhorbitant Land Grants in New York" of 1708–1709 (and reissued for New York and Virginia in 1727–1728), the governor from issuing "any grant of Land . . . unto any person whatsoever . . .

without an obligation upon the grantee to plant, settle, and effectually cultivate at least three acres."[8] The governors were concurrently ordered to "lay out townships of a convenient size" for "it has been found by experience that the settling planters in townships hath very much redounded to their advantage, not only with respect to the assistance they have been able to afford each other in their civil concerns, but likewise with regard to the security they have thereby acquired against the insults and incursions of neighboring Indians or other enemies."[9] Land should be set aside for the support of a church, minister, and schoolmaster, as well as for "fortifications and barracks."[10] Finally, a town would acquire the "immunities and privileges" of "any other parish or township of said province" (such as the right of representation in the provincial assembly) when it contained one-hundred families or "householders."[11] Thus not only would towns facilitate conquest, they could also provide the basis of civilized society as well as security in a new and alien environment.

Moreover, the Crown evidently envisioned colonial towns primarily as centers serving a traditional agrarian society. All instructions relating to towns contain some provision for ensuring that each town be surrounded by adequate and good farmlands, including "common and herbage," as well as "laid out upon or as near as conveniently may be to some navigable river or the sea coast."[12] However, the Crown did not envision a colonial realm of rural grandees; rather, the provinces were to be populated by independent farmers possessing a "quantity" of land upon which they were to build a "dwelling house" "in proportion to their ability to cultivate," usually regarded as one-hundred acres for each householder plus fifty acres for each member of the household.[13]

Whether as military nodes of defense and social control, or as spearheads of civilization in a new society, the fate of actual towns in Virginia toward the end of the seventeenth century hung by the twisted threads of tobacco culture and mercantile policy.[14] The Crown might, as a general rule, favor towns in the New World colonies, but Virginia proved a special case. Virginia's planters might themselves desire the establishment of towns, and they would attempt to legislate them into existence in a series of acts passed in the House of Burgesses between 1662 and 1705. But the Privy Council through its standing committee, the Lords of Trade and Plantations, was loath to countenance any development that would reduce the flow of tobacco profits into the king's revenues or the pockets of English importers, while encouraging colonial artisans and tradesmen, a possibility "inimical to the trade of English merchants." So long as projected towns served solely as export centers, reducing shipping costs and facilitating customs collections, the Crown would smile on the assembly's efforts. But the bottom line was reached when it feared, as Queen Anne explained in her disavowal of the Ports and Towns Act of

1705, that towns would be "detrimental by drawing the inhabitants off from their planting tobacco in the country to the cohabiting and setting up handicraft trades."[15]

The Virginia planters too, as they passed act after act to establish towns, were often working at cross-purposes. As tobacco prices rose and fell so too did their enthusiasm for limiting tobacco production, and as Sir William Berkeley and Lord Thomas Culpeper maintained throughout, the success of any town-planting scheme hinged on the success of economic diversification. Moreover, the development of Jamestown for example, a project adopted by both Berkeley and the assembly in an act of 1662, would have required a considerable outlay of public and private funds to finance the erection of houses and public buildings, as well as the bounties offered to induce economic diversification. But public funds alone were inadequate and excess private capital went back into tobacco culture or sought investment opportunities in England. Then, too, the location of proposed towns, a factor critical to their viability, was governed by the speculative interests of owners of large tracts like the Byrds, Carters, Fitzhughs, and Wormeleys.[16] Finally, whatever interest the planters had in the establishment of towns—whether for personal profit or to nurture local trade, manufactures, and society—was soon dissipated by the centrifugal momentum of plantation agriculture.

The movement in seventeenth–century Virginia to establish towns as ports and market centers may have died of material causes, but the desire for the cultural benefits of urban life did not. The ambitious names given struggling little settlements in the Tidewater during the first decade, such as "Rochdale Hundred" and "Bermuda City," are an indication that urban aspirations preceded the vagaries of the tobacco trade as a source of town–planting efforts. Governor William Berkeley, in his desire to promote the building of towns in the 1660's, had his eye on the character of Virginians as well as tobacco prices. Towns might protect the settlers "from savage enemies without," but they could also protect them "from the savage nature that lurked within." And "only towns and cities could nourish the arts and skills that distinguished civil men from barbarians."[17]

James Blair, the bishop of London's commissary in Virginia from 1689 to 1743, blamed the absence of towns in Virginia on the settlers' habit of settling "without any Rule or Order in Country Plantations" and rusticated members of the general assembly who, never having "seen a Town, nor a well improv'd Country in their lives, cannot therefore imagine the Benefit of it." If only Virginians, like New Englanders, had established towns they might be enjoying "convenient Ports and Markets . . . well improv'd Trades and Manufactures . . . well educated Children . . . an industrious and thriving People . . . an happy government in Church and State . . . in short . . . all the other Advantages of human improvements." Lacking these advantages, Virginia was "one of the poorest, miserablest, and worst Countries in all *America*, that is inhabited by Christians."[18] Francis Makemie, a Presbyterian clergyman from Accomack County, was more blunt:

> When I have considered the Antiquity of Towns and Cities, known to as many as are conversant with Sacred and Profane History, and the Universal Copy cast us by the whole Christian and Pagan World, I have been justly amazed to see the unaccountable Humour and Singularity of Virginia and Maryland, who have so patiently, and for so long a time, sat down with a kind of stupid satisfaction under those pressing and Innumerable Disadvantages both they and their Posterity must still endure, by their scattered and remote Settlements, without Towns and Cohabitation.[19]

William Berkeley and James Blair, and Blair's sometime political conspirator Governor Francis Nicholson, shared an appreciation of urban places as providing something more than convenient centers of trade, manufacture, and revenue collection. Each grasped implicitly what Aristotle had meant when he wrote that the city exists not simply to satisfy "the bare needs of life" but "for the sake of the good life." Each evidently perceived that a city could become what it had for Giovanni Botero—a theater of culture and power. And where Berkeley and Culpeper had failed, Blair and Nicholson would succeed, for it was largely as a result of their efforts that two important centers of eighteenth-century culture in Virginia were finally established. Within a decade the College of William and Mary received its charter (1693) and the new capital city of Williamsburg was created by an act of the assembly (1699). Both were the result of a single ambition to assure Virginia the vital instruments of an elite culture. It was the special role assigned to Williamsburg that made it possible for the Virginians to attempt to establish a "city," while they had failed to establish "towns." The Virginia planters succeeded in describing in 1699 and 1705 a city intended primarily neither as market, manufacturing center, nor port, but as a political and cultural center. Whereas every other enactment to promote towns had spoken of "towns" and "ports," the legislation which created Williamsburg spoke of a "city."[20] No doubt the continued interest in urban places, directed now less toward ports than toward the erection of a true capital city, was affected by the changing composition of the House of Burgesses. The assembly of 1699 was, for the first time, dominated by second-generation, Virginia-born planters.

The arguments made on behalf of the new capital were similar to those made on behalf of the new college, and they reveal the common perceptions of an urbane culture that underlay the founding of Williamsburg.

An indication of how Virginians understood the connection between the city and cultivated life was offered by the students of the College of William and Mary who had been enlisted by Governor Nicholson not only to promote support for the college but for his scheme to move the colonial capital to Middle Plantation (where the general assembly had been meeting since 1676 when Nathanial Bacon and his cohorts burned Jamestown). On May 1, 1699 the students presented an assemblage of the governor, the council, and the House of Burgesses with five orations on the benefits to be expected from removing the capital to Middle Plantation, the location of the college. "If we make scholars," warned one youthful orator, ". . . in such a retired Corner of the world, far removed from business, and action," they would remain "meer scholars, which make a very ridiculous figure: made up of Pedantry, disputaciousness, positiveness, and a great many other ill qualities which render them not so fit for action and conversation." By providing the college with "a good Town . . . and filling it with all the selectest and best company that is to be had within the Government," the Muses would acquire "a decent confidence by seeing & conversing among men, and being acquainted with action and business." The blight complained of by Commissary Blair could be overcome if Virginia only had a town attractive to "Tradesmen, Labourers, Shopkeepers . . . Printers, Booksellers, Bookbinders, Mathematical instrument makers, nurses for the sick and . . . men of fashion and business." In fact, the Virginians might even "retrieve the reputation" of their colony, "which has sufferred by nothing so much as by neglecting a seat of trade, wealth and Learning," by establishing "such a Town as may equal if not outdo Boston, New York, Philadelphia, Charleston and Annapolis" in "trade and commerce . . . mind and manners."[21]

When James Blair set out to write the preface to the "Statutes of the College of William and Mary in Virginia," the same contrast between rusticity and urbanity that informed his indictment of Virginia society in *The Present State of Virginia* served as his *apologia* for the college. In the colony's early days, he argued, the first planters had been understandably preoccupied with the effort to wrest "a mean Livelyhood" from a "Country over-run with Woods and Briers, and . . . infested with the Incursions of barbarous Indians." How could such men be expected "to read and write" or have "commerce with the Muses, or learned Sciences" when their lives were spent "ignobly at the Hoe and Spade, and other Employments of an uncultivated and unpolished Country?" The study of "good Letters, and the liberal Sciences" have ever been essential for "the cultivating the Minds of Men, and rectifying their Manners." It was the

study of letters and the liberal sciences which distinguished "those famous Nations the Hebrews, Egyptians, Greeks, and Romans." Happily
"these studies" were "at last retrieved" following "a great Interruption
and almost Destruction of them, through the Incursions of the barbarous
Nations." Likewise the colonies would be saved from another dark age
through the efforts of "a small Remnant of Men of better spirit, who had
either had the Benefit of better Education themselves in their Mother-
Country, or at least had heard of it from others." Thanks to their vision
and determination the college could attempt to fulfill its duty to promote
"the Study of the learned Language, and liberal Arts."[22] Among the
statutes to which Blair affixed his signature in 1727 was a provision requiring the separation of biblical and liberal studies into separate depart-
ments; the former, it was casually written, "we leave to the Divinity
School."[23]

James Blair's commentary on Virginia and his prescription for the
recovery of English civilization on the western shores of the Atlantic suggests the meaning of urbanity to some Englishman in Virginia. The kind
of life that only a city could provide for the college's first president and its
students was a life of learning and conversation with the "best company,"
a life of refinement achieved through the on-going intercourse of scholars
with men of fashion and men of affairs. Such a life was being pursued on
the remote plantations of Virginia's gentlemen planters. Transported to
Middle Plantation, it would remain an elite culture. Furthermore, in the
improvement of "mind and manners" expected of education in an urban
setting was the application of the formalizing imagination not only to the
physical environment but to thought, expression, and conduct. Not only
did men refine what they saw, but what they did, what they thought,
what they said, and the personality that they showed to the world. The
urbane man and woman, as had been true since antiquity, were as much
works of art as the buildings they erected and the musical instruments
they played, and the key to an understanding of their urbanity is fundamentally aesthetic.

The Act of 1705 confirming an earlier act creating the capital city of
Williamsburg must be one of the more instructive documents in the history of urban design. The reason for the construction of the new city is
made explicit at the start. A setting had to be provided for the erection of
"another building . . . for the convenient setting and holding of the
general assemblies and courts, at a healthy, proper and commodious
place, suitable for the reception of a considerable number and concourse

of people." The Middle Plantation had been selected as the site for it

> hath been found by constant experience to be healthy and agreeable
> to the constitutions of the inhabitants of his majesty's colony and do-
> minion, having the natural advantage of a serene and temperate air,
> dry and champaign land [a quality which Jamestown had sorely
> lacked], and plentifully stored with wholesome springs, and the con-
> vening of two navigable and pleasant creeks, that run out of James
> and York rivers, necessary for the supplying the place with provisions
> and other things of necessity.[24]

The Act specifies that the new capital should be incorporated into "one
body politic and corporate, by the name of mayor, aldermen, and commonality of the city of Williamsburg." What is remarkable about the Act is
the care taken to determine, as a matter of law, the total appearance of the
city. It is here that Governor Francis Nicholson's (1690–1694, 1698–1705)
influence is most probable, for this Cambridge-educated gentleman
soldier, who served as governor or lieutenant–governor of six of their majesties' colonies in North America, was well acquainted with the urban
milieu of London and Paris and was undoubtedly familiar with the work of
Christopher Wren, architect and chief exponent of baroque urban design
in England.[25]

The Act of 1705 begins by describing carefully how the new capitol
building should be built. Little is left to the creative impulses of the colonial carpenters and masons as the Act prescribes every detail of the
handsome brick building from the flagstone flooring of each "great room"
in the two wings of the structure to the "sash windows" to the "cupola to
surmount . . . the building, which shall have a clock placed on it." Provision is made for a committee to supervise the maintenance of the building the uses of which, even to particular rooms, is specified in the Act.
Furthermore, houses built on Duke of Gloucester street had to meet
certain requirements of size and construction; they should stand no closer
to the street than six feet, should all "front alike" and be at least "ten foot
pitch." Similar specifications governed construction on side streets.[26]

The earliest extant plan of colonial Williamsburg is a 1782 map of the
city. One can readily recognize a rectilinear plan with its emphasis upon a
long, broad central avenue, aesthetically rewarding vistas, and the large
central open space or square.[27] In evidence also are the two diagonal
streets converging at the College of William and Mary, creating a dynamic setting for the college building. These streets, Jamestown Road
and Richmond Road on the map of 1782, not only form the central V of
either the letters "W" or "M", but function to direct the flow of traffic
from the western end of the city directly down the long Duke of
Gloucester Street to the capitol building. A similar arrangement, com-

pleting the initials of their majesties William and Mary, is on the eastern end of the city directly down the long Duke of Gloucester Street on a later map. John W. Reps argues persuasively that the two sets of diagonals form two separate monograms composed of a "W" and its mirror image which also, of course, appears as an "M" (Figure 17).[28] In this instance mannerist motive and baroque diagonals serve not only to provide long vistas culminating in visual interest; they also direct the very movements of pedestrians and carriages into a dynamic vista itself which only contributes to the dramatization of the public buildings. This effect is enhanced by the termination of the streets paralleling the Duke of Gloucester Street (Francis Street and Nicholson Street) at the Palace Green and its King Street extension, rather than their continuation for the length of the city. The location of the George Wythe house (c. 1750) takes full advantage of this arrangement; fronting on the Palace Green it faces the length of Nicholson Street and is itself visible along the length of that street. Added to another quality of the Williamsburg plan—the appropriateness of its scale to the number of people the city would have to accommodate—these applications of baroque principles to the colonial capital assured Williamsburg a human dimension sometimes lacking in later European cities.

Colonial Williamsburg mirrored those characteristics of urban design which have their ultimate roots in the civic consciousness of the Renaissance. While Renaissance building was essentially static in its studied imitation of Roman architecture, Renaissance culture nurtured the secularized civic pride which would eventually transform the neoclassicism of the earlier period into the plastic and dynamic, if occasionally grandiose, design of the baroque. The use of long avenues ending in elegant buildings, monuments, or fountains combined with a concern for the third dimension—the architecture of public and, less predominantly, private buildings—declare the planned city of the sixteenth and seventeenth centures a work of art. Sweeping diagonals radiating from large squares or ovals, more in evidence in Nicholson's Annapolis than in Williamsburg, emphasize the dynamic potential of a "commodious place, suitable for the reception of a considerable number and concourse of people." "If the City is noble and powerful," wrote Leo Battista Alberti, "the Streets should be strait and broad, which carries an Air of Greatness and Majesty."[29] Above all the baroque city is a setting and celebration of authority—secular, spiritual, and cultural. Giovanni Botero's counsel on the origins of great cities is echoed throughout the streets of the colonial capital. As a model of urban design Williamsburg declared itself the center of a civilization. Small in scale, it befitted the society it was meant to serve.

Williamsburg's town plan also reflected the architectural aesthetic of harmony through mathematical proportions. Excavations at Williamsburg during its restoration revealed that the dimensions of the principal streets and buildings had been determined according to the systems of mathematical ratios, which dominated both Renaissance and baroque architectural design.[30] The aesthetic of mathematical proportions had originated with the sixth-century Greek philosopher, Pythagoras, whose astronomical and musical systems, based upon the "perfect numbers" of four and ten and those figures which could be constructed out of geometric divisions of these harmonic numbers, were preserved in the medieval treatises of Boethius (482–525). Mathematical harmonies persisted as exemplar of the universe into the Renaissance, whether in the cosmology of Dante's *Divine Comedy*, drawn from Boethius, or Alberti's *Ten Books on Architecture*, in which he acknowledged Pythagoras as the author of the principle that "the same numbers, by means of which the agreement of sounds affects our ears with delight, are the very same which please our eyes and our mind."[31]

English Renaissance and Neo-Classic architecture mirrored the doctrine of mathematical proportions which it received primarily through Sebastino Serlio's *Book of Architecture* (1537–1547; first English edition, 1611) and Andreas Palladio's *Four Books on Architecture* (1570; first English edition, 1715). The persistence of the aesthetic of mathematical harmony could be seen in the work of Inigo Jones (1573–1652) and Sir Christopher Wren (1632–1723), both of whom served as Surveyor of His Majesty's Works. And it was the Office of His Majesty's Works under Wren, who was as avid a student of mathematics as of architecture, that was the most probable source of the Williamsburg plan. Whether Wren was the actual source of the Williamsburg plan, or indeed of the "Wren building" of the College of William and Mary or the Capitol building, matters less than that the principal public buildings of Virginia's second capital city were in the Wren-baroque style.[32] Virtually all of the major public and private buildings of Williamsburg were constructed according to systems of mathematical proportions, the most common of which were multiples of the square or geometric divisions of the square, such as the equilateral triangle, or $\sqrt{2}$ and ½ : 1 : 1½ (Figures 18–20). These systems, or geometric sections, were prescribed by the Act of 1705 itself, which limited the minimum size of any house on Duke of Gloucester street to 20 feet by 30 feet (1 : 1½). They also provided the basic dimensions of the main building of the College of William and Mary, Bruton Parish Church (both rebuilt by Alexander Spotswood c. 1710, after the fire of 1705), Brafferton Hall at the College of William and Mary, the Courthouse, the Governor's palace, the George Wythe House, the Archibald Blair House, and, a few miles up the James River, that loveliest of colonial buildings, William Byrd's "Westover."[33]

The public and private buildings that housed Virginia's ruling elite and the landscaped gardens and parks of virtually every other aspiring "country seat" of the period reflected the stress on "harmonick proportions" found in such contemporary colonial builders' treatises as William Halfpenny's *Practical Architecture, or a Sure Guide to the true Working according to the Rules of that Science* (London, 1730) and Robert Morris' *Lectures on Architecture* (London, 1734).[34] "True proportions," wrote Halfpenny, "are the Fundamentals, the Beauty and the very Life of Architecture," in a manual complete with diagrams based on Palladio and Inigo Jones.[35] "True proportions," Morris explained, were "arithmetical & harmonick" and give pleasure to the eye not because of some arbitrary external standard but because

> beauty, in all Objects, spring [sic] from the same unerring Law of Nature. . . . The joint Union and Concordance of the Parts, in an exact symmetry, forms the whole a compleat Harmony, which . . . is agreeably blended through the whole, and diffuses itself to the Imagination by some sympathising Secret to the Soul, which is all Union, all Harmony, and Proportion.[36]

In its rationalism and formalism, the Williamsburg aesthetic was a pervasive quality not only of design but also of refined living in that colonial society. Art was not simply an imitation of nature which, in turn, was articulated in mathematics; nature and the soul were mirrored in art. The soul, created of a mathematically conceived cosmos, responded to an aesthetic of harmony, symmetry, and proportion. That was true of music, for example, a social art in which every eighteenth-century gentleman and gentlewoman was expected to be accomplished. Morris demonstrated the fundamental nature of this aesthetic by deriving his principles of proportion in architecture and music from a common mathematical source. "The Affinity between Architecture and Musick," he explained, is due to the fact that just as "in Musick [there] are only seven distinct Notes, in Architecture likewise are only seven distinct Proportions, which produce all the different Buildings in the Universe, viz. The Cube,—the Cube and half,—the Double Cube,—the Duplicate of 3, 2, and 1, —of 4, 3, and 2—of 1, 4, and 3,—and of 6, 4, and 3, produce all the Harmonick Proportions or Rooms."[37] Readers of the *Virginia Gazette* received similar instruction in aesthetics from "The Monitor" in 1736 when the author of this eighteenth–century "Talk of the Town" advised that music gives pleasure not by "the Tickling of the Ear, and a mere Delight of the Sense." It is not the perception of sound by the ear or of color by the eye that gives us pleasure in music and painting; rather we delight in those things through "the Perception of Harmony, Beauty or Symmetry arising from them; the Perceiving of Harmony between [sounds]

. . . is an Act of the Mind. . . . The Ear, the Eye and the Hand, furnish the Materials; but it is The Operation of the Mind upon those Materials that gives the Delight."[38] The aesthetic of harmony, symmetry, and proportion pervaded all forms of artistic expression, not the least of which was the styling of life itself.

❦

The principles of conduct and delineations of the constructed self—not only of the city, but of its citizens—as a work of art which governed Virginia's urbane planters were derived from the world of Renaissance England. On the one hand was the example of London, herself become the stage for profound social changes, not the least of which was the urbanization of the country gentry. Already a city of tradesmen and artisans, attributable to the fact that the city was corporately organized into gilds and companies (membership in which was a prerequisite to obtaining the priveleges of freemen) London became a mecca in the late seventeenth century for gentry seeking political power, economic influence, seasonal amusement, or, not infrequently, good matches for their daughters. The newcomers demanded fine residences and amusements—parks, clubs, coffeehouses, theaters—and thus stamped upon the face of the city a character which it retains to this day. City officials grew alarmed as it appeared the influx would only promote idleness and dissolution; meanwhile even the French would be attracted to London's lively, cultivated and diverse ambiance, full of stimulating novelties and contradictions.[39]

London served not only as a magnet for the English gentry but it provided standards of taste and culture for the Virginia planter as well. He sent to London for his clothing and household furnishings, for his books and his musical instruments. Robert Carter of Nomini Hall reproached his London tailor peevishly for sending him a suit of clothes that didn't fit as well as his neighbor George Wythe's fit *him*. The tailor could make amends, however, by making him a scarlet waistcoat lined in silk and scarlet breeches, "the Button holes of the suit of clothes to be embroidered with gold and hansom double gilded Buttons."[40] A revealing instance of the manner in which a planter's tastes were formed is a letter which this son of "King" Carter wrote a London merchant asking that "an Armonica" be procured for him. "Mr. Pelham," wrote Carter, "is just returned from New York, he heard on his journey Mr. B. Franklin of Phila. perform on the Armonica: The Instrument pleased Pelham amazingly . . . ." What Carter wanted precisely was "an Armonica as played by Miss Davies in the great Room in Spring Gardens, being . . . musical Glass with Out Water: Formed into a complete Instrument . . .

never out of tune." This was no common requisition; "Charles James . . . near Gray's Inn London is the only maker of the Armonica in England."[41] Among the events of Sabine Hall that Robert Wormeley Carter thought to report to his father, Landon, then at Williamsburg, was the arrival of a shipment from England which contained "Beer . . . with but little life" and "Cloathes vastly genteel . . . with velvet waistcoat & Breeches; to be sure," promised the son, "you will be very fine."[42]

Not all Virginia planters regarded the latest in London fashion as the sum and substance of urbane gentility (nor, for that matter, did Robert Carter). Robert Beverly insisted that all the furniture at Beverley Park be made on the plantation,[43] and even "King" Carter preferred the household's shoes—which he ordered by the dozens—to be plain and sturdy rather than "made of black leather, which always proves rotten."[44] The Virginia planter, like all newcomers to the higher reaches of society, walked a narrow line between refinement and vulgarity. He was most secure if he outfitted his family, as William Fitzhugh instructed George Mason, charged with the care of his young son in England, "with what is fit & decent, as befits an honest planter or farmer's son, not with what's rich or gaudy."[45] Woe to him who mislocated that boundary, as William Dawkins, London factor to "King" Carter learned when he tried to tantalize his employer with the mention of a Mrs. Heath's £1000 earrings. "I esteem her more for the ornaments of her mind," pontificated Carter; he then admonished Dawkins to "remember I was your master's equal and all along have lived in as good rank and fashion as he did, even when you were something like Graves's cabin boy, and am old enough to be your father, not to mention any more reasons that justly give me a title to your deference."[46]

The distinction between gentleman and commoner, which in its subtlety had escaped William Dawkins, lay, of course, not in what this new gentry wore but in its way of life; not in its sociability, but in the form it took. While London vied with Paris in setting the standard for stylish dress, it did set the standard against which genteel refinement was measured. Hugh Jones, who early recognized the importance of speech in the proper social location of Englishmen, warned "no Englishman . . . can make any tolerable figure" unless he could "read, write, and talk" English as it was mastered in London. Jones, himself an urbane Anglican who traveled in the same circles as William Smith, Benjamin Franklin, and James Logan, was pleased to note that Virginians residing in Williamsburg "live in the same neat manner, dress after the same modes, and behave themselves exactly as the gentry in London." That "the habits, life, customs," and speech were "much the same as about London" Hughes attributed to colonial ties "with persons belonging to trade and navigation" from the city on the Thames.[47]

The *Virginia Gazette,* which began publication at Williamsburg in 1736, reflected a conscious effort at urbanity in style and content. Its issues contained regular reports from various European capitals of the state of politics and the life of royalty in those places as well as satires and periodic essays, styled after the *Spectator* and the *Rambler,* under the caption "The Monitor." Intriguing to the modern reader is the frequent appearance in those early eighteenth-century pages of mathematical puzzles (and subscribers' solutions) which were confidently proffered readers as a means by which "the Learned of our own Country, may be rais'd to a Spirit of Emulation, in a Science equally Useful, and . . . full as Entertaining" as "Pieces of Poetry."[48] The *Gazette's* readers were as concerned with society as with the improvement of the mind, however, for the newspaper regularly carried announcements of subscription dances and weddings, the later revealing full well what constituted "society" in Virginia. The 1736 announcement of the union in marriage of two first Virginia families was typical in the attributes it memorialized: "Williamsburg, Novemb. 19 . . . Ralph Wormeley, of Middlesex County, Esq.; a young Gentleman of fine Estate, was married to the celebrated Miss Salley Berkeley, a young Lady of great Beauty, and Fortune."[49]

Occasionally the *Gazette* offered advice on how to become, or at least appear, well bred. The obnoxious story-teller, warned "Cato," is "fatal to good Society." "The Delightful story-teller is one, who speaks not a Word too much, or too little, who . . . shows . . . a delicate Turn of Wit in every Thing which comes from him; who can entertain his Company better with the History of a Child and its Hobby-Horse, than one of the Soporoficks can with an Account of Alexander and Bucephalus." ("Better never be born," cautioned William Fitzhugh, "than ill bred.")[50] The paramount injunction was to acquire "a proper Education." The best foundations of that education, as first suggested by "the School of Sparta," were "to form the Mind, and regulate the Manners; to instruct the Understanding; and exercise the Affections."[51] The purpose of an education, and thus its character, was less to expand the intellect than to complete and refine the man. Translated into the Renaissance values of the period that meant that men who would be educated for social leadership must acquire "fortitude, temperence, prudence and justice." As Christian gentlemen the new gentry had also to display "liberality and courtesy."[52] The essential element in this drawing out and shaping of one's social personality was the Aristotelian mean—moderation and proportion in all things. Thus it was that the aesthetic which determined the design of the physical city was not confined to the arts alone, but was wholly pervasive, extending as well to an aesthetic of civility and sociability, or urbanity.

Edmund S. Morgan, in his portrait of homelife in eighteenth–century

Virginia, remarks upon the gregarious hospitality of plantation life, attributing it largely to the isolated and self-sufficient nature of rural
existence.[53] It is worth asking, however, whether the dancing-classes and
balls, barbecues and fish-feasts, and endless visits by horseback and carriages over rough country roads were a necessary accompaniment of
plantation life. The isolated rural life of the American west in the
nineteenth century produced no such phenomenon as the distinctive
social life which moved from plantation to Williamsburg and back on a
seasonal calendar. Obvious differences lie in the relative scales of wealth
enjoyed by an individual "homesteader" in each respective time and
place, and the fact that the earlier society had the benefit of bond labor to
relieve it of much of the drudgery of frontier life. The explanation of the
particular style of sociability which the Virginia planter strove for can be
found in the fact that that society strove to emulate, on its country seats,
the mode of life of the urbanized gentry of England, for whom highly
cultivated social intercourse was essential to their sense of status and
dignity. The people of Williamsburg could not accept their new parish
"Reader," complained Governor William Gooch to the bishop of London
in 1728, not because of his "Shape or Make," but because of "his igno-
rance of the World.[54]

An interesting glimpse of the success with which the new Virginia
gentry strove for urbanity is left to us in the form of the journal Philip
Vickers Fithian kept while he served as tutor to the children of Robert
Carter of Nomini Hall in 1773–1774. The good people of Cohansie, New
Jersey, whence Fithian had come, were not unsociable; but at Nomini
Hall and Williamsburg the young tutor was confronted with a society
quite unlike anything he had known before. When Fithian took his leave
from Princeton for Virginia he had been so amply warned against the
"corrupted . . . manners of the people" and their "promiscuous
assemblies" that one of the earliest entries in his journal was a prayer that
the Almighty "save me from being corrupted, or carried away with the
Vices which prevail in that Country."[55] But from that moment forward his
journal is a record of the re–education of that earnest youth into a way of
life which, with the exception of slavery, charmed and tantalized him.
Again and again an honest conscience moved Fithian to such confessions
as "I am situated . . . in a most delightful Country; in a civil, polite
neighborhood; and in a family remarkable for regularity, and economy."
"The People are extremely hospitable," conceded another journal entry,
"and very polite both of which are most certainly universal Characteristics
of the Gentlemen of Virginia—some swear bitterly, but the practise
seems to be generally disapproved—I have heard that this Country is no-
torious for Gaming, however this be, I have not seen a Pack of Cards, nor
a Die, since I left home, nor gaming nor Betting of any kind except at the

Richmond-Race." Inevitably Fithian had to write home, gently reproach-
ful of ill-founded northern notions, a glowing description of the sound
learning, magnificent library, incomparable manners and great diligence
which prevailed in the Carter household.[56]

Fithian's southern journey, however, was not without its torments; tu-
tors were expected to participate as equals in the social life of the
family, accompanying it in its travels to other plantations and to
Williamsburg. For this he had not been prepared. One of the favorite
amusements of the gentry was dancing; a good dancing master could expect regular employment in instructing the art to budding gentlemen and
ladies whose education would have been incomplete without it. But for
Fithian, balls were an ordeal. "Ben [Carter] came with a Message for me
to go to a Ball, but poor fellow, I cant dance!" Again: "the young Ladies
tell me we are to have a Ball, of selected Friends in this Family—But I,
hard Lot, I have never learn'd to dance!" "Poor me! I must hobble, or set
quiet in the Corner!" More than circumstance was at fault acknowledged
Fithian as he complained of his own education which had failed to teach
him "what I think is an innocent and an ornamental, and most certainly,
in this province . . . necessary qualification for a person to appear even
decent in Company!"[57]

Each English immigrant coming to Virginia with aspirations to wealth
and gentility brought with him, or acquired, at least one of the several
"courtesy books" written in the seventeenth century, among which
Henry Peacham's *The Complete Gentleman* (1622) was "one of the best
known."[58] If men like William Fitzhugh, Ralph Wormeley, or William
Byrd II, and the men who sought to emulate them, took Peacham's advice
seriously then the old stereotype of the Virginia planter as frivolous and
immoderate must be definitively dispelled, for Peacham's advice was
sobering indeed. Fear of God and "good learning," or the humanists'
program as laid out by Vergerio, Guarino da Verona, and Vittorino da
Feltre, were the foundations of a true gentleman's character and conduct.

William Byrd II honored well the precription for the gentleman provided by Henry Peacham and other Renaissance writers on gentlemanly
breeding. He spent virtually all of his adult life in the service of Virginia,
as agent for the colony in London, member of the House of Burgesses and
the Council of State, receiver-general for the colony, and colonel of the
militia of Henrico County. He took care to say his prayers regularly (in
which he often admittedly failed), to read his daily portions of Greek, Hebrew, and French, practice his drawing, exercise, and engage in sociability with his neighbors or, if in London, the various court luminaries,
business acquaintances and ladies who made up his London circle.
Fashion was important to him, but no substitute for genuine accomplishment or feeling. His daily studies in Greek and Latin were sufficiently
sincere undertakings that they would yield classical allusions throughout

the *History of the Dividing Line, The Progress to the Mines* and *The Journey to the Land of Eden,* not to mention the charm of a stylized marriage proposal composed in Greek.[59] His literary style may have been somewhat conventional, as a recent biographer intimates; it is the nature of this conventionality—its adherence to the stylized expression of the London literati—which matters here. His library shared with Cotton Mather's and James Logan's the distinction of being one of the finest in the colonies and his pride in his membership in the Royal Society was justified by the sincerity of his enthusiasm for natural science, if not his actual output of scientific treatises.[60] But let Byrd describe the sort of gentleman *he* thought he was:

> His conversation was easy, sensible and inoffensive, never bordering either upon profaneness, or indecency. He was always tender of the modesty of those that were present, and of the reputation of those that were absent. . . . He was the never failing friend of ye unfortunate, and good nature was the constantest of all his virtues. He pay'd his Court more to obscure merit, than to corrupt Greatness. He never cou'd flatter any body, no not himself, which were two invincible bars to all preferment. . . . His religion is more in substance than in form, and he is more forward to practice virtue than profess it. . . . He never interlopt with anothers wife or mistress, but dealt altogether where the Trade was open & free for all Adventurers. . . . He loved retirement, that while he is acquainted with the world, he may not be a stranger to himself. . . . He often frequented the company of Women, not so much to improve his mind as to polish his behavior. . . . All the ingenious tortures of the Inquisition cant force him to betray either his Faith, or his Friend.[61]

William Byrd II was undoubtedly as urbane as any of Virginia's "first gentlemen." And yet his writings reveal less a thorough commitment to urbanity than an ambiguous attitude toward city and country; unlike his brother-in-law Robert Beverley, Byrd could never become completely absorbed in provincial life. He proclaimed the virtues of "retirement" to country life often enough and honored literary convention by creating for his London friends a pastoral setting for himself in which he led a life of simplicity, independence, and hospitality, "attended" only by the trouble of keeping all his "people to their duty." "A library, a garden, a grove, and a purling stream are the innocent scenes that divert our leisure," he wrote. "Thus, my Lord, we are very happy in our Canaans if we could but forget the onions and fleshpots of Egypt."[62] Byrd could not forget. His love for the country was slightly less for its substance than a matter of style, and no less significantly, for what it would yield. Byrd was, like most of his contemporaries, a land speculator as well as farmer, full of schemes to settle immigrants on his properties or to exploit possible iron deposits. His plan for the town of Richmond was, unlike Williamsburg's, an undistinguished grid which lent itself primarily to surveying into regular lots for ready sale.[63]

Meanwhile this Virginia gentleman made the long journey to London frequently not only in the service of his colony, but to carry on at the Spanish Ambassador's, be entertained at the restoration theater or Will's Coffeehouse, "haunt of poets and critics," or to entertain a number of ladies whose indentities were confessed not always even to the secret diaries.[64] In the end, Byrd probably agreed with his daughters who complained that "they like everything about the country except the retirement: they can't get the plays, the operas, and the masquerades out of their heads. However, the lightness of our atmosphere helps them to bear all their losses with more spirit." While standing on an ocean bluff on the Virginia coast he heard "the breakers rise mountains high with a terrible noise . . . cast a longing eye toward England and sighed."[65]

The tension between the city and the country which Byrd experienced was not peculiar to himself; it appeared in the Latin literature he read and in Henry Peacham's warning that too much time spent in London leads to dissolution.[66] Opposing conceptions of city and country had become literary convention, as in *The Ladies Complete Letter-Writer,* a manual of epistolary style which was among the books Robert Carter required his daughter, Nancy, to read.[67] Among the subjects in this compilation of letters for emulation were "From Wives to Husbands, in many Situations; From Sisters to their Brothers; On Death; . . . Female Economy; Hiring and Management of Servants; Dress, Balls, Assemblies"—and "On the Pleasures of the Country and the Joys of the Town." Just what those pleasures and joys were supposed to be was engagingly revealed for young ladies who would express in felicitous style the sentiments appropriate to the gentlewoman. "Clora" was advised that retirement "to Country Shades for sake of heavenly Contemplation" was "the most certain way to Happiness," for "the Gay and Ambitious" would be left behind "to divide the Honours and Pleasures of the World" and the mind disengaged "from those Interests and Passions which mankind generally pursue." Besides, queried "An Invitation to the Country for the Summer," "what can you do all the dull Season in London?"[68]

Judging from one letter the sentiments to be expressed by the young lady who did in fact retire to country shades were somewhat mixed:

> I am now I don't know how many Miles distant from dear London,
> the Seat of your Joys, and must not expect to see again those Places

of Diversion and gaiety to which, alas! I have been too much endeared. . . . in a Month or two I shall be reconciled to gloomy Shades, tall Trees, and murmuring Brooks, and all the Sylvan Scenes which surround me; and even cease to regret my Distance from the Genteel Entertainments of the gay and polite World. . . . Here are no powdered Beaus, or gilt Equipages, none of the splendid Allurements with which Ladies of your Vivacity are apt to be captivated: But, for my Part, a natural Tincture of Gravity may possibly make me more easily support the Absence of what your gayer Disposition may induce you to consider as the very Essence of Happiness.[69]

Another letter, an illustration of what one mother might write another on the education of daughters, expressed less condifidence in the instructive potential of contemplation by the side of murmuring brooks when compared with exposure to "the Humours of the Town." The more a young lady "is acquainted with what you so carefully hide from her," promised this letter, "the more her Good-Sense, and the excellent Rudiments you have given her, will teach her to despise it."[70] The conceptions of city and country modeled here were those in which only a gentry class could indulge: the city was a place of gaiety and worldliness while the country was a place of innocence and contemplative appreciation of nature as sublimity itself.

These stylized conceptions were not, of course, wholly without some reinforcement from experience. When he arrived in Virginia in 1710 Alexander Spotswood wrote his cousin that he expected to live "contentedly" in Williamsburg, for "if I have not the diversions of London (which I do not in the least hanker after) neither have I the perplexitys of that Town." He looked forward to a release from "a Crowd of Company . . . a Throng of Business" and a life led "after a quiet Country manner . . . with planting orchard & gardens, & with furnishing a large House which is designed . . . for the reception of their Governor".[71] Attitudes remained equivocal, nonetheless, for country life, whatever its charms, remained a solitary way; and these first gentlemen of Virginia were reared for the public life and society of the city. As the storm clouds of revolution began to gather over the Atlantic, Landon Carter would find himself chided for wanting to stay at Sabine Hall when his country and constituents had summoned him to Williamsburg.[72]

The innocence and self-sufficiency of rural life would continue to nourish the young country's imaginings. Once London was lost to the Virginians as exemplary of the way of life proper to gentlemen rulers, they were forced to turn back upon themselves and only then did the country, as much a literary motif as a wide reach of earth, begin to become their true and proper habitat. But it was an uncomfortable transformation; the agricultural society which John Taylor of Caroline summoned from memory to inspire republican virtue in the young nation belonged not to the yeoman farmer, as Jeffersonian idealogy would have it, but to a small group of fortunate men who lived the paradox of urbane gentility, with its attendant political sophistication, in an unlettered wilderness. The passing into time of their influence entailed more than the displacement of a colonial aristocracy by an American democracy; with them passed a pervasive aesthetic of harmony and symmetry, of proportion and balance, of formalism and refinement, in life as well as art.

✻

Unlike Boston or Philadelphia, which emerged in the eighteenth century as colonial cities in spite of their founders' hopes that they would remain no more than modest towns serving the limited market needs of a rural colonial society, Williamsburg failed to become the "city" envisioned in the acts of 1699 and 1705. Her vitality was dependent upon the seasonal political congregations called fourth by the meetings of the General Assembly. Those gatherings, and the quarterly "public times" or meetings of the General Court and the Oyer and Terminer Court, occasioned a flurry of social activity, whether at the governor's palace, neighboring plantations, or Raleigh Tavern. They provided audiences for Williamsburg's first (and the colonies' first) theater, erected in 1751, and customers for her booksellers and craftsmen, if only to repair or copy articles imported from London. Four times a year the town became a colonial financial market as well. But as often as not the town remained a "sleepy little village" as the "men of fashion and business" returned to their plantations, leaving behind the college students who hoped to benefit from their company, a small population of regular residents—tradesmen, printers, officials, innkeepers—and the enslaved negro domestics who served them.[73]

Governor Nicholson's new capital had hardly received the charter of incorporation (1722) promised in the Act of 1705 before William Byrd II began to lay out a town on a piece of land at Shocco he inherited from his father, which he would rename Richmond, after Richmond on the Thames. That enterprising planter, whose heart was always torn between London and Virginia, was succeeding in mastering the arts of the American urban entrepreneur as well as those of the urbane gentleman. His efficient if aesthetically uninspired grid town plat at the first falls of the James River soon became the seat of Henrico County and, as Virginia's population center began to move westward, so too did its capital city. As the Continental Congress prepared in 1799 to send John Adams to negotiate peace with Great Britain, Byrd's town was chosen as the new capital of the Commonwealth of Virginia, to become hereafter the meeting place of the Virginia General Assembly. Williamsburg, created largely as a "commodius" setting for the assembly, lost, with the assembly, her chief purpose in the colony. Better sited as a regional manufacturing and distribution center, Richmond would supplant James Blair's theater of urbane culture whose primary legacy, as indeed its original conception, would remain symbolic and aesthetic in nature.

Williamsburg's significance lies not so much in what the city became, as in what it came to represent. Seventeenth-century Virginia's many ill-fated towns had been conceived to serve limited market functions in an agrarian setting within an empire governed by the rules of mercantilism. But the purpose of Williamsburg had been to represent political and social sovereignty, to provide a setting worthy of the periodic assemblies of those who ruled. Precisely because Williamsburg's function was largely ceremonial, the city was conceived as a work of art much in the same way that the cultural style she embodied was a work of art. This was Williamsburg's, and Virginia's, inheritance from the Renaissance. In contrast to Boston or Philadelphia, the capital city of Virginia was in its conception an aesthetic statement. The principles of that aesthetic, the principles of formalized and rationalized harmony achieved through mathematically contrived proportions, were a projection of a cultural style adopted by and for an elite planter class to enhance its own aspirations toward social and political ascendancy. Derived from a European tradition of the constructed, refined, and cultivated self it became identified, in the context of its origins, with the city.

What may seem a curious anomaly—the statutory creation of a Renaissance city in the midst of an intensely agrarian landscape—was not, so anomalous after all. The particular conception that created Williamsburg may have been the only viable urban conception possible at the close of Virginia's first century. As we have seen, the seventeenth-century Englishman's perception of the city was closely intertwined with his perception of the country. John Winthrop and William Penn had feared the city because it represented to them the disruption of a rural world in which industrious husbandry and righteousness would be perpetuated under the rule of the "better sort." The city, with its commerce and manufacturers, represented economic and social dislocations which could be perceived but ominously by men predisposed through their religious convictions to measure all change in moral terms. The wealth of the city seemed to bear little relation to economic probity, just as the presence of its impoverished rabble threatened not only social stability, but the virtue of industrious labor itself. At the heart of the conflict between the country and the city, in the minds of men like Winthrop and Penn, lay the problem of the relationship of labor to land, virtue, wealth, and influence.

Because of Virginia's special social, political, and economic development toward the close of the seventeenth century, the moral conditions of work and leadership became substantially altered from what they had been for the founders of Massachusetts Bay and Pennsylvania. As a result, the symbolic and actual significance of the country and the city were also altered. To begin with, the elite planter class whose aspirations created Williamsburg were largely the scions of middle-class immigrant families into Virginia of the 1640's and 1650's. They had been less personally engaged in the toils of settlement themselves, resting their claims to their lands in Virginia on titles derived from original investments in the Virginia Company. Their economic ties were with the commercial world of London rather than the rural world of the remote English counties.[74] Thus gentility, with its urbane refinements, was an object of ambition, a means to dignity and status, rather than a condition naturally acquired through the immediate experience of social and moral leadership in the English countryside. They had less to fear from the city so long as the city continued to represent for them the stage on which the successful acted out their roles of political and cultural authority.

Moreover, as a rural aristocracy, Virginia's planters at the turn of the century were in significant ways unlike the rural aristocracy whose survival was challenged, in the minds of a John Winthrop or a William Penn, by the increasing capacity of the city to reward the corrupt and slothful as it relegated the industrious to oblivion. While Virginia's aristocracy managed its own estates, keeping their "people to their duty"—and some, like Landon Carter, did so with "scientific" care—their financial success depended less on their own husbandry than upon their ability to accumulate increasing amounts of land and later slaves, a circumstance in which tobacco cultivation conspired with the relative availability of land. Furthermore, the inheritance of patriarchal status and responsibility which had constituted an essential element in rural social stability in old England, gradually dissappeared in Virginia as primogeniture and entail were abandoned in order to provide generations of offspring with the principal form of livelihood and wealth in Virginia—land.[75] If the country in England represented the continuation of social stability and virtue through the symbiotic perpetuation of virtuous hubandry and morally accountable patriarchal leadership, it acquired a lesser moral significance as it came to symbolize, through the accumulation of landed wealth, success for Virginia's planters of middle-class origins eager for acccoutrements of gentility which were in fact urban in nature. The country became for them not an end in itself, but a means to an end.

Finally, the country lost its moral content in Virginia as the seventeenth century drew to a close because of the peculiar way in which Virginians had resolved the problem of labor in their tobacco economy. The period 1689 to 1705 was remarkable not only because it produced the establishment of the College of William and Mary and the statutory creation of Williamsburg, but because it saw the beginning of the importation in earnest of negro slaves into the colony. The same year that saw the passing of the Act of 1705 to build Williamsburg was also the year in which almost double the number of slaves was imported over any previous year, and in which the colony's growing number of slave regulations was codified into law.[76] Meanwhile Virginia's assemblies, magnates, and her governor were learning to court the small freemen of the colony in their political contests, thus deepening the chasm between white labor and black.[77] As the number of small property owners increased in the last quarter of the seventeenth century, the size of their properties decreased with the remaining available amount of unclaimed land. But as the price of tobacco rose, so too did the small white farmer's economic position and, more importantly, his political influence as the burden of exploitation was shifted to the backs of black enslaved laborers.[78]

Virginia's "peculiar institution" may then help to explain the difference in her manifest perceptions of the city and the country. Having transferred the drudgery of rural toil to a growing population of negro slaves, the planter also denied himself the moral satisfaction of self-sufficiency through industrious husbandry. However conscienciously he might manage his land and his slaves, he could not himself fully enjoy the satisfactions of Livy's Cincinnatus. His love of the country would necessarily become the stylized love of "a garden, a grove, and a purling stream . . . the innocent scenes that divert our leisure." If he could not find moral self-justification on the strength of his husbandry, he would have to seek it elsewhere. He found it in the theater of political and cultural leadership represented by the city that was to have been Williamsburg, as well as by the urbane way of life he pursued at Westover, or Carter's Grove, or Nomini Hall, or Berkeley Plantation, or numerous other "country seats." And the city as a cultural theater could become all the more attractive for the city of the Virginia planter was free of the "scruff and scum" of humanity that swarmed the depths of London and alarmed men like Winthrop and Penn; the dispossessed of Virginia society, because of her economy and her peculiar institution, remained imprisoned in the countryside. Virginia's urbane first gentlemen, and the city they conceived to symbolize their cultural ambitions, depended for their existence upon their release from righteous toil made possible by the colony's special place in the economic and social history of early America.[79]

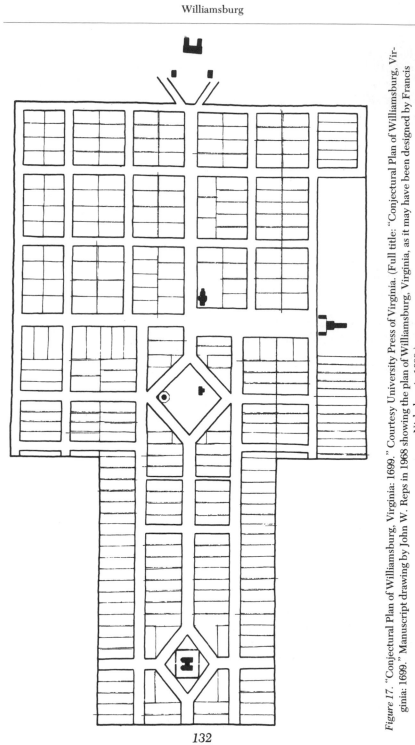

Figure 17. "Conjectural Plan of Williamsburg, Virginia: 1699." Courtesy University Press of Virginia. (Full title: "Conjectural Plan of Williamsburg, Virginia: 1699." Manuscript drawing by John W. Reps in 1968 showing the plan of Williamsburg, Virginia, as it may have been designed by Francis Nicholson in 1699.)

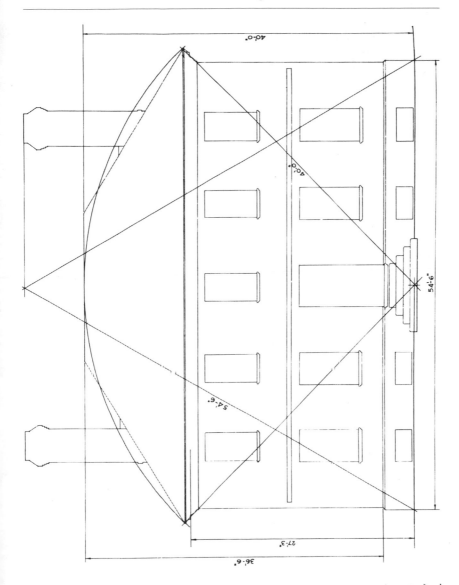

Figure 18. The Wythe House. Diagrammatic elevation, showing system of proportion, as analyzed by Marcus Whiffen. Courtesy Holt, Rinehart & Winston.

133

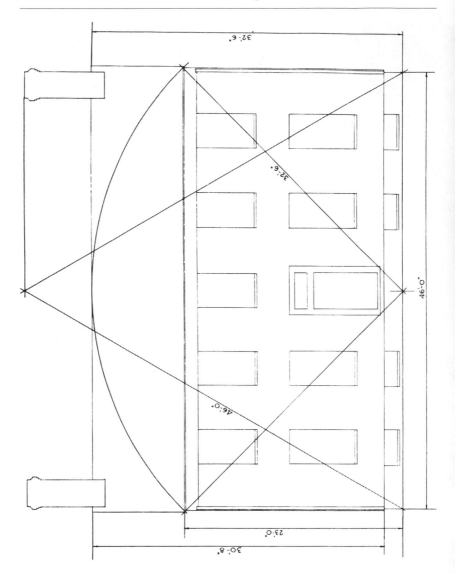

Figure 19. The Archibald Blair House. Diagrammatic elevation showing system of proportion, as analyzed by Marcus Whiffen. Courtesy Holt, Rinehart & Winston.

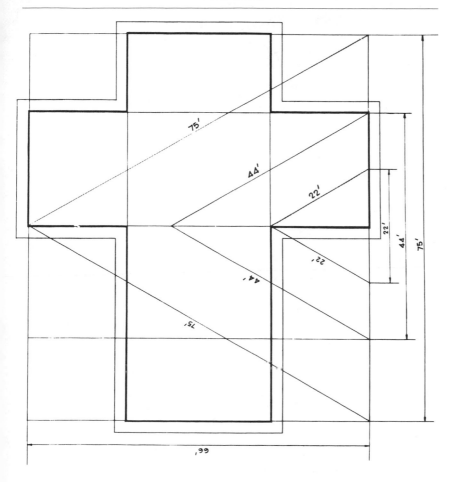

Figure 20. Bruton Parish Church. Diagrammatic plan of the building as originally designed, showing system of proportion, as analyzed by Marcus Whiffen. Courtesy Holt, Rinehart & Winston.

5

Savannah: The City in the Country

꘎

In the summer of 1729, while James Edward Oglethorpe was gathering the support of "several parliament men, clergy, &c." for a project to settle "a colony of a hundred English families on the river Savannah," William Byrd of Westover confided to John Percival, Earl of Egmont, his reservations about Bishop George Berkeley's plan to establish a college in Bermuda for the conversion of the Indians to Christianity. Berkeley's "pious design," wrote Byrd, was the "romantic . . . visionary scheme" of a "Don Quixote."

> Is it not a wild undertaking to build a college in a country where there
> is no bread, nor anything fit for the sustenance of man, but onions
> and cabbages. . . . Then when this college is built, where will the
> Dean find the Indians to be converted?

The only way Berkeley could procure his Indians, presumed Byrd, would be to seize them "upon the coast of Florida," a measure "as meritorious, as the Holy War used to be of old" and, if they proved recalcitrant in conversion, "take the French way, and dragoon them into Christianity."[1] Percival's reply to Byrd was that he would "not undertake to dispute with you the feasibleness of the execution." He would later caution Berkeley that "the design seems too great and good to be accomplished in an age where men love darkness better than the light, and nothing is considered but with a political view."[2] The key to an understanding of the Georgia Trustees' vision for Georgia and their plan for the city of Savannah lies not in the utopianism conventionally ascribed to the Trustees, but in Percival's weary assessment that "men love darkness better than the light."[3]

Much had changed since John Winthrop's earnest company settled the Massachusetts Bay. The England of Elizabeth and John Foxe had endured the ordeal of civil upheaval to become the complacent Britain of latitudinarianism, the parliamentary settlements of 1689–1701 and the Hanoverian succession, and the ministerial government of Robert Walpole. The distinction between the country and the city had likewise, with the national purpose, undergone a loss of clarity. The inevitability of trade and commerce impinged upon the belief of a John Winthrop or a William Penn that a traditional feudal rural society could be preserved, protected from the social, economic, and moral dislocations of the city. Common to the perceptions of the city held by the founders of Boston and Philadelphia was a fundamental set of presumptions about the relationship between labor, land, and virtue. For Winthrop and Penn the nurture of virtue was measured in terms of uniformity in religious conviction, economic probity through labor and wealth in the land, and the preservation of an hierarchical, traditional rural world. Thus, for them, the imminence of the heterogeneous and commercial city became antipodal to the triumph of virtue. In Virginia the increasing reliance on slavery upset the formula for virtue contained in the social expectations that had underlain the founding of Massachusetts Bay and Pennsylvania. Righteous toil on the land as the basis for political responsibility, and hence the possibility of civic if not religious, virtue, no longer could yield traditional moral authority; the burden of rural labor had been passed to men and women bonded in interminable servitude and subjection. Virginia's planters, as a result, could look upon the city more positively. Not only might their city of Williamsburg be immune from the social upheaval of the dispossessed, but upon the city was placed greater emphasis as the locus of the exercise of virtue—a virtue which to the Virginia elite of necessity had become the political virtue of public service in the city. The setting of their self-justification was transferred from the righteous assemblies of the country to the theater of political power at Williamsburg.

The attainment of virtue remained a problem for the public-spirited persons of Augustan England, but the terms of the problem had changed since the Puritan Revolution sought to assure England its place in sacred history as the Elect Nation. Not the least of the casualties of the crisis of the 1640's and 1650's had been the belief that public virtue was dependent upon religious virtue. Religious virtue had required an acceptance of descending authority and ascending allegiance in matters political as well as spiritual. Thus the notion of the "ancient constitution" as descriptive of a political harmony derived through the hierarchical balance of royal authority and the liberty of a loyal people was bound to undergo a transformation as well.[4]

It was at this juncture that James Harrington's restatement of English history in *Oceana* (1656) provided the parties to the debates of 1658–1689 over the relative roles of the monarchy and parliament with a new frame of historical reference, a reinterpretation of the "ancient constitution," and a new definition of civic virtue. For Harrington, and the neo-Harringtonian Independent Whig publicists of the half century after 1689, the essence of political harmony upon which the survival of any commonwealth was seen to depend, was conceived not in hierarchical but in lateral terms. That is, the enduring commonwealth rests upon a Polybian balance of power elements against one another. The terms of the problem of virtue had been shifted from a Christian and traditional view of the public world to a neoclassical interpretation of politics. Virtue became less a religious problem than a political one; it inhered in the ability of a people to maintain the balance of power within the English constitution, and their capacity to do so depended upon their independence relative to the power of the monarchy. This independence was, according to Harrington, the result of two conditions: freehold tenure and the right to bear arms.[5]

The Harringtonian redefinition of civic virtue bore fruit in the Court-Country controversies of the early eighteenth century. At issue was the potential "corruption" of the balance of the ancient constitution, a balance perceived, in Machiavellian terms, as necessary to the preservation of English liberties. The sources of this corruption, and hence loss of civic virtue, were alleged to come, in the view of Country proponents, from the emergence of standing armies and the incursion of ministerial patronage into the deliberations of parliament. The growth of a professional standing army, the product of Britain's military conflicts with France and Spain, was seen to threaten the independence of an arms-bearing citizenry. At the same time, the use of patronage and the appearance of the king's placemen in Parliament appeared as a subversion of parliamentary independence. Added to the debate was the increasing anxiety among Country ideologues over the growth of commerce and the national debt. The "opposition" to the Walpole Whigs did not reject outright trade and commerce in favor of land; rather, they feared the dependence of the moneyed interests on the government. Furthermore, if wealth, whether it came from the land or from commerce, could become a marketable commodity, so also could political independence, or civic virtue.[6]

The motivations for the Georgia Trustees' plan for Georgia were military and mercantile as well as philanthropic. Yet the full significance of the Georgia enterprise can be understood only in the context of the Augustan concern for, and analysis of, civic virtue. The Georgia Trustees' design for the colony entrusted to them was overwhelmingly agrarian in character; but it did not, at the same time, represent a rejection of the city. The antithesis between the country and the city which had seemed so clear to the founders of Boston and Philadelphia had become blurred in the contemporary debate over public virtue in the context of the new realities of money, trade, and credit—necessary to national prosperity, and located in the city. Thus what was attempted in Georgia by the Trustees was not simply a scheme to restore a wholly agrarian society of independent arms-bearing yeoman proprietors, although that was an important element in the Georgia plan. In the design of Savannah they revealed an acceptance of the city—but they sought to cleanse the city of its economic dislocations and political corruption by reintegrating the city with the country into a social whole which, once achieved, might restore a viable polity sustained by the public virtue of an independent citizenry. Theirs was a complex and ambiguous vision framed in the context of a quarrel among Englishmen. But the failure of their enterprise in material terms should not obscure its success in symbolic terms. The Georgia plan and the plan of Savannah introduced a uniquely American conception of the city, one which was explored repeatedly by nineteenth-century utopian communities and the "new town" planners of the twentieth century. Savannah represented an attempt to create a city—accepted as a cultural necessity—while purifying it through the integration with it of rural proprietorship, and thus civic virtue.

❧

Both supporters and opponents of the Walpole ministry, as well as Independents, could be found among the most active of the seventy-one members elected or appointed to the Georgia Trust. Indeed, the very lack of agreement on the question of loyalty to Walpole among the Trustees, many of whom were members of Parliament, was a frequent source of contention, much to the dismay of John Percival.[7] Percival himself was in intimate of the king and queen and tended to support Sir Robert, who had engineered his advancement to the rank of Earl. Nonetheless Percival was capable of passing harsh judgment on the first minister who, he alleged, had incurred much of the "ill-will" against himself on account of his "meanness . . . the prostitution of the character of a first minister in assisting and strenuously supporting the defence of dunghill worms, let their cause be ever so unjust, against men of honour, birth, and fortune."[8] Percival and James Oglethorpe, who regarded himself as a mild High Tory, might disagree on fine points of politics, but they shared a profound unease that luxury—to which wealth and position had entitled them both—was dangerous to moral character.

Oglethorpe's second marriage to the heiress Elizabeth Wright would assure him a firm place in the social life of London. Yet he was known to lecture his regular dinner guests—Samuel Johnson, James Boswell and

Oliver Goldsmith—on the evils of luxury. "The best depends much upon ourselves," he declaimed, "and if we can be as well satisfied with plain things, we are in the wrong to accustom our palates to what is high-seasoned and expensive."[9] Percival had addressed similar scruples to the Queen Caroline, lamenting the "cheating and overreaching [of] our neighbors . . . occasioned by riches, trade, and the great increase of the city." He had been sorely stung by the extravagance of his own son in Ireland and was hardly less displeased by the prince's amours with the royal chambermaids. The queen replied with some perception, "may be you are for reducing people to poverty to make them honest." Percival demurred, explaining "I would not have the nation poorer, yet it were better if riches were more equally divided . . . if the nation were richer we should never be better, because everything we bought would be dearer, and then the poor would be scarce able to live."[10] Oglethorpe's and Percival's concern that luxury entailed moral deblitation, their solicitude for the poor, and Percival's suspicion that "it were better if riches were more equally divided," would be mirrored in their expectations of Georgia.

We are never likely to know the full extent and nature of the poverty that pursued the day laborers and displaced farmers of late seventeenth- and early eighteenth-century England. But the growing contrast of vagabond and pauper with the wealth of a nation prospering from imminent commercial hegemony was no where more pronounced than in London. The city played an ungenerous host to multitudes of the unemployed, their ranks increased by veterans of England's Continental wars.[11] In his first proposals to the Pennsylvania "adventurers" of 1681 William Penn had blamed the fact that "the land swarmed with beggars" to the flight of the country people to the city, where men are "effeminated by lazy and luxurious living," and the resulting "decay of country manufactures." "Formerly, it was rare," observed the founder of Pennsylvania,

> to find any asking alms but the maimed or blind, or very aged, now thousands of both sexes run up and down both city and country, that are sound and youthful and able to work . . . nor is there any care taken to employ or deter such vagrants.[12]

Vagrants might have found work in the "Union" houses after 1723, whence they would be hired out to be exploited by manufacturers; but neither workhouse nor an inadequately functioning Poor Law served to ameliorate the desperate condition of the poor. The prevailing tendency in the seventeenth century was to attribute poverty, itself an uncomfortable suggestion of national failure, to vice and idleness. John Locke had been content to blame the poverty of the working classes on "nothing else but the relaxation of discipline and corruption of manners."[13] An augury of declining republican virtue was manifest not only in the "effeminated" urban rich, but in the dependent urban poor; both ends of the economic spectrum of the city were an affront to the moral integrity of the nation.

How different from Penn's and Locke's approach to poverty was that which appeared in "A New and Accurate Account of the Provinces of South Carolina and Georgia," written for the Georgia Trustees in 1732 by their secretary, Benjamin Martyn:

> Let us . . . cast our Eyes on the Multitude of unfortunate People in the Kingdom of reputable families, and of liberal . . . Education. Some undone by Guardians, some by Law–Suits, some by Accidents in Commerce, some by Stocks and Bubbles, and some by Suretyship. . . . What various Misfortunes may reduce the Rich, the Industrious, to the Danger of a Prison, to a moral certainty of Starving![14]

Martyn's poor deserved sympathy because many seemed to be innocent victims of an unscrupulous commercial world that rewarded connivance before it bowed to sober industriousness. The well-to-do to whom the Georgia Trustees turned for subscriptions to finance their undertaking might readily sympathize with victims of "Stocks and Bubbles" and "Law-Suits" who, but for the grace of God, might include one of themselves.[15] But those "industrious" poor, not "our Common Run of Old-Baily Transports," and occasional "Emeriti" of the State[16] who were to benefit from the second chance being offered them in Georgia did not simply include the middling sort who drew losing numbers in the city's lottery of success. The undeserving poor would also include those "wretched creatures" who "infested" the roads of England and who were referred to with great anxiety throughout the sermons delivered before the Trustees at their annual London meetings.[17]

The anniversary sermons served, along with the express promotional literature penned by Benjamin Martyn and Oglethorpe, as the principal vehicle of persuasion for support for the Georgia colony. Discreetly printed and distributed, the sermons reflected the range of avowed purposes for which the Georgia project had been designed and mirrored in the charter of 1732: to relieve unemployment, to Christianize the native Indians, to enhance Britain's colonial defenses against the Spanish, to increase Britain's mercantile wealth, and to provide a place of refuge for the persecuted Protestants of the Continent.[18] But the most anxious phrases were reserved for the problem of the poor. Typical of the sermons was Samuel Smith's assurance that

> Plantations, in proportion to the kind and Quantity of Goods imported from them, are Supports to the Dignity and Revenue of the Sovereign, and Conveyances of Wealth to the People. But this Design may perhaps appear to affect our Interests more nearly in other Lights. The annual Resort of Multitudes to this Town, unless they could be rendered serviceable in proper Employments, must be attended with Inconveniences to the publick Tranquility. Most Crimes at least . . . may be justly charg'd to Poverty, or its common Parent, Idleness. But from whatever cause they are found to proceed . . . a Deluge of wickedness seems to have been breaking upon us.[19]

If the Poor Laws were only properly executed, explained Philip Bearcroft, there would be no problem. But "do not our streets swarm, and are we not daily stopped, and pestered by these Vagrants? "[20] The poor have "not only become a Burden to the Publick," warned William Berriman, "but [they] endanger the common Peace by their Disorders."[21] Fulfillment of the Trustees' aims, promised Lewis Bruce, would reduce the danger to the public peace of those "turbulent men" who have not been quieted by "coercive or penal laws" and could be found in great numbers "in this great City, the Refuge and Asylum of luxurious Vices, which enervate Mankind."[22]

What concerned the supporters of Georgia was not primarily the economic causes, and hence possible economic remedies for, poverty. Their preoccupation was with the *moral* effects of poverty, just as they were concerned with the moral effects of commercial wealth.[23] They could speak, as did Percival and Samuel Smith, simultaneously of the vices of luxury and the vices of poverty. What disturbed them was an apparent loss of virtue entailed in an economic environment in which wealth was dissasociated from "industry." This disassociation became all the more problematic in the city which seemed to foster it, and not only that, displayed it with the vast discrepancies of wealth which threatened not only virtue, but the civil peace. If there was to be a solution to the related imbalances of industry and wealth, and rich and poor, it would come about only through a restoration of that harmonious order in which men and women could achieve independence through their own labor, and thus recover their capacity for moral conduct and public virtue. Percival may not have actually sought to reduce "people to poverty to make them honest," as the queen charged. But he did envision their return to a form of labor in which their economic independence would be a measure of their industry and thus moral probity would become the fruit of material effort. The only form of labor that seemed to allow for such a restoration of economic harmony and hence civic virtue, was the cultivation of land equitably distributed.

The authors of the promotional tracts published by the Georgia Trust turned for the validation of their purposes not only to scripture, but to history. Their choice of the Roman republic of Livy and Machiavelli as a model of the exemplary society reveals their concern for civic virtue as the foundation of liberty and their association of civic virtue with independent proprietorship. Moreover, that virtue and independent proprietorship could be achieved through colonization enhanced the value of the republic as a guiding image in their conception of Georgia. The applicability of the example of the colonizing activities of republican Rome to imperial Britain had been suggested by Walter Moyle, a close associate of the Independent Whig publicists of the turn of the century. Through colonization Rome under the republic had extended her citizenship with its rights and her civilization throughout the Mediterannean world. Choosing colonies rather than garrisons as her instruments of expansion, Rome was not only able to preserve her liberties among newly acquired territories, but provide for her expanding population and veterans through the acquisition of land. "Merit and virility," not brute conquest was the means by which colonial expansion served to increase, rather than deplete, her human and material resources. Moreover, the civic virtue of the Romans, which might have been a casualty of imperial expansion, was preserved in the figure of the citizen-warrior.[24]

The example of Rome was heralded not only by Independent Whigs defending colonization, but by the clergymen who delivered the anniversary sermons before the Georgia Trustees. Virtually every sermon cited the example of republican Rome in its defense of the Georgia undertaking. Perhaps the clearest evocation of the memory of Rome as it shaped the Trustees' vision of Georgia was offered by Philip Bearcroft in his anniversary sermon of 1737. "An equal Quantity of Land is given to every Planter sent over," he explained,

> that they may apply with Pleasure and Alacrity, to the Cultivation of their Farms . . . which will naturally raise such a general Industry, and virtuous Emulation through the Colony, that with the free-born Romans of Old, they will quit the Plough only to transact the Business of their rising State; and that finished, hasten back to the Labors of the Field, and at the Close of them, sit with their Wives and Children, under their own Vines and Fruit-Trees, and enjoy Themselves, in a virtuous Frugality, under the happy Influence of this Agrarian Law.[25]

Here, at the meeting of the contemporary Augustan concern for public morality in a world in which extremes in wealth threatened the civil peace as well as civic virtue, the neo-Harringtonian veneration of the independent, arms–bearing yeoman proprietor, and the memory of republican Rome engaged in extending her liberties throughout an expanding empire,[26] lay the intellectual foundations of the Georgia plan. These elements were embodied in a land policy designed to achieve what amounted to the Harringtonian formula for a durable commonwealth: an equitable distribution of land among a population of independent freehold proprietors with safeguards against the conversion of land into a marketable commodity, and the protection of liberties within the setting of imperial expansion through the maintenance of a citizen army. That such a formula was compatible with the needs of actual mercantile policy in the 1730's no doubt enhanced its appeal.

∗

What the Georgia Trustees envisioned for their colonial enterprise was the restoration of a society of modest farm households, each family working industriously a parcel of land within its honest capacity and adequate to sustain itself. The Trustees themselves were not to profit from their undertaking. Their disinterestedness would be insured by a provision in the Charter of 1732 prohibiting members of the Corporation from receiving any "salary, fee, perquisite, benefit or profit" or grant of land and reserving "all rents and profits" for "the development of the colony."[27] Land should not become a marketable commodity either for the Trustees or for the beneficiaries of their philanthropy. They suspected rightly that absentee ownership as well as real-estate speculation would undermine their vision of a society of industrious freehold proprietors. Percival, who with Oglethorpe was the most likely draftsman of the social and economic outlines of the Georgia plan, had been admonished by his uncle and guardian, Sir Robert Southwell, not to allow his Irish tenants any more than each, with his own stock, could manage. Otherwise "some Irish gentleman that has nothing of his own . . . may bring in his followers, and while he makes them pay double the rent, he lives idly upon the over-plus himself."[28] Each grantee in Georgia was required to cultivate his lot himself and forbidden to lease his lot without a special license "that the Colony may not be ruined by Absentees Receiving and Spending their Rents elsewhere."[29]

Each person sent to Georgia on charity was to receive a fifty-acre lot. Those settling in villages were to be given fifty-acre lots each, "to lie all together," while those settling in towns would have a sixty by ninety square foot town lot plus "as much Land in the Country as in the whole will make up Fifty Acres." At the risk of forfeiture, all grantees were to clear their lands, build defences and "habitations" within twelve months and work, as directed, "for the Common Good and publick Weal of the Colony."[30] They were required to inhabit and cultivate their lands for two years afterwards. Land could not, at first, be alienated. Although lots were granted "in Tail Male" to "Descend to the Heirs Male of their Bodies for ever," if there was a "failure of Issue Male," lots would revert to the Trust.[31]

The Georgia colony, from the point of view of the British government, was intended not only to relieve the distress of the poor, but to serve as a military buffer against the Spanish. The Lords Proprietors of South Carolina had given up their claims to the territory later called Georgia in 1729 in despair of protecting the region successfully against the assaults of the Spanish, pirates, and Yamasee Indians. The charter granted to the Georgia Trustees had included imperial defense as one of the purposes of the grant. Thus the Trustees were empowered to commission "any Commander or other Officer . . . to Train, Instruct, Exercise, and Govern, a Militia for the special Defence and Safety of the . . . Colony." In order to maintain "the Military Strength of the Province" the Trustees resolved "to Establish such Tenures of Lands as might most effectually preserve the Number of Planters, or Soldiers, equal to the Number of Lots of Lands, and therefore each Lot of Land was to be considered as a Military Fief."[32]

Georgia's expected role in the imperial defense, and the determination with which Oglethorpe pursued his military obligations, were in no way incompatible with the Trustees' social vision. A colony of yeoman proprietors under arms was in keeping with the ideological context in which Georgia was conceived. Oglethorpe's forces were not to be the professional "standing army" which Independent Whigs feared as potentially subversive of English liberties, but a citizen militia composed of Georgia's settlers. One version of the several "Accounts" of Georgia published by the Trustees lays out in considerable detail how civil and military considerations should combine in the organization of the colony. Georgia should be populated by three "sorts": townsmen, yeomen, and gentry. Each township would contain one town and twenty dependent villages, and together they would provide 625 foot-soldiers, 125 dragoons, and 100 horse. Here, again, antiquity was summoned as the authority for the conception and plan of Georgia. The Trustees' officers were described as having been given the powers of Roman officers in charge of Roman colonies, while the proposed form of colonial government—to be based on English tithings and hundreds—would be according to the "ancient English laws" by which Britain's Anglo-Saxon ancestors had transformed the English isle into a great and freedom-loving nation. Georgia was to become what England had been in the days of her "ancient constitu-tion."[33] As arms-bearing freemen, the yeomen proprietors of Georgia could recover the independence believed necessary to the restoration of public virtue in the commonwealth.

Military and ideological, if not humanitarian, considerations also underlay the Trustees' determination to exclude negro slavery from Georgia. While the Trustees had no scruples against engaging in the slave trade themselves,[34] they had cast a wary eye toward South Carolina and not liked what they had seen. There was another Barbados of large plantations worked, necessarily it was believed, by negro and Indian slaves. Not only did the possibility of slave insurrection pose a great danger in time of war, but the existence of negro slavery would hardly provide a hospitable setting for the society of modest freehold farms the Trustees sought to create in Georgia. Where large plantations were found slavery was more than likely to occur, and the Trustees wanted neither. Thus the "Rules for the Year 1735" and one of the two laws enacted by the Trustees prohibited the use of negro slaves in the colony.[35]

A society composed of self-sufficient families, "masters of houses and lands," could but slowly (and perhaps never) be created out of a popula-tion of dependent servants and large landowners. Originally the Trustees had hoped that by soliciting contributions they might provide passage and initial support for each settler so that "poor Adventurers" could go to Georgia without binding themselves "to Servitude."[36] But solicitations for gifts of money brought disappointing results. There was great public enthusiasm in response to the Trustees' unprecedented propaganda cam-paign, but too large a proportion of benefactions came from many well intentioned "Ladies" (each discretely desiring to remain anonymous as an "Unknown Hand") who gave several thousand bibles, tracts, testaments, catechisms and other assorted nourishment for the soul.[37] Failing an initial outpouring of gifts and support from Parliament in the first year to inaugurate the enterprise, the Trustees were forced to turn to the wealthy London merchant community. However, men like Sir Gilbert Heathcote, Sir Joseph Eyles, and Sir William Chapman were interested only in trade. The Trustees had to persuade such men that support for Georgia constituted a promising commercial investment. Nor was Parliament likely to extend its purse strings for the mere purpose of charity, espe-cially when it was argued by some that Georgia would draw off labor needed in England. Support from the merchant community and Parlia-ment was finally forthcoming—indeed, the government ultimately bore 90 percent of the financial cost of Georgia. But in order to receive ade-quate funding the Trustees, by the end of 1732, had to open the colony to financially independent settlers. The Georgia experiment was thus barely launched before a critical part of the Trustees' plan was subverted by the entry of "private adventurers" and indentured servants. [38]

The Trustees nonetheless struggled to preserve the character of their intended society by devising regulations which, they hoped, would speed and insure the restoration of servants to independence on the one hand, and prevent the worst excesses of large-scale land ownership, on the other. Private adventurers going to Georgia and taking with them ten servants (at their own expense) were granted five hundred acres in tail male. Land left without a male heir reverted to the Trust except for the main house and one-half of the improved land, which were allowed to the widow. Private adventurers, like the charity grantees, were initially forbidden to alienate land and were required to build upon and cultivate their lands within three years. But there was another important requirement too: holders of five hundred–acre grants would have to plant, within ten years, 1,000 mulberry plants for every hundred of the five hundred acres cleared; the Trust would provide the plants. [39] As for indentured servants, the Trustees had to concede that "for the better to Enable the said Persons [settlers sent on charity] to Build the new Town [Savannah], and clear the Lands," it would allow each Freeholder to take with him one male servant "or apprentice" at least eighteen years of age, bound in service for no more than four years. The Trust would pay for the servant's passage and provisions as a loan to the freeholder and allow three years from the date of embarkation from England for repayment. At the end of a servant's term he was assured of a grant of twenty acres of land. [40]

⁂

Speculative greed, large scale land-holdings and absentee ownership were not, however, the only possible impediments to the Georgia Trustees' restoration of "the integrity of the Primitive Times." Given the conditions from which many of the settlers would have come, their manners could be expected to improve only with a little "discipline." Once again the town came to symbolize social order. The "Rules for the Year 1735" specified that the settlers should live in towns or villages, where each settler's lands should "lie all together." Benjamin Martyn's prospectus for 1733 promised that those "unfortunate persons" given a second chance in Georgia would be re-established "in an orderly manner, so as to form a regulated town." [41] That town was to be the city of Savannah. Moreover, as James Oglethorpe promised Bishop George Berkeley in May of 1731, "the Society will use their utmost endeavours to prevent luxury and oppression in the officers, and idleness and vice in the people."[42] Since everyone knew that one sure way to render a man worthless and destitute was to allow him to console himself with rum, and since rum was causing havoc among the Indians whom the Trustees sought to befriend, the "Rules for the Year 1735" forbade the use and sale of rum in the colony without license.

Englishmen in Georgia were largely left to their own devices in matters of spiritual discipline. Some assistance was offered in the pious exhortations of ministers who volunteered to go to Georgia, including John and Charles Wesley, and the countless volumes of *Duty of Man* and *Christian Monitor* sent over to them.[43] And yet it was not primarily through spiritual milk that the Trustees hoped to nurture Christian conduct. Benjamin Martyn probably echoed their own assumptions when he assured potential supporters of Georgia that

> Christianity will be extended by the execution of this design; since, the good discipline established by the Society, will reform the manners of those miserable objects [sic], who shall be by them subsisted; and the example of the whole colony, who shall behave in a just, moral, and religious manner, will contribute greatly toward the conversion of the Indians, and taking off the prejudices received from the profligate lives of such who have scarce anything of Christianity but the name.[44]

Seeing Christianity among the common people more as a problem of "good discipline" than as a matter of spiritual wealth, and committed to the preservation of religious liberty, partly out of consideration for the German Protestants in Georgia, the Trustees did not, significantly, require regular religious worship as a part of their design to extend Christianity by means of the new colony.[45]

Good discipline, however, proved to be one of Georgia's greater problems. Unlike the other English colonies in North America, Georgia was not created with a specific group—such as the New England clergy or the Virginia planters—to assume and exercise social control. In so far as each settler was required to serve guard duty and to respond to a call to arms one could say that the small military hierarchy in Georgia led by Colonel Oglethorpe was a source of authority. But there is nothing to suggest that the settlers saw themselves as a surrogate army subject to military rule, however elementary or sporadic. Indeed, what positive influence Oglethorpe had over the civilian life of Georgia seems to have been on the strength of his personality rather than his military commission.[46] Nonetheless the Trustees were not "so intent on the Utopian social experiment that they had neglected to study governmental needs."[47] The Trustees, all men of affairs, were hardly so naive.

Oglethorpe, ever watchful for the perils of luxury, wrote George

Berkeley that "the Society . . . intend to send no governour to prevent the pride that name might instill. The power of government they intend to invest in an overseer and council of honest and discreet men. The division of the people is to be in hundreds and tithings under constables and tithing men, the men to be regularly armed and exercised."[48] This formula had the constitutional sanction of antiquity and by no means precluded an elective officer and court with the right to sue on behalf of each "hundred." Within six months after the signing of the Charter (April 21, 1732) the Board of Trustees

> resolved a Civil Government should be established in Georgia, and the town to be erected should be named Savannah, and the lands thereto belonging to be 5,000 acres. The government to be by bailiffs, constables and tithing men, a court to be erected of Oyer and Terminer, with a judge, jurats, justices of the peace, etc. We are not particular in establishing the constitution, because till we come to that the laws of England take place.[49]

If there was no provision in the Charter for the colonists' consent to the laws (as had been the case with the Maryland, Carolina, and Pennsylvania charters), it was probably because the Trustees had no intention of having any laws made in Georgia and very few by themselves. They were incorporated "one body politic and corporate" and were, in fact, empowered to make all laws, "constitutions, orders and ordinances" not in violation of the laws of England. The Trustees were not deluded by an innocent expectation that the grateful Georgians would more or less run things successfully on their own. Yet Percival and his associates were members of a generation which had been instructed by John Locke and James Harrington and their followers to look upon government as the creature of society.

The Georgia Trustees had calculated that the size and nature of the population hardly would sustain an elaborate system of self-government. Moreover, any law passed in Georgia, or by the Trustees, would be subject to review, like the Trust's expenditures, by Parliament and the government. That, Percival feared, could prove disastrous.[50] The Trustees had objected strenuously to the original draft of the Charter, fearing that its provisions for the periodic election and rotation of members of the council would soon take control of the Trust from those who had come to it with philanthropic aims and, as Oglethorpe put it, "convert the scheme to a job." They had also been apprehensive that if the military affairs of the colony were placed in the hands of the governor of South Carolina, as the original draft provided, "he at his pleasure may distress our people."[51] Rather than to administer the colony by such ready targets for parliamentary scrutiny as a governor and formal statutes, they chose instead to make do with a resident trustee (after 1740, president) and regulations made by themselves.

Though the Georgia Trustees tended to equate the reform of manners with Christianization, there were no regulations made in Georgia to equal the statutes regulating conduct which were to rule in early Philadelphia. The principal exception was the prohibition against the sale of rum, but its purpose was not wholly moral. Beer was plentiful, and the conviction that rum was physically harmful was a commonplace of the day. Oglethorpe feared that the costly attire of those settlers who came at their own expense would arouse resentment among the humbler people and therefore, as might be expect of him, advocated sumptuary laws for Savannah; but none are on record.[52] Committed to religious freedom the Trustees could do little more than provide for an Anglican ministry and see that countless donated guidebooks to Christian virtue found their way to Georgia. There being no ruling class to provide leadership and impose norms of conduct, security and social order depended all the more on the pattern of settlement. Once again a central town would be anticipated as the principal instrument of social cohesion. For the duration of the Trust's responsibility for the colony the same form of civil government—"by bailiffs, constables and tithingmen"—would serve in Georgia as had been functioning in the English countryside since the beginning of time. The Trustees took for granted that the seat of this government would "be the new town to be erected . . . named Savannah."

John Percival had equated the creation of a civil government for Georgia with the establishment of the town of Savannah. The Trustees may have never aspired to re-create London, which "Metropolis," sang Benjamin Martyn, would inspire visiting Indians with "the high Idea . . . of the Grandeur of Empire." Nonetheless they were intent upon settling "such unfortunate persons" as could not subsist in England in Georgia "in an orderly manner" through the establishment of "a well regulated town."[53] One of the oldest existing maps we have of Savannah is a map dating from 1735, published with a German account of the emigration of the Salzburgers to Georgia (Figure 21). Savannah lies near the center of the map, at the mouth of the Savannah River, and protected by a ring of forts including fortified settlements at Purisburg, Abercorn, and Ebenezer. The city itself appears as an expansive grid facing north by northeast. On February 1, 1733, a week after his arrival in Georgia, Oglethorpe and a surveyor from South Carolina, Colonel William Bull, "marked out the Square, the Streets, and 40 Lots for houses for the town," having satisfied themselves that the site was dry, supplied with fresh water and "sheltered from the western and southern winds." Construction of the first house, "ordered to be made of clapboards," began on the same day.[54] Oglethorpe's achievement in the Savannah plan was unique for its originality and sophistication, reflected in its neighborhood sized wards or squares, the key element in the plan of the town itself, and in its attempted functional integration of the urban and rural landscapes.

Perhaps the first thing one notices in Peter Gordon's handsomely illustrated engraving of Savannah in 1734 (Figure 22)[55] is the geometrical coherence of the city's plan, a quality characteristic of eighteenth–century academism in design. The focal point of Gordon's illustration is the long central street of the city leading southward from the waterfront and indefinitely into the pine forests. There is no city center as such; rather the central street appears merely as the means of connecting the four wards which flank it, two opposite each other on either side. These wards, each of which contained forty house lots, permitted the city to expand through the addition of neighborhoods with their own centers of activity, rather than a scattered filling out of isolated individual lots. The principal characteristic of the original Savannah plan was its integration of town and country into what John W. Reps has praised as a "true regional plan."[56] This integration, a singular formalization of rural-urban ecology, was accomplished by the method of granting lands which Oglethorpe followed. As we have seen, each fifty-acre land grant was granted in portions of one sixty-by-ninety-foot town lot, one five-acre garden lot, and one forty-four– acre farm lot. Oglethorpe's arrangement was confirmed by the Trustees' "Rules for the Year 1735."[57] Nor did this integration end with the town proper. "Where the town lands end," observed Francis Moore, a visitor to Georgia in 1735, "the villages begin;

> four villages make a ward without, which depends upon one of the wards within the town. The use of this is, in case a war should happen, the villages without may have places in the town, to bring their cattle and families into for refuge, and to that purpose there is a square left in every ward, big enough for the outwards to camp in.[58]

Granting lands in combined urban and rural units was not in itself novel; this practice had been followed in New England and in the "liberty land" farm lots allowed Philadelphia residents by William Penn. What is novel is the confirmation and geometric ordering of these essentially regional land use arrangements within the actual physical design of Savannah itself. The town as originally planned, composed of its rectangular wards, is surrounded on three sides by contiguous, square-shaped double garden plots; each plot was ten acres square and consisted of two adjoining five-acre triangular garden plots. This area was, again, surrounded on its sides by the much larger, rectangular and contiguous farm lots. Still beyond this area lay thirty-nine contiguous, rectangular lots of approximately one square mile each. These were undoubtedly the large 500-acre grants reserved for "private adventurers" and for the Trustees' use for the benefit of the colony. A common surrounding the town itself insured the orderly expansion of the town, through the farther accretion of wards and related garden lots, into the surrounding country region without disruption of the arrangement of successive and contiguous rectangles of lots of one kind.[59]

Contemporary visitors to Savannah admired the town for the regularity and straightness of its streets and the uniformity in "Models and Dimensions" of its houses; for the "lightsome prospect" afforded by its open, surrounding land; for its "wide and commodious streets" and "several large Squares;" for the air and garden room permitted by the placement of the houses "at some distance from each other." These qualities had been intended by the Trustees, one of whom laid out the town and surrounding area and who advertised that the houses were built "for the sake of Air, and to prevent the spreading of any Fire . . . Some Distance from each other" and that the streets were wide and formed "several spacious Squares."[60] Even Patrick Tailfer, who had little good to say about Georgia, had to concede that he found Savannah "beautifully laid out in wards, tythings, and publick squares left at proper distances for markets and publick buildings; the whole making an agreeable uniformity."[61] Happily the Savannah plan, which was generally imitated at Ebenezer, Frederica, George Town, and Darien, was honored in Savannah's growth until the middle of the nineteenth century when the pressure of land speculators to develop the greatest number of lots consumed its landscape, as it did that of so many other American towns.

There are a number of plausible explanations for the Savannah plan. Turpin Bannister, relying heavily on Oglethorpe's military background and the military role Georgia was expected to fulfill, sees the origins of Savannah's wards and squares in the Roman art of castrametation. Machiavelli's *Arte della Guerra* (1521), based upon Vegetius and Livy, stresses the importance of uniformity in camp layout and the availability of safe or protected places for rest. Machiavelli's treatise was widely distributed, having gone through three London printings in 1560, 1573, and 1588. Oglethorpe's father's library at Westbrook contained a copy of a leading English campaign manual by Robert Barret, *The Theorike and Practike of Modern Warres* (1598) which called for "an outer line of fortifications" enclosing "a square area on three sides with the river forming the fourth." A rampart with corner bastions was to form a second line enclosing "the camp proper." Open areas around the perimeter of the camp proper were intended for "auxiliary craftsmen" and a "parade ground." A "transverse street" bisecting the central, square area should be flanked by "three sets of four blocks . . . each arranged around large squares." The likelihood that Oglethorpe may have drawn upon Machiavelli and Barret is increased, according to Bannister, by "the underlying military purpose of the Georgia Trustees" which they "minimized in their formal charter for reasons of diplomacy."[62]

There is, however, very little evidence besides the circumstances Bannister points to to confirm an essentially military design as the basis of Oglethorpe's Savannah plan. Bannister relies upon William De Brahm's plan of Savannah included in his *History of the Province of Georgia*, first printed in 1849, which shows Savannah as containing six wards surrounded by fortifications (Figure 23). The De Brahm map, however, was made in 1757, as the appearance of two further wards indicates, and the fortifications shown are those ordered by De Brahm himself, British surveyor general, in 1757.[63] Gordon's 1734 engraving pictures a small fort at the southeast corner, a guard house and battery at the northeast corner and a minimal palisade under construction on the eastern side. These would hardly have served as Barret's ramparts and bastions. The principal protective fortifications for Savannah most probably were projected as the same as those for the colony itself, a ring of forts surrounding the city as shown on the Urlsperger map of 1735. Secondly, the Georgia Trustees had no underlying military purposes which they were secreting for diplomatic reasons. Indeed, in 1737 the Trustees called a halt to fortification building at Savannah since "the People . . . were not so immediately exposed to Danger" and "this took off the People from their Cultivation," not to mention that "the work would be very Chargeable."[64]

Had the urban design of Savannah been purely military in intent, it is probable that the ancient art of castrametation may have served as its source. But the design reflects a much larger purpose—to incorporate within the actual physical arrangements of the city a society of a distinct nature and sustained by a clear integration of urban-rural functions. Each resident would have had a nearby garden and a more distant farm large enough to support himself and his family. Some might be tradesmen and some not, but no portion of the population would be at the mercy of the other for its support. There might be a few very large landowners, but these would constitute only a small proportion of the whole. The town would function as a location of services, sociability, and authority which would embrace and effect all parts equally. While agriculture was necessarily a paramount consideration, the design was not innocent of the needs of trade. The squares within each ward were intended for use as markets, as well as other "Publick Uses," and, as the Trustees often advertised, the town was "excellently situated for Trade, the Navigation of the River being very secure and Ships of Three Hundred Tons can lie within Six Yards of the Town and the Worm does not Eat them."[65]

Another contender for the source of the Savannah plan is Sir Robert Mountgomery's Margravate of Azilia, a province designed in 1717 for the southernmost portion of South Carolina by Mountgomery by permission of the Carolina proprietors. Mountgomery's promise that the new colony was in "the Most Delightful Country of the Universe" was not enough to lure sufficient investors to speculate in his scheme and he was unable to promote enough settlement within three years, as his grant stipulated, in order to retain claim to the area. But Mountgomery had an adventuresome imagination and tried to show that civilized men, settled according to his scheme, could "at once defend, and cultivate a Territory, with the utmost satisfaction and security, even in the Heart of an Indian Country." Like the later Georgia the Margravate of Azilia was also intended to benefit "honest and qualified Gentlemen in *Great Britain*, or elsewhere, who having Numerous and well-educated Families, possess but little Fortunes, other than their Industry," who would be settled gratis. The beneficence of the earlier scheme did not depend upon charity or Parliament, however. Instead, settlement of impoverished gentlemen would await the arrival of prosperity to the colony which was, for Mountgomery, almost a foregone conclusion. The first settlers, after the soldiers and builders of fortifications, would be the "Gentry" who would acquire their estates of "640 Acres in a Square" by subscription.[66]

Mountgomery's proposed fortress settlement, another offering to geometric academism in design, was in the shape of a large square divided into four square quarter sections. Between the fortification line and the inner square formed by the quarter squares, was a broad belt of farm and forests. The quarter sections were constituted of "116 squares, each of which has a house in the middle . . . [and is] 640 acres in a square, bating only for the highways which divide them. These are the estates." Each quarter section enclosed yet another square, four miles square, which was intended to serve as game forests and for raising cattle. At the joining of the quarters and in the geometric center of the whole stood "the City" at the center of which "stands the *Margravate's House*, which is to be his constant Residence, or the Residence of the Governour, and contains all sorts of publick Edifices for Dispatch of Business." Here was a perfect instance in which government and public business are the essential purposes of a "city" and that purpose is expressed by the placement of the city in the physical and focal center of the surrounding area. The city, intended to be "full of streets crossing each other," was then to be surrounded by a greenbelt separating it from the surrounding country estates and "affording a fine Prospect of the Town in Drawing near it."[67]

The reappearance of a system of squares and the integration of rural-urban functions at Savannah naturally lead one to suspect that Mountgomery's plan for the Margravate of Azilia may have influenced the Trustees of Georgia in drawing up their plan if, indeed, anyone other than Oglethorpe and Bull are responsible for the town plan of Savannah. But it seems improbable that "the Georgia trustees simply reduced the size of the Azilia plan in keeping with the more modest land grants contemplated for their own colony,"[68] because there are some fundamental conceptual differences between the two plans. To begin with, the difference in land grants was not simply one of size. Azilia is portrayed diagrammatically as an almost feudal community in which large estates are the principal sustaining elements. Similarly, the margravate was intended to be founded and sustained by its "gentry." In the Georgia plan large estates figured not only on the periphery of Savannah's layout, but in the periphery of the Trustees' conception of the kind of society they were bringing about. Second, the town-country integration in the Savannah plan is much more complete than it was in Mountgomery's plan. In the former residents are tillers of the soil as well as town-dwellers. In the latter plan a complete segregation of country-dwellers and the town is quite possible and there is little to suggest an interdependence, except political, between the two. Third, Savannah, in the original plan, lacks the single distinctive town center as a source of authority and locus of civic activity indicated for the Margravate of Azilia. Rather, the squares in the city's wards served that function; the ultimate source of authority being in London, centers of civic activity could be more dispersed and, accommodating smaller numbers of settlers, were so planned.

Finally, the projected Margravate of Azilia is far more the fortified settlement, possibly influenced by the Roman art of castrametation, than was early Savannah. The band of fortifications surrounding Mountgomery's margravate is a prominent determinant of the interior, which reflects the simple rectilinear crossing of two princial arteries typical of Roman planning for colonial towns. Moreover, these axial avenues lead from nowhere in particular to the center of the city; their sole function seems to have been to accommodate the geometric requirements of Mountgomery's plan and otherwise to serve the politico-aesthetic function of accentuating the authority of the central city. The streets of Savannah's grid, on the other hand, connect all of the town's neighborhoods with each other, with the waterfront, and with the expandable hinterland.

The principle of the urban square had also been used in English colonial town-planning in the Ulster plantation towns of northern Ireland. In the preface to Benjamin Martyn's "New and Accurate Account of the Provinces of South Carolina and Georgia" he asked leave "to mention a Precedent of our own for planting Colonies," whereupon he described the building of Londonderry in Colerain "in the Days of King James the First" by "the twelve companies constituting the London Society for the Plantations of Ulster". The town plans of Coleraine and Londonderry, and probably for the six counties generally, followed the walled grid plan with central market square typical of the *bastide*. The plan of Londonderry pays greater heed to geometric order with its large open square set in the center of a rectangular grouping of square blocks of house lots and entered at the mid-points of each of the four sides.[69] Yet Savannah's plan with its neighborhood squares resembles more closely the urban designs for the rebuilding of London after the Great Fire of 1666 proposed by Robert Newcourt and Richard Hooke than it does the centralized fortified towns of Ulster.

The most likely inspiration for the Savannah plan was a gradual development with which all the Trustees were undoubtedly well acquainted. This was the growing popularity in London of residential squares. One of the eight plans proposed for the rebuilding of London was offered by Robert Newcourt. Newcourt's plan was a large grid containing four symmetrically placed open squares. These elements were not untypical in some of the other plans offered; but Newcourt's use of them was unusual and did reappear in the Savannah plan. Each of the five principal squares (the fifth being at the center) was surrounded by blocks each of which, in itself, contained an open center with space set aside for a parish church. Each block formed a separate parish, thus combining neighborhood intimacy with the larger framework of an expanding city.[70] A similar symmetrical arrangement of residential squares appears in a rebuilding proposal for London of 1666(?) commonly attributed to Richard Hooke, which even more closely resembles the Savannah plan in its avoidance of a large central square as it affirms the heterogeneous life of the city (Figure 24). Newcourt's and Hooke's plans thus bear a closer conceptual resemblance to the Savannah design than do Mountgomery's Margravate of Azilia, Roman encampments, or the Ulster plantation towns.

Residential squares became quite popular in late seventeenth- and early eighteenth-century London. Because of the presence of originally vast estates private and corporate land developers had large areas at their disposal which enabled them to plan in terms of units of parks enclosed by rows of adjoining houses of a fairly uniform plan—adjoining to maximize the income from the real estate and uniform because of the rationalism of the age's aesthetic. The squares themselves had the added virtues of providing seclusion, neighborhood, and exclusiveness. At least two Georgia Trustees—Sir William Heathcote and George Carpenter—were active in the development of such residential squares in London.[71]

The singularity of the Savannah plan and its historical significance lie in the fact that the surveyor's lines sought to integrate the intimacy of urban life with the sustaining activities of the countryside. Moreover, the plan was designed so that its essential features would be preserved as the city expanded. The society thus defined was one in which virtue could be recovered through a righting of the alienation of the country and the city. The city would no longer embody moral and political corruption once the nation's citizens could affirm their independence as public persons. That they could do as yeomen proprietors, whose own land, labor, and right to bear arms would become once again the foundation of their moral integrity, liberty, and future security. Citizen soldier, freehold proprietor, virtuous citizen—gathered in one civic person and in one city: this was the meaning of Savannah.

❧

On June 23, 1752, one year before their Charter was due to expire, the Trustees for Georgia surrendered it "taking into consideration the present State of the Colony and the total inability of the Trustees to defray the Expenses of the Civil Government . . . to furnish the Troops stationed in Georgia with Provisions, or to give any Encouragements for the Produce of Raw Silk, without a further Supply."[72] The Trustees' vision for Georgia thus abandoned had long since been depleted of its distinctive character. Only roughly one-half of the population of Georgia consisted of Englishmen, and never more than half of the settlers were sent and maintained on charity because of inadequate benefactions and support from Parliament. Moreover, of the 827 settlers sent on charity whose occupations are known, only ninety were identified as "farmers" or "husbandmen."[73] In this the Trustees had not erred; that the overwhelming number of charity settlers should be small craftsmen and tradesmen was in keeping with the Trustees' intention that a new opportunity in Georgia should relieve the plight of the urban poor. Where they erred was in their evident assumption that successful husbandry was a moral pursuit, requiring only industriousness, rather than an acquired skill. This may be one of the most revealing aspects of the execution of the Georgia plan, for its suggests the persistence of an attitude which may have viewed differentiation in economic roles and success in terms of "virtue" rather than learned abilities or functional specialization.

Too many of the Englishmen who sailed for Georgia went as private adventurers, and thus it was inevitable that they would begin to press for changes in the Trustees' regulations on land inheritance and the alienation of property, and so they did, with eventual success. The presence of large plantations with negro slavery across the Savannah River in South

157

Carolina only enticed the Georgians into further acceptance of the notion that a white man could not do hard labor in that warm quarter of the universe, although more than one Georgian testified to the fallacy of that argument.[74] More to the point was the claim that negro labor being cheaper, the South Carolinians would always undersell the Georgians. A small but vocal group of "malcontents" led by Patrick Tailfer and the regulars of the "Scotch Club" at Savannah got the ear of the Trust's opposition in Parliament with that argument in 1742 and by 1750 pressure from within the colony and pressure from London—by that time the Trustees were desperate for sustaining funds from Parliament—succeeded in forcing them to repeal their prohibition of negro slavery. The rum prohibition, from the first moment more honored in the breach than in its observance, had been abandoned in 1742.[75]

No one had pretended that Georgia could be self-liquidating from the start, and because of her military value to Britain it could have reasonably been expected that the government would bear some of the expenses. As benefactions dwindled and the costs of transportation, provisions, and public works grew, after 1736 the Trustees had to plead with Parliament annually for a grant of money to carry them through the year. Georgia thus became a victim of the political factionalism that plagued the undertaking from its inception. The machinations upon which depended the Trust's precarious fortunes were recorded by Percival in his *Diary*. The ministry was "jealous" of the Trust, Percival wrote, lest there should be "too great an union of so many Parliament men as we consist of in sundry cases, where they may combine in votes not pleasing to the Administration." "Court members of the House" opposed the Trustees, in the meantime, "because they see such as are Parliament men among us hang together, and generally in opposition to Court measures. They say we give a turn to elections, and if encouraged will ruin the Whig cause.[76]

In so far as there were any real complaints in Parliament against the colony, other than those provided by Tailfer's group, they were typified by the assertions that, first, everyone having abandoned the colony, the land there was worthless, to the loss of those who invested their own money; and, second, there was no pecuniary or commercial advantage to England, so the maintenance of a military barrier was enough. These were bitter objections indeed, for Georgia had been designed expressly for the cultivation of the soil, not its conversion into a marketable commodity. Furthermore, the Georgia Charter had been granted on the condition that the colony remain a philanthropic enterprise.[77] For every testament that the people of Georgia were miserable, starving; that silk culture was a failure; that the Trustees' officials were rogues and scoundrels; that the climate was sending every other Georgian to his grave—an equal number of contradictory "evidences" were given to the

Trustees.[78] To their discredit not one of the Trustees, except Oglethorpe, ever visited the colony. Thus the Trustees simply could not themselves assess whether their project was succeeding. If the failure of Georgia under the Trustees was due to the folly of their plan, one could expect to see some improvement in the colony's fortunes after the Trustees abandoned, first, their prohibitions against land alienation and slavery, and second, their Charter. But the colony remained as small, poor, and dependent upon the British government after 1752 as before.[79]

John Percival resigned in 1741 claiming illness, but more probably in despair over the failure of Parliament to vote adequate funds and the realization that some of the Trustees were politicking with the opposition in Parliament to admit negro slaves as "the price of money for Georgia."[80] In the end Percival had probably been right in the reflection which had led to his involvement with the Georgia colony a decade before: "men love darkness better than the light, and nothing is considered but with a political view."

Clarence L. Ver Steeg, in a graceful review of the interpretative issues raised by contemporary and historical accounts of colonial Georgia under the Trustees, concludes with the view that early Georgia foundered among a confusion of purposes, on the lack of a unifying image.[81] That Georgia's first settlers and those to whom the Trustees, led by Percival and Oglethorpe, turned for support, did not share a common vision for Georgia, can not be argued. That is not to say, however, that the conception of Georgia lacked an image which might have unified the colony had the Trustees' original scheme been faithfully executed. Nor is it accurate to dismiss the Georgia plan as the consequence of the utopian musings or philanthropic dogmatism of a handful of noble-spirited but innocent gentlemen in Parliament.[82] As the sophisticated design of Savannah, with its attempted reintegration of the country and the city in a durable regional plan, suggests, the vision of Georgia was not limited to mere philanthropy sustained by a utopian belief in the corrigibility of human nature.

The Trustees' design for Georgia, like their design for Savannah, was deeply rooted in a contemporary ideological controversy and cannot be wholly understood apart from that controversy. Its essence was whether the nation could survive without a recovery of her ancient virtue, allegedly on the decline, and what, in fact, constituted that virtue. This issue was not fundamentally different than the issue which resulted in the founding of Boston and, perhaps less ostensibly, Philadelphia. The two northern cities were conceived as testaments to the belief that virtue is ultimately the source and succor of the commonwealth. Where Savannah differed in conception from Boston or Philadelphia was in the altered terms of the issue. "Virtue" for the leaders of Massachusetts Bay and Pennsylvania colonizations meant primarily religious virtue, a spiritual condition from which all social virtues were derived. Virtue for men like John Percival or James Oglethorpe, for the Independents of Robert Walpole's England, was primarily a political condition. That is, the attainment of virtue became a problem in the origins and distribution of power. The pious saint of England in the 1630's became the independent citizen of the 1730's. In both instances the perception of the country and the city was affected by the extension of the controversy into the social and economic spheres. Earlier, religious virtue was best nurtured where consensualism, uniformity, and the deferential harmony of an hierarchical society could prevail. Such a place was, and only could have been, the traditional world of the English countryside. The city was, in turn, perceived as a source of a change which, as it fostered heterogeneity, moral innovation, and social and economic dislocation, could only be apprehended as a threat to the nation's "virtue." The fact, widely acknowledged since the Elizabethan Renaissance, that the city's commerce in ideas as well as things enriches civilization, only served to heighten the tension between the two as Englishmen found themselves, in the shadow of the city, confronted with a moral dilemma.

The conception of Georgia expressed in the Trustees' promotional literature and diagramed in the plan of Savannah represents an attempt to solve that dilemma. The city, with its unique capacity for government, society, and neighborhood—the city as a vehicle of civilization—might be preserved from the corruptive influence of a world in which all things, including one's civic personality, might become a commodity of exchange and profit. The solution to their dilemma came, as did so many ideas in that neoclassical age, ultimately from Rome. There, then, in the days of the Roman republic when liberty was secured through the studious balance of contending political groups and functions, could be found a model for emulation. Rome, the glorious city of the imminent empire, supposedly preserved her economic equilibrium by sending her excess people and her veterans to her colonies, as she protected her liberty through the character of her citizens, independent as they cultivated their own land, free as they bore their own arms in the defense of the state. The memory of Rome became suffused into the Harringtonian prescription for a restored true commonwealth. Through an "agrarian law" let land proprietorship be more evenly distributed so that the political power derived therefrom would likewise be more balanced. Through the restoration to the commonwealth of a preponderance of arms-bearing freehold proprietors, civic virtue might once again return to the English nation. The city could serve its civilizing role without auguring corruption if the foundations of its wealth were relocated in the land, not to be bartered away for the baubles of political power. What was sought at Savannah, then, was a reintegration of the country with the city, not only as focal points in the landscape, but in the development of public character.

Whether at Boston, New Haven, Philadelphia, Williamsburg, or Savannah, the city in colonial America was conceived within a rich tradition of historical and contemporary meanings. These meanings were never independent from the social, religious, or ideological preoccupations of the societies which accepted them and in so doing transplanted them into the American landscape. Perhaps the most pervasive conception, the one that binds each of our foundings into a common theme, is that the city, with its counterpart the country, is above all a moral phenomenon. Ambiguity thus necessarily arose: if the city was the seat of social discipline and civilization, how was it that it also spawned so much corruption? If the Almighty had dictated that his church be represented as a city, while the devil roamed the wilderness, how was it that the city could foster all the vices of Vanity Fair? The imagistic solution had lain, of course, in the parallel cities of the New Jerusalem and Babylon, the City of God and the earthly city. But had Babylon created sinners, or had sinners created Babylon? Did man's moral condition inhere in his inward self, or was it the bitter fruit of his environment? The colonial American perception of the city and the country, each as a moral place, and the concurrence of attempts to articulate expectations of the city while being engaged in an effort to recover primitive virtue, suggest an attempt to free the self and society from the burden of evil, resting it instead in the environment.

Furthermore, the effort to relocate the origins of the moral condition of society and hence its amelioration in the environment, with its attendant restoration of rural virtue to the public life of the city, entailed a subtle but significant alteration in expectations of the city. This alteration was the result of a changed perception of the transurban landscape necessitated by the presence of a real wilderness, hitherto unknown to the European experience except as a metaphor of the poetic and religious imagination. The frontier that the many Englishmen who looked to America found there was a place of darkness and evil, devoid of traditional restraints upon human conduct. The secure countryside of the English landscape with its manors, farms, pastures and villages, had been transformed into an alien and potentially malign environment. Likewise the city, which in the Old World had come to represent the forces of social disintegration as well as civilization, underwent a conceptual transformation as well. As the transurban landscape lost its capacity to sustain social cohesion and continuity, transplanted Englishmen retreated into the city. But because their social vision was rural in nature, the city was reconsidered less as the source of civilization than as an instrument of social order and stability. Denied by that expectation those attributes of diversity and variety which make of true urban places centers of cultural vitality and change, the city became confined within the perimeters of a constricted and apprehensive social vision; cities came to be conceived as "well-ordered vineyards" surrounded by an untamed wilderness.

In spite of the gradual domestication of the wilderness, the continued presence in the American experience of uncertain frontiers—be they social, moral, or spatial—rendered the condition of imminent dislocation an enduring one; thus the quest for cohesion and stability has never wholly subsided. Nineteenth century social reformers and landscape architects might have sought to recover a sense of community as they strove to cleanse the urban setting of brute poverty and political corruption while they graced it with parks and winding lanes.[83] But when all is said and done, they sought no more than did William Penn for Philadelphia, or James Oglethorpe for Savannah. The "city beautiful" and "garden city" movements of the late neneteenth century, Jane Jacobs correctly argued, were attempts to impose upon the city an aesthetic inherently at odds with the world of the city, enlivened by diversity, in terms of both its visual and social ambience, as its necessary dynamic. Lamenting the sterile urban renewal efforts of the post-World War II decades, another critic had concluded "what passes for city planning . . . is fundamentally a rejection of the big city and of all it means—its variety, its peculiarities, its richness of choice and experience—and a yearning for a bucolic society."[84] If the American city has, inappropriately, been expected to provide the cohesion and stability of rural memory, it is because the city must yet answer to the unmet needs of a frontier society.

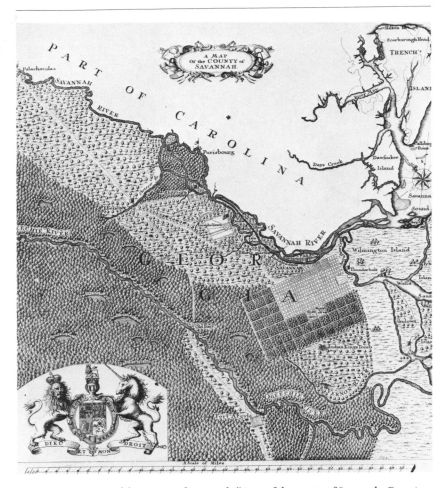

Figure 21. "A Map of the County of Savannah." Map of the county of Savannah, Georgia, from Samuel Urslperger, *Ausfulrliche Nachricht von den Saltzburgischen Emigranten,* vol. I, part 4, Halle, 1735. Courtesy John Carter Brown Library, Brown University.

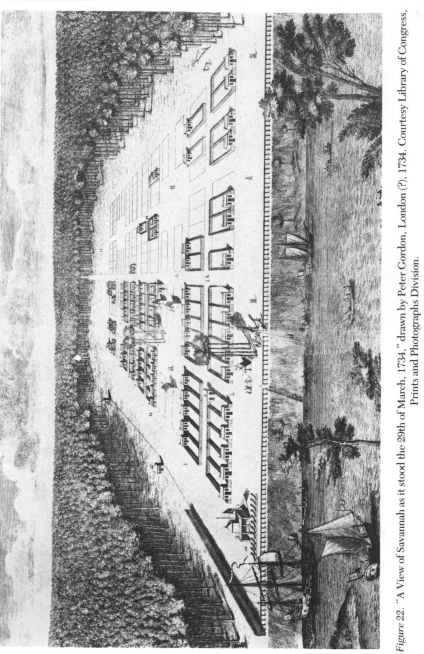

Figure 22. "A View of Savannah as it stood the 29th of March, 1734," drawn by Peter Gordon, London (?), 1734. Courtesy Library of Congress, Prints and Photographs Division.

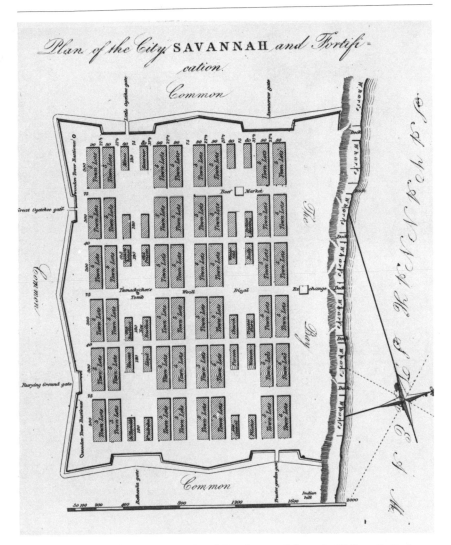

Figure 23. "Plan of the City Savannah and Fortifications," drawn by William De Brahm, 1757. Courtesy Tracy W. McGregor Library, University of Virginia.

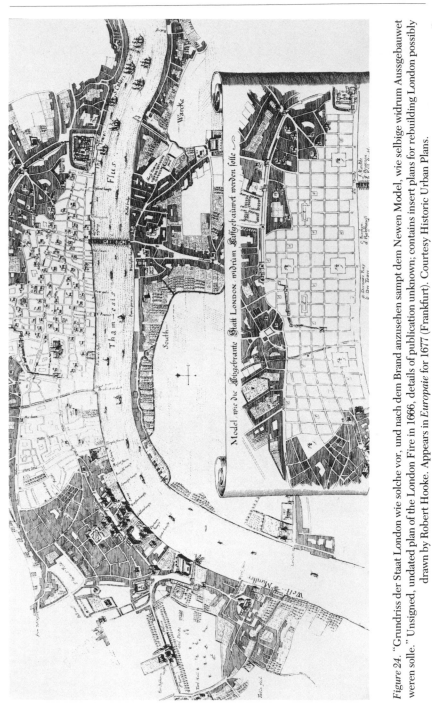

Figure 24. "Grundriss der Staat London wie solche vor, und nach dem Brand anzusehen sampt dem Newen Model, wie selbige widrum Aussgebauwet weren solle." Unsigned, undated plan of the London Fire in 1666, details of publication unknown; contains insert plans for rebuilding London possibly drawn by Robert Hooke. Appears in *Europaie* for 1677 (Frankfurt). Courtesy Historic Urban Plans.

Notes

※

Preface

[1] Morton S. and Lucia White, *The Intellectual versus the City* (Cambridge, Mass., 1962); Lewis Mumford, *The City in History: Its Origins, Its Transformations, and Its Prospect* (New York, 1961).

[2] Henry Nash Smith, *Vergin Land: The American West as Symbol and Myth* (Cambridge, Mass., 1950); Leo Marx, *The Machine in the Garden: Technology and the Pastoral Ideal in America* (New York, 1964).

[3] Blanche Housman Gelfant, *The American City Novel* (Norman, Okla., 1954). This study focusses largely on twentieth-century novels. For an analysis of the fictional treatment of the city in American in the pre–Civil War period see Janis P. Stout, *Sodoms in Eden: The City in American Fiction before 1860* (Westport, Conn., 1976).

[4] David R. Weimer, *The City as Metaphor* (New York, 1966). Weimer's interpretations are based on a study of the writings of Walt Whitman, Henry James, Stephen Crane, Theodore Dreiser, E. E. Cummings, F. Scott Fitzgerald, William Carlos Williams, and W. H. Auden.

[5] Anselm Strauss, *The American City: A Sourcebook of Urban Imagery* (Chicago, 1968); Charles N. Glaab and A. Theodore Brown, "The City in American Thought, 1790–1850," in *A History of Urban America* (New York, 1967, rev. 1975); Frank Freidel, "Boosters, Intellectuals, and the American City," in Oscar Handlin and John Burchard, eds., *The Historian and the City* (Cambridge, Mass., 1963).

[6] Robert E. Park, "Magic, Mentality, and City Life," in Robert E. Park and Ernest W. Burgess, *The City* (Chicago, 1925, reprt. 1967), p. 130.

7   Valuable beginnings have been made in Jorge Hardy, *Urban Planning in Pre-Columbian America* (New York, 1968); John W. Reps' chapters on French and Spanish town planning in the new world in *The Making of Urban America: A History of City Planning in the United States* (Princeton, 1965); and Dan Stanislawski, "Early Spanish Town Planning in the New World," *Geographical Review* 47, no. 1 (Jan. 1947), 94–105.

8   Reps, *The Making of Urban America;* Anthony N. B. Garvan, *Architecture and Town Planning in Colonial Connecticut* (New Haven, 1951).

9   Carl Bridenbaugh, *Vexed and Troubled Englishmen, 1590–1642* (New York, 1967).

1

Introduction

1   Mildred Campbell, "Social Origins of Some Early Americans," in James Morton Smith, ed., *Seventeenth Century America: Essays in Colonial History* (Chapel Hill, 1959).

2   E. M. W. Tillyard, *The Elizabethan World Picture* (New York, 1944); William Haller, *The Elect Nation: The Meaning and Relevance of Foxe's Book of Martyrs* (New York, 1963); William M. Lamont, *Godly Rule: Politics and Religion, 1603–1660* (London, 1969).

3   Lidia Staroni Mazzolani, *The Idea of the City in Roman Thought: From Walled City to Spiritual Commonwealth* (Bloomington, 1970), pp. 99–124, 173–181, and passim.

4   Augustine, *City of God*, Trans. Marcus Dods, intro. by Thomas Merton (New York, 1950), Book XI, xxxiii, p. 377; Book XIV, iv, p. 445; xxviii, p. 477.

5   Ibid., Book XIX, xxi, pp. 699–700. One historian finds, however, that Augustine conceded "a limited degree of genuine moral probity to historical societies not favored by divine revelation." Jeremy D. Adams, *The Populus of Augustine and Jerome: A Study in the Patristic Sense of Community,* (New Haven, 1971), p. 134.

6   Augustine, *City of God*, Book XII, i–viii, pp. 380–388.

7   Ibid., Book XIX, xvii, pp. 695–696.

8   Ibid., Book XXII, xxxix, pp. 859–860.

9   Rex Martin, "The Two Cities in Augustine's Political Philosophy," *Journal of the History of Ideas* 33, no. 2 (Apr.–June 1972), 195–216.

10   James Kendall Hosmer, ed., *Winthrop's Journal: "History of New England, 1630–1649,"* 2 vols. (New York, 1908), 2:238–239, entry for May 14, 1645.

11   Lamont, *Godly Rule*, pp. 14–26.

12   Ibid., p. 95.

13   John Goodwin quoted in ibid., p. 180.

14   See, for example, Charles F. Mullett, "Classical Influences on the American Revolution," *Classical Journal* vol. 35 (Nov. 1939), and H. Trevor Colbourn, *The Lamp of Experience: Whig History and the Intellectual Origins of the American Revolution* (Chapel Hill, 1965).

15   For illustrations see Richard M. Gunmere, *The American Colonial Mind and the Classical Tradition: Essays in Comparative Culture* (Cambridge, Mass., 1963).

16   Thucydides, *The Complete Writings of Thucydides: The Peloponnesian War*, ed. John H. Finley (New York, 1951), pp. 102, 104.

17   Ibid., p. 385.

18   Mason Hammond, *City-State and World State in Greek and Roman Political Theory until Augustus* (Cambridge, Mass., 1951), p. 29 and passim. See also Mason Hammond, *The City in the Ancient World* (Cambridge, Mass., 1972), pp. 241–319.

19   References are to *The Dialogues of Plato*, trans. Benjamin Jowett (New York, 1920).

20   References are to Aristotle, *The Politics of Aristotle*, trans. Ernest Barker (Oxford, 1948).

21   "Nicomachean Ethics," *Introduction to Aristotle*, ed. Richard McKeon (New York, 1947), Book II, chaps. 1 and 6.

22   Mazzolani, *The Idea of the City in Roman Thought*, pp. 34–67.

[23]   Livy, *The Early History of Rome*, Books I–V, trans. Aubrey de Selincourt (London, 1960), p. 105 and passim.

[24]   Marcus Tullius Cicero, *On the Commonwealth*, trans. and ed. George H. Sabine and Stanley B. Smith (New York, 1929).

[25]   George H. Sabine, *A History of Political Theory* (London, 1951), p. 129.

[26]   Henri Pirenne, *Medieval Cities: Their Origins and the Revival of Trade*, trans. Frank D. Halsey (Princeton, 1952).

[27]   Ibid., chap. 7.

[28]   John E. Stambaugh, "The Idea of the City: Three Views of Athens," *Classical Journal* 69, no. 4 (1974), 309–316.

[29]   Chester G. Starr, *A History of the Ancient World* (New York, 1965), pp. 413–431; Edwin S. Ramage, *Urbanitas: Ancient Sophistication and Refinement* (Norman, Okla. 1973), chap. 1.

[30]   Ramage, ibid., chaps. 3–5, pp. 79–138, passim; Raymond Williams, *The Country and the City* (New York, 1973), pp. 14–17, 47.

[31]   Hans Baron, *The Crisis of the Early Italian Renaissance* (Princeton, 1966), pp. 196–207.

[32]   Quoted in A. G. Dickens, *The Age of Humanism and Reformation: Europe in the Fourteenth, Fifteenth and Sixteenth Centuries* (Englewood Cliffs, N.J., 1972), p. 25.

[33]   Giovanni Botero, *A Treatise Concerning the Causes of the Magnificence and Greatness of Cities*, trans. Robert Peterson (London, 1606), pp. 4, 12–13.

[34]   Ibid., pp. 30–31, 36, 41–42.

[35]   Ibid., pp. 45, 60, 98, 9.

[36]   Ruth Kelso, *The Doctrine of the English Gentleman in the Sixteenth Century*, University of Illinois Studies in Language and Literature, no. 14 (Urbana, 1929), pp. 18–25, 38.

[37]   Henry Peacham, *The Complete Gentleman, The Truth of Our Times and The Art of Living in London*, ed. Virgil B. Heltzel (Ithaca, 1962), p. 22. Mechanics and

artisans, however, could not qualify, for "their bodies are spent with labor and travail, and men that are at their work *assidui et accubui umbratiles esse coguntur* [are busily occupied and are forced to remain in the shadows]" (p. 23).

[38]   Kelso, *Doctrine of the English Gentleman*, p. 50.

[39]   W. Lee Ustick, "Changing Ideals of Aristocratic Character and Conduct in Seventeenth Century England," *Modern Philology* 30, no. 2 (Nov. 1932), 147–166.

[40]   Peacham, *The Complete Gentleman*, pp. 4, 24.

[41]   Peacham, *The Art of Living in London*, pp. 245, 250.

[42]   Peacham, *The Complete Gentleman*, p. 36.

[43]   Sir Walter Ralegh, *The History of the World* (London, 1621), p. Al.

[44]   George Rudé, *Hanoverian London, 1714–1808* (Berkeley, 1971); chap. 4, pp. 64–81.

[45]   Francois Marie Arouet de Voltaire, "Charlatan," *The Philosophical Dictionary*, trans. H. I. Wolf (New York, 1924), p. 71.

[46]   Bonamy Dobrée, ed., *The Letters of Philip Dormer Stanhope, 4th Earl of Chesterfield*, 6 vols. (London, 1932), vol. 1, chap. 1.

[47]   Ibid., 4:1295, 1259–60, 1223–24.

[48]   Ibid., 4:1275–76, 1240, 1231.

[49]   Thomas Cassirer, "Awareness of the City in the Encyclopédie," *Journal of the History of Ideas* 24, no. 3 (1963), 387–396.

[50]   See Isaac Kramnick, *Bolingbroke and His Circle: The Politics of Nostalgia in the Age of Walpole* (Cambridge, 1968), and Maynard Mack, *The Garden and the City: Retirement and Politics in the Later Poetry of Pope, 1731–1743* (Toronto, 1969).

[51]   C. A. Doxiadis, *Architectural Space in Ancient Greece* (Cambridge, 1972), pp. 3–21.

[52]   R. E. Wycherley, *How the Greeks Built Cities* (Garden City, N.Y., 1969), p. 142 and passim.

[53] The *groma*, a cross mounted horizontally on a staff, was a surveying instrument designed to determine straight lines and right angles. O. A. W. Dilke, *The Roman Land Surveyors: An Introduction to the Agrimensores* (New York, 1971). See also Ferdinando Castagnoli, *Orthogonal Town Planning in Antiquity* (Cambridge, Mass., 1971), pp. 15–88.

[54] Dan Stanislawski, "Early Spanish Town Planning in the New World," *Geographical Review* 47, no. 1 (Jan. 1947), 94–105.

[55] Vitruvius, *Ten Books on Architecture*, trans. Morris Hicky Morgan (New York, 1960), pp. 30–32, 72–85, 141–142, passim. See also Dan Stanislawski, "The Origin and Spread of the Grid-Pattern Town," *Geographical Review* 36, no. 1 (Jan. 1946), 108–115.

[56] Helen Rosenau, *The Ideal City in Its Architectural Evolution* (London, 1959), pp. 25–28.

[57] Raphael du Fresne, "The Life of Leone Battista Alberti," in Leone Battista Alberti, *Ten Books on Architecture*, trans. James Leone, from the Italian trans. of Cosimo Bartoli (London, 1755), p. xiv.

[58] Ibid., Book IV, chap. 3, p. 72; Book V, chap. 1, p. 83.

[59] Ibid., Book V, chap. 1, p. 33; chap. 6, p. 89.

[60] Ibid., Book VII, chap. 1, p. 134.

[61] Ibid., Book IV, chap. 3, p. 81; Book VII, chap. 1, pp. 133–34.

[62] "An Act Continuing the Act directing the Building the Capitol and the City of Williamsburg; with Additions," in William Waller Henig, ed., *The Statutes at Large: Being a Collection of all the Laws of Virginia*, 13 vols. (New York, 1819–1823), 3:419. The original act for the building of Williamsburg was passed in 1699.

[63] Sigfried Giedion, *Space, Time and Architecture: The Growth of a New Tradition* (Cambridge, Mass., 1974), pp. 42–100.

2
The Two Cities of Massachusetts Bay

[1] Darrett B. Rutman, *Winthrop's Boston: A Portrait of a Puritan Town, 1630–1649* (Chapel Hill, 1965), pp. 278–279.

2   E. M. W. Tillyard, *The Elizabethan World Picture* (New York, 1944), passim.

3   Herbert Butterfield, *The Origins of Modern Science* (New York, 1965), p. 43.

4   Perry Miller, *The New England Mind in the Seventeenth Century* (New York, 1939), p. 217.

5   The Englishman's confrontation with the wilderness, his attraction to and repulsion from it, and its effects on the colonial American imagination have been the subject of numerous studies. Among the more useful are: George H. Williams, *Wilderness and Paradise in Christian Thought* (New York, 1962); Peter N. Carroll, *Puritanism and the Wilderness: The Intellectual Significance of the New England Frontier, 1629–1700* (New York, 1969); Roderick Nash, *Wilderness and the American Mind* (New Haven, 1967); and Richard Slotkin, *Regeneration through Violence: The Mythology of the American Frontier, 1600–1860* (Middletown, Conn., 1973). Still suggestive is Howard Mumford Jones' *O Strange New World: American Culture, the Formative Years* (New York, 1952). For a critical discussion of some of the literature dealing with the role of undomesticated nature in America see Thomas A. Krueger, "The Historians and the Edenic Myth: A Critique," *Canadian Review of American Studies* vol. 4, no. 1 (1973).

6   Ramist logic and its use by Puritans is discussed in Perry Miller, *The Puritan Mind in the Seventeenth Century*, chap. 5, and somewhat more concisely by Edmund S. Morgan in *The Puritan Family: Religion and Domestic Relations in Seventeenth Century New England* (New York, 1966), chap. 1.

7   James Kendall Hosmer, ed. *Winthrop's Journal: History of New England, 1630–1649* (New York, 1908), 2:239; John Winthrop, "A Declaration in Defense of an Order of Court Made in May, 1637," *Winthrop Papers*, Massachusetts Historical Society, 4 vols. 3:424; Edmund S. Morgan, *The Puritan Family*, pp. 20–25.

8   John of Salisbury, *Policratus*, trans. John Dickinson (New York, 1927); William Bradford, "Of Boston in New England," Massachusetts Historical Society, *Collections*, 3rd ser. (Boston, 1838), 7:28.

9   "The Company's Second General Letter of Instructions to Endicott and His Council," in Alexander Young, ed. *Chronicles of the First Planters of the Colony of Massachusetts Bay, from 1623 to 1639* (Boston, 1846), p. 187. "This feudal tenure," remarked Young, "was never established. Land was too plentiful and cheap to authorize it, or render it practicable; and accordingly it was all held in fee simple" (pp. 187ff).

10   Justin Winsor, *The Memorial History of Boston*, 4 vols. (Boston, 1882), 1:483–485.

[11]   Hosmer, ed., *Winthrop's Journal*, 2:99.

[12]   John Cotton's reply is reprinted in Edmund S. Morgan, *Puritan Political Ideas, 1558–1794* (New York, 1965), pp. 161–173. See also Arthur Percival Newton, *The Colonising Activities of the English Puritans* (New Haven, 1914), p. 181.

[13]   Our use of term "feudal" refers simply to a view of society that regards it as hierarchical and cohering in a network of mutual dependencies and obligations determined by rank or status. Whether or not such a view was actually mirrored in a political or economic system common to any part of medieval Europe is a question more adequately debated elsewhere. See Elizabeth A. R. Brown, "The Tyranny of a Construct: Feudalism and Historians of Medieval Europe," *American Historical Review* vol. 79, no. 4 (Oct. 1974).

[14]   "Experiencia," *Winthrop Papers*, 1:209.

[15]   Economic values in colonial America are explored in J. E. Crowley's *This Sheba, Self: The Conceptualization of Economic Life in Eighteenth-Century America* (Baltimore, 1974). See especially chap. 2, "The Legacy of the Calling" pp. 50–75.

[16]   Bernard Bailyn, *The New England Merchants in the Seventeenth Century* (New York, 1964), pp. 21, 41–44.

[17]   There is no better testimony to the social conservatism of the Puritan merchants than the fact that those who dominated the London City government in 1644 affirmed, in their proposals to Parliament of that year, traditional chartered privileges. See Valerie Pearl, *London and the Outbreak of the Puritan Revolution* (Oxford, 1961), pp. 281–284.

[18]   John Stow, *A Survey of London*, 2 vols. (1603; reprt. ed., Oxford, 1908), 2:207–213.

[19]   For a sensitive portrait of Winthrop as he gradually came to the decision to join the Puritan migration to New England, see Edmund S. Morgan, *The Puritan Dilemma: The Story of John Winthrop* (Boston, 1958), chaps. 1–3.

[20]   John Winthrop to Thomas Fones, 29 Jan. 1621[22], *Winthrop Papers*, 1:268; Richard S. Dunn, *Puritans and Yankees: The Winthrop Dynasty of New England, 1630–1717* (Princeton, 1962), p. 5; John Winthrop to Sir William Springe, 8 Feb. 1629[30], *Winthrop Papers*, 2:204; "General Considerations for the Plantation in

New-England; with an answer to several objections," in Alexander Young, ed., *Chronicles*, pp. 272–278. Additional manuscript versions of Winthrop's "Considerations" are reprinted in *Winthrop Papers*, 2:106–149.

[21] William Bradford, *Of Plymouth Plantation, 1620–1647*, ed. Samuel Eliot Morison (New York, 1952), pp. 11–16.

[22] John White to John Winthrop, 16 Nov. 1636, in Massachusetts Historical Society, *Collections*, 5th ser. (Boston, 1871), 1:231–232.

[23] Lawrence Stone, *The Causes of the English Revolution: 1529–1642* (London, 1972), pp. 68–71.

[24] The English "revolution" has received detailed study and analysis in Christopher Hill, *The Century of Revolution, 1603–1714* (Edinburgh, 1961); Stone, *The Causes of the English Revolution;* and Perez Zagorin, *The Court and the Country: The Beginnings of the English Revolution* (New York, 1970).

[25] Lord Say and Sele to John Winthrop, 9 July 1640, in Massachusetts Historical Society, *Collections*, 5th ser. (Boston, 1871), 1:297–301.

[26] The fourth Earl of Lincoln, Lord Say and Sele, John Humphry and Thomas Dudley, for example, were all related to one another. Valerie Pearl, *London and the Outbreak of the Puritan Revolution* (Oxford, 1961), pp. 161–169; Newton, *The Colonising Activities*, pp. 2–3, 35–58, passim; Zagorin, *The Court and the Country*, p. 101.

[27] Stone, *The Causes of the English Revolution*, pp. 105–106.

[28] Zagorin, *The Court and the Country*, p. 33.

[29] Stone, *The Causes of the English Revolution*, pp. 72–75, 99, 106–107.

[30] T. H. Breen, "Persistent Localism: English Social Change and the Shaping of New England Institutions," *William and Mary Quarterly* 32, no. 1 (Jan. 1975), 3, 27 and passim.

[31] Christopher Hill, *Society and Puritanism in Pre-Revolutionary England* (New York, 1964), pp. 483–489.

[32] Nathaniel B. Shurtleff, ed., *Records of the Governor and Company of the Massachusetts Bay in New England*, 5 vols. (Boston, 1853), 1:43.

33 Massachusetts Bay *Records*, 1:64–65; Marshall Harris, *Origin of the Land Tenure System in the United States* (Ames, Iowa, 1953), pp. 275–277; Rutman, *Winthrop's Boston*, p. 88.

34 The proprietary right of land distribution in Boston which inhered in the General Court was transferred in 1635 to a committee of seven selectmen. The right of land distribution fell to the town proprietors in New England as the original grantees or purchasers of the land. Winsor, *Memorial History of Boston*, 1:173; Roy H. Akagi, *The Town Proprietors of the New England Colonies* (Philadelphia, 1924), p. 3; Rutman, *Winthrop's Boston*, pp. 72–77, 87, 90.

35 Bailyn, *The New England Merchants in the Seventeenth Century*, p. 102; Akagi, *Town Proprietors*, p. 12; Massachusetts Bay *Records*, 1:43; Edna Scofield, "The Origin of Settlement Patterns in Rural New England," *Geographical Review* 28, no. 1 (Oct. 1938), 653–654; Akagi, *Town Proprietors*, pp. 12, 16, 45.

36 Deputy Governor Thomas Dudley to Lady Bridget, Countess of Lincoln, 12 March 1631, in Young, ed., *Chronicles*, p. 314.

37 John W. Reps, *The Making of Urban America: A History of City Planning in the United States* (Princeton, 1965), chap. 5. Sumner Chilton Powell, in his study of Sudbury, Mass., points out that three types of English land settlement were known to the founders of that town, established in 1638: the open-field manorial village, the incorporated borough, and the enclosed farm village common to East Anglia. The essential characteristic of the agricultural community centered in the nucleated village, however, was the one that prevailed in New England. *Puritan Village: The Formation of a New England Town* (New York, 1965), pp. xvi, passim.

38 Massachusetts Bay *Records*, 1:30; "Essay on the Laying Out of Towns, & c.," Massachusetts Historical Society, *Collections*, 5th ser. (Boston, 1861), 1:480.

39 Although actual apportionments varied considerably according to the basis used in determining their size—need or estate—Graves' figures seem to have been fairly standard. The Massachusetts Bay Company initially regarded fifty acres as the minimum size required for a single household while the General Court at first required that each dwelling be located within one-half mile from a meeting house. Edward Johnson described Watertown and Ipswitch as containing 160 and 140 families respectively in 1650. The typical township land plot was laid out at six to eight miles square. Harris, *Origins of the Land Tenure System*, p. 279; William Haller, *The Puritan Frontier: Town-Planning in New England Colonial Development, 1630–1660* (New York, 1951), p. 36; Scofield, "The Origin of Settlement Patterns in Rural New England," pp. 654, 663; J. Franklin Jameson, ed.,

Johnson's Wonder-Working Providence of Sion's Saviour in New England (New York, 1910), pp. 74, 96. See also Douglas R. McManis, *Colonial New England: A Historical Geography* (New York, 1975), pp. 41–84, for a general discussion of colonial New England's settlement and demographic patterns.

[40] "New Englands Plantation, or, A Short and True Description of the Commodities and Discommodities of that Countrey," in Peter Force, ed., *Tracts and Other Papers, Relating Principally to the Origin, Settlement and Progress of the Colonies in North America* (New York, 1947), p. 14; John Josselyn, Gent., "An Account of Two Voyages to New-England," in Massachusetts Historical Society, *Collections*, 3rd ser. (Cambridge, 1838), 3:318, 321; William Wood, *New Englands Prospect: A True, Lively, and Experimentall Description of That Part of America, commonly called New England* (London, 1634), pp. 40–43; Jameson ed., *Johnson's Wonder-Working Providence*, pp. 68–96.

[41] Morgan, *Puritan Family*, passim; and John Demos, *A Little Commonwealth: Family Life in Plymouth Colony* (New York, 1970).

[42] "Experiencia," *Winthrop Papers*, 3:213; "A Declaration in Defense of An Order of Court Made in May, 1637," ibid., 3:423–424.

[43] Haller, *Puritan Frontier*, p. 38; Harris, *Origins of the Land Tenure System*, p. 287.

[44] Hosmer, ed., *Winthrop's Journal*, 1:323–324; Winsor, *Memorial History of Boston*, 1:129, 136, 234–235: George H. Sabine, *A History of Political Theory* (London, 1937), pp. 383–385.

[45] Samuel Sewall, "Diary of Samuel Sewall, 1647–1729," Massachusetts Historical Society, *Collections*, 5th ser. (Boston, 1878), 1:460; John Cotton, "An Abstract of the Lawes of New England as they are now established," in Force, ed., *Tracts*, 3:6; Massachusetts Bay *Records*, 1:79.

[46] "New-Englands Plantation," in Force, ed., *Tracts*, p. 14.

[47] Bradford, *Of Plymouth Plantation*, pp. 253–254; "A Descriptive and Historical Account of New England," Massachusetts Historical Society, *Collections*, 1st ser., 3:81.

[48] Jameson, ed., *Johnson's Wonder-Working Providence*, pp. 59, 32, 29.

[49] Josselyn, "Account of Two Voyages to New–England," p. 331.

[50]   Wood, *New Englands Prospect,* p. 42; Rutman, *Winthrop's Boston,* pp. 26–32.

[51]   Early Boston is described in Walter Muir Whitehill, *Boston: A Topographical History* (Cambridge, 1959). See also Reps, *The Making of Urban America,* pp. 140–146.

[52]   Bailyn, *The New England Merchants in the Seventeenth Century,* pp. 36–37.

[53]   Wood, *New Englands Prospect,* p. 42; Rutman, *Winthrop's Boston,* pp. 166–167, 181–201.

[54]   Rutman, ibid., pp. 185–201.

[55]   The transformation of Winthrop's Boston from "the ideal of the medieval community . . . into the reality of modern society" forms one of the themes of Rutman's *Winthrop's Boston* and is summarized in the Epilogue. That the "idea of the covenant" constituted "fertile ground" for "Lockean doctrine," as Rutman suggests, is, however, debatable. See Michael Walzer, "Puritanism as a Revolutionary Ideology," *History and Theory* vol. 3, no. 1 (1963), especially pp. 63–66.

[56]   Bailyn, *The New England Merchants in the Seventeenth Century,* pp. 38–41; Rutman, *Winthrop's Boston,* pp. 181–182; Winsor, *Memorial History of Boston,* p. 291.

[57]   Jameson, ed., *Johnson's Wonder-Working Providence,* pp. 71, 247; Cotton Mather, "The Boston Ebenezer" (Boston, 1698), p. 7.

[58]   Josselyn, "An Account of Two Voyages," pp. 318–320, 330–331.

[59]   Sewall, "Diary", p. 116. For a critique of the notion of Puritan "declension" in the later half of the seventeenth century in New England see Robert C. Pope, "New England versus the New England Mind: The Myth of Declension," *Journal of Social History* vol. 3, no. 2 (Winter 1969–1970).

[60]   Bradford, "A Descriptive and Historical Account of New England," pp. 78–84; "Of Boston in New England," pp. 27–28.

[61]   Mather, "The Boston Ebenezer," pp. 1–11, 29–42, passim.

[62]   Peter Gay, *A Loss of Mastery: Puritan Historians in Colonial America* (Berkeley, 1966), p. 11.

63   Willaim Haller, *The Elect Nation: The Meaning and Relevance of Foxe's Book of Martyrs* (New York, 1963), pp. 66–69.

64   Haller estimates that roughly ten thousand copies of the *Actes and Monuments* were in circulation by 1600; *The Elect Nation*, pp. 13–14. Over 120 editions of the Geneva Bible appeared in England between 1560 and 1611, almost five times as many as the official Bishop's Bible of 1568; Introduction to *The Geneva Bible* (1560; Facsimile ed., Madison, Wisc., 1969), p. 14.

65   See Lamont, *Godly Rule;* Gay, *A Loss of Mastery;* Haller, *The Elect Nation;* Sacvan Bercovitch, *The Puritan Origins of the American Self* (New Haven, 1975), especially chap. 2; J. F. Maclear, "New England and the Fifth Monarchy: The Quest for the Millenium in Early American Puritanism," *William and Mary Quarterly* vol. 32, no. 2 (Apr. 1975).

66   Augustine, *City of God*, trans. Marcus Dods, intro. Thomas Merton (New York, 1950), Book XIV, xxviii, p. 477. For a discussion of the identity of church and state in Augustine's *City of God* see Rex Martin, "The Two Cities in Augustine's Political Philosophy," *Journal of the History of Ideas* 33, no. 2 (Apr.– June 1972), 195–216.

67   Winthrop, "A Modell of Christian Charity," in *Winthrop Papers*, 2:289, 292, 295; "John Davenport's Confession of Faith," in Isabel MacBeath Calder, ed., *Letters of John Davenport* (New Haven, 1937), p. 74.

68   Augustine, *City of God*, Book XI, xviii, p. 362.

69   Jameson, ed., *Johnson's Wonder-Working Providence*, p. 22; Deputy-Governor Thomas Dudley to the Lady Bridget, Countess of Lincoln, 12 March 1631, in Young, ed., *Chronicles*, p. 324; Winthrop, "General Conclusions" and "Reasons to be Considered, and Objections with Answers," in *Winthrop Papers*, 2:138, 143; John White, "The Planters Plea, or the Grounds of Plantations Examined and Usual Objections Answered," in Massachusetts Historical Society, *Proceedings* 62 (Boston, 1930), 374–380.

70   "The Humble Request," in *Winthrop Papers*, 2:232; Increase Mather, "A Brief Relation, The State of New England, from the Beginning of that Plantation to The Present Year, 1689," in Force, ed., *Tracts*, 4:3–4.

71   "The Humble Reqest," in *Winthrop Papers*, 2:232.

72   Jameson, ed., *Johnson's Wonder-Working Providence*, pp. 26–27, 270.

73 Hosmer, ed., *Winthrop's Journal*, 2:37, 83–84.

74 "Modell of Christian Charity," in *Winthrop Papers*, 2:294–295; *Winthrop's Journal*, 1:144.

75 See Sacvan Berkovitch's discussion of the *Magnalia Christi Americana* in *The Puritan Origins of the American Self*, pp. 35–72, passim. William Lamont has explored the struggle over godly rule, what that meant and how it was to be achieved, in England, 1603–1660. He argues that it was not the collapse of English Calvinism, but its strength, that led to the abandonment of Godly Rule through princes, bishops, and presbyters, for God's unintelligibility precluded the presumption of knowing His purposes or identifying His instruments. In this context Mather's *Magnalia* seems more akin to Foxe's *Actes and Monuments*, for both make that presumption as they turn sacred history into national history. Lamont, *Godly Rule*, passim.

76 John Bunyan, *The Pilgrim's Progress from this World to That Which is to Come*, ed. James Blanton Wharey (Oxford, 1928), p. 103.

77 Ibid., p. 172.

78 Nathaniel Ward, "The Simple Cobler of Aggawam in America," in Force, ed., *Tracts*, 3:25.

79 Actually both interpretations of the text are plausible; Ezekiel 48:15 describes the "profane place for the citie, for housing, & for suburbes" as a 5,000 by 25,000 "rede" portion to the east of the 25,000 reed square "holy portion of the land" (45:1), while subsequent verses describe the city and suburbs as 4,500 reeds square and 250 reeds square, respectively. Ezekiel's reed, a Hebrew standard of measurement, was equal to six cubits, at 18 inches to 22 inches a cubit. For an illustrated discussion of Castalion's and Villalpandus's reconstructions see John Archer, "Puritan Town Planning in New Haven," *Journal of the Society of Architectural Historians* 34, no. 2 (May 1975), 146–149.

80 The surveyor need not attempt to measure a right angle, for opposite sides of equal length and two diagonals of equal length will produce a rectangular formation.

81 Isabel MacBeath Calder, ed., *Letters of John Davenport*, pp. 10–11.

82 Davenport to Mary, Lady Vere, 28 July 1639; Davenport to John Winthrop the Younger, 24 May 1654, in Calder, ibid., pp. 77, 94.

[83] Possible biblical precedents for New Haven's plan are explored by John Archer in "Puritan Town Planning in New Haven," passim.

[84] Anthony N. B. Garvan, *Architecture and Town Planning in Colonial Connecticut* (New Haven, 1951), pp. 45–46. John W. Reps has commented that Garvan's argument is "at best tortured." For Rep's discussion of the New Haven plan see *The Making of Urban America*, pp. 128–130.

[85] Rutman, *Winthrop's Boston*, pp. 29–32.

3
William Penn's "Greene Country Towne"

[1] Richard B. Morris, ed., *Encyclopedia of American History* (New York, 1965), "Population and Immigration," p. 467; Gabriel Thomas, "An Historical and Geographical Account of Pennsylvania and of West New-Jersey," in Albert Cook Meyers, ed., *Narratives of Early Pennsylvania, West New Jersey, and Delaware, 1630–1707* (New York, 1912), pp. 317–331; Ruth L. Springer and Louise Wallman, eds., "Two Swedish Pastors describe Philadelphia, 1700 and 1702," *Pennsylvania Magazine of History and Biography* 84, no. 2 (Apr. 1960), 207.

[2] Jacob M. Price, "Economic Function and the Growth of American Port Towns in the Eighteenth Century," in Donald Fleming and Bernerd Bailyn, eds., *Perspectives in American History* vol. 7 (1974), passim; Carl and Jessica Bridenbaugh, *Rebels and Gentlemen: Philadelphia in the Age of Franklin* (New York, 1942); J. Thomas Scharf and Thompson Westcott, *History of Philadephia*, 3 vols. (Philadelphia, 1884); E. P. Oberholtzer, *Philadelphia: A History of the City and Its People*, 4 vols. (Philadelphia, 1911); Thomas J. Wertenbaker, *The Golden Age of Colonial Culture* (New York, 1942), passim; Frederick B. Tolles, *James Logan and the Culture of Provincial America* (Boston, 1957); and George B. Tatum, *Penn's Great Town* (Philadelphia, 1961).

[3] William Penn has been the subject of numerous biographical studies. Among the most valuable are Bonamy Dobrée, *William Penn: Quaker and Pioneer* (London, 1932); William I. Hull, *William Penn: A Topical Biography* (London, 1937); William Wistar Comfort, *William Penn, 1644–1718: A Tercentenary Estimate* (Philadelphia, 1944); and Catherine Owens Peare, *William Penn: A Biography* (New York, 1957). While not a biography, Melvin Endy's *William Penn and Early Quakerism* (Princeton, 1973) is a useful study.

[4] David Hawke, *The Colonial Experience* (Indianapolis, 1966), p. 231; Edward C. O. Beatty, *William Penn as Social Philosopher* (New York, 1959), pp. 5–7;

Hugh F. Russel-Smith, *Harrington and His Oceana: A Study of a Seventeenth Century Utopia and Its Influence in America* (Cambridge, Eng., 1914), pp. 165–166.

5 W. Lee Ustick, "Changing Ideals of Aristocratic Character and Conduct in Seventeenth Century England," *Modern Philology* 30 (1932–1933), 155–158 and passim. See also Ruth Kelso, *The Doctrine of the English Gentleman in the Sixteenth Century*, University of Illinois Studies in Language and Literature, vol. 14 (Urbana, 1929).

6 Alison G. Olson, "William Penn, Parliament and Proprietary Government," *William and Mary Quarterly*, 3rd ser. 18, no. 2 (Apr. 1961), 176–195.

7 William Penn, "No Cross, No Crown," in *The Witness of William Penn*, ed. Frederick B. Tolles and E. Gordon Alderfer, (New York, 1957), pp. 47, 53, 60.

8 William Penn, "Fruits of Solitude," in William Penn Tercentenary Committee, *Remember William Penn* (Philadelphia, 1944), p. 74.

9 Ibid., pp. 70, 75.

10 William Penn to Robert Turner, 5 Jan. 1681, in John F. Watson, ed., *Annals of Philadelphia and Pennsylvania*, 3 vols. (Philadelphia, 1887), 1:82.

11 The flight of country people to town would have been as likely to encourage large families to provide extra "hands" as to discourage them. William Penn, "Some Account of the Province of Pennsylvania," in Meyers, ed., *Narratives of Early Pennsylvania*, pp. 204–205.

12 William Penn to Gulielma Penn, 4 Aug. 1682, in William Penn Papers, Historical Society of Pennsylvania, Philadelphia, Pa.

13 See Raymond Williams' discussion of this theme in *The Country and the City* (New York, 1973, reprd. 1975), pp. 46–54 and passim.

14 "Fruits of Solitude," in *Remember William Penn*, pp. 22, 29, 33.

15 Edwin B. Bronner, *William Penn's "Holy Experiment": The Founding of Pennsylvania, 1681–1701* (New York, 1962), pp. 59–60; Marshall Harris, *Origin of the Land Tenure System in the United States* (Ames, Iowa, 1953), pp. 121–125. Penn's charter did lack the bishop of Durham clause granting the proprietor complete sovereignty excepting only that he remain loyal to the king.

16 For a discussion of the successive drafts of the First Frame of Government of 1682 see Gary B. Nash, *Quakers and Politics: Pennsylvania, 1681–1726* (Princeton, 1968), pp. 33–47; and Gary B. Nash, "The Framing of Government in Pennsylvania: Ideas in Conflict with Reality," *William and Mary Quarterly* vol. 22, no. 2 (Apr. 1966).

17 "Some Account of the Province of Pennsylvania," in Meyers, ed., *Narratives of Early Pennsylvania*, p. 5.

18 Staughton George, ed., *Charter to William Penn, and Laws of the Province of Pennsylvania* (Harrisburg, 1879).

19 Ibid., p. 99.

20 Nash, *Quakers and Politics*, p. 43.

21 Russell-Smith, *Harrington and His Oceana*, pp. 161–179.

22 Ibid., p. 51.

23 As it turned out, land in Pennsylvania was bought, with a reservation of modest quitrents to the proprietor by which he hoped to secure an income for his family, in varying parcels. The most common was 500 acres, and only sixty-nine colonists originally acquired estates of 5,000 acres or more. Penn's land policy in Pennsylvania is described in Bronner, *William Penn's "Holy Experiment,"* pp. 59–65. See also John E. Pomfret, "The First Purchasers of Pennsylvania, 1681–1700," *Pennsylvania Magazine of History and Biography* vol. 30, no. 2 (Apr. 1956).

24 Frederick B. Tolles, "William Penn and Private Affairs, 1686: An Important New Letter," *Pennsylvania Magazine of History and Biography* 30, no. 2 (Apr. 1956), 242.

25 Caroline Robbins, *The Eighteenth-Century Commonwealthman: Studies in the Transmission, Development and Circumstance of English Liberal Thought from the Restoration of Charles II until the War with the Thirteen Colonies* (New York, 1959, 1968), pp. 3–48.

26 "First Frame of Government," in George, ed., *Charter to William Penn*, pp. 91–92.

27 Ibid., pp. 92–93. See William Lamont, *Godly Rule: Politics and Religion, 1603–1660* (London, 1969). Valuable discussions of Penn as a political and social thinker are to be found in Beatty, *William Penn as Social Philosopher;* Mary Maples, "William Penn, Classical Republican," *Pennsylvania Magazine of History and Biography* vol. 81 (Apr. 1957), and Mary Maples Dunn, *William Penn, Politics and Conscience* (Princeton, 1967).

[28] "The Great Law, or The Body of Laws," George ed., *Charter to William Penn*, p. 107.

[29] The General Assembly was empowered only to assent to or negate laws passed by the Council. It was confined to a nine-day annual session and could neither debate nor amend measures submitted to it.

[30] "The Great Law," in George, ed., *Charter to William Penn*, pp. 102–103.

[31] Ibid., p. 108 and passim.

[32] James T. Lemon has provided the best discussion of Penn's plan for the disposal of land in Pennsylvania in his *The Best Poor Man's Country: A Geographical Study of Early Southeastern Pennsylvania* (Baltimore, 1972), pp. 98–109 and passim; "Certain Conditions and Concessions," *Colonial Records of Pennsylvania* (Philadelphia, 1852), 10th provision, 1:27; William Penn, "A Further Account of the Province of Pennsylvania," in Meyers, ed., *Narratives of Early Pennsylvania*, p. 263.

[33] "A Further Account," in Meyers, ed., *Narratives of Early Pennsylvania*, p. 263; James T. Lemon, *The Best Poor Man's Country*, p. 100.

[34] "The Frame of Government," in George, ed., *Charter to William Penn*, p. 95; "Certain Conditions or Concessions," *Colonial Records*, 1:26.

[35] "Instructions Given by Mee William Penn Proprietor and Governor of Pennsylvania," Sept. 30, 1681, William Penn Papers. Thomas Holme was appointed to replace Crispin, who died on his way to Pennsylvania in 1681. Holme was then appointed Surveyor-General for the province on Apr. 18, 1682. Oliver Hough, "Captain Thomas Holme, Surveyor-General of Pennsylvania and Provincial Councillor," *Pennsylvania Magazine of History and Biography* 19 (1895), 414, 418.

[36] "A Short Advertisement upon the Situation and Extent of the City of Philadelphia and the ensuing Platform Thereof. By the Surveyor General," in William Penn Papers.

[37] "Instructions Given by Mee William Penn," in William Penn Papers; "A Short Advertisement," in William Penn Papers. John W. Rep identifies the map

of 1683 as "Philadelphia in 1683 as planned by Penn and Holme" and commends the plan as "Penn's great accomplishment in city building" in "William Penn and the Planning of Philadelphia," *Town Planning Review* 27, no. 1 (Apr. 1956), 28; Reps, *The Making of Urban America: A History of City Planning in the United States* (Princeton, 1965), p. 158; William E. Lingelbach, "William Penn and City Planning," *Pennsylvania Magazine of History and Biography* 68, no. 4 (Oct. 1944), 398; Tatum, *Penn's Great Town*, 19; Peare, *William Penn: A Biography*, pp. 225–226, 249–250; and Gary B. Nash, "City Planning and Political Tension in the Seventeenth Century: The Case of Philadelphia," *Proceedings of the American Philosophical Society* 112 (1968), 60.

[38] A Short Advertisement," in William Penn Papers; Reps, "William Penn and the Planning of Philadelphia," pp. 30–32; Hough, "Captain Thomas Holme," p. 414; Gilbert Gamblin, *The Town in Ulster* (Belfast, 1951), pp. 19–29.

[39] "A Short Advertisement," in William Penn Papers; "Instructions," 15th provision, in William Penn Papers.

[40] "A Short Advertisement," in William Penn Papers.

[41] "Instructions," 2nd provision, in William Penn Papers. By "First Purchasers" Penn meant the buyers of the first 500,000 acres in Pennsylvania, or the purchasers of the first one hundred 5,000-acre shares.

[42] "Certain Conditions or Concessions," 5th provision, in William Penn Papers, p. 27. The same document contains a curious stipulation that roads "from City to City" be laid out before first purchasers' dividends in Philadelphia. It is, however, likely that Penn was merely responding to his charter obligation to provide for principal roads and did not actually expect the location of cities to determine the spatial arrangements of land in Pennsylvania. Access roads from city to city could not in fact have been laid out until the cities themselves were located, and that could not have occurred until purchasers' lands, whether in townships or individually, were granted or sold and laid out.

[43] Pomfret, "The First Purchasers of Pennsylvania, 1681–1700," *Pennsylvania Magazine of History and Biography*, p. 149; "A Further Account," *Narratives of Early Pennsylvania*, p. 262.

[44] Nash, *Quakers and Politics*, p. 52.

[45] "Instructions," 4th provision, in William Penn Papers.

[46] Ibid., 12th and 16th provisions.

[47]   Ibid., 15th provision.

[48]   Ibid., 12th, 13th, and 14th provisions.

[49]   Reps, *The Making of Urban America*, pp. 138–139. I am indebted to Russell I. Fries for valuable suggestions of how Penn's "Instructions" would most probably have been interpreted by a contemporary surveyor.

[50]   Hannah B. Roach, "The Planting of Philadelphia: A Seventeenth Century Real Estate Development," *Pennsylvania Magazine of History and Biography* 92, nos. 1 and 2 (Jan. and Apr. 1968), 11 and passim.

[51]   "A Letter from William Penn . . . to the Committee of the Free Society of Traders," in J. Sowle, ed., *A Collection of the Works of William Penn* (London, 1726), 2:706.

[52]   Gary B. Nash, "City Planning and Political Tension in the Seventeenth Century," *Proceedings of The American Philosophical Society* 112 (Philadelphia, 1968), 57, 70–72. A city charter was issued in 1691 over Deputy Thomas Holme's signature "erecting 'the said Town & Borough of Philadelphia into a city' " but it is unknown whether any government actually operated under that earlier document. Judith M. Diamonstone, "Philadelphia's Municipal Corporation, 1701–1776," *Pennsylvania Magazine of History and Biography* 90, no. 2 (Apr. 1966), 186.

[53]   The Free Society of Traders, a London-based joint stock company composed largely of Quaker merchants, was "from the outset . . . an integral part of his plans for the colony." Nash, *Quakers and Politics*, pp. 19–22.

[54]   "A Further Account," p. 262. The "Charter of Property" passed in 1701 by the Pennsylvania assembly guaranteed landowners the right to alienate their lands and "revoked the proprietor's power of escheat," which made it virtually impossible for the proprietors to enforce their settlement provisions once land had been deeded. Lemon, *The Best Poor Man's Country*, pp. 105–106.

[55]   Price, "Economic Function and the Growth of American Port Towns in the Eighteenth Century," pp. 138–140, 151–153.

[56]   Nash, "City Planning and Political Tension in the Seventeenth Century," p. 56; Roach, "The Planting of Philadelphia," p. 22.

[57]   "Certain Conditions," 1st provision, p. 26.

[58]   Ibid., 9th provision, p. 27.

[59]   For a breakdown of the specific sizes of Philadelphia lots see Nash, "City Planning and Political Tension in the Seventeenth Century," p. 61.

[60]   Ibid., pp. 62–64.

[61]   Edward Armstrong, ed., *Correspondence between William Penn and James Logan*, 2 vols. (Philadelphia, 1840), 1:60, 70, and passim. James T. Lemon has argued that the disintegration of the medieval open-field system in Pennsylvania was due less to the cheapness of land, the weakenss of proprietary control, or imported European patterns among the English Quakers or the Scotch-Irish, than to the "fundamental force . . . [of] the rise of individualism over peasant values in western Europe." Lemon, *The Best Poor Man's Country*, pp. 101–108.

[62]   Tatum, *Penn's Great Town*, p. 19.

[63]   T. F. Reddaway, "The Rebuilding of London After the Great Fire: A rediscovered Plan," *Town Planning Review* 39, no. 3 (July 1939), 155–161.

[64]   "A Short Advertisement," in William Penn Papers.

[65]   Anthony N. B. Garvan, "Proprietary Philadelphia as Artifact," in Oscar Handlin and John Burchard, eds., *The Historian and The City*, (Cambridge, Mass., 1963), p. 193.

[66]   Ibid., p. 191.

[67]   Sam Bass Warner, Jr., *The Private City: Philadelphia in Three Periods of Its Growth* (Philadelphia, 1968), pp. 9–10; Diamondstone, "Philadelphia's Municipal Corporation, 1701–1776."

[68]   Reps, *The Making of Urban America*, p. 120.

[69]   Robbins, *The Eighteenth-Century Commonwealthman*, p. 45 and passim.

[70]   "William Penn, Speech to the Assembly of Pennsylvania," in William Penn Papers.

[71]   Scharf and Westcott, *History of Philadelphia*, 1:160–163; J. Francis Fisher, "A Discourse delivered before the Historical Society of Pennsylvania, the 9th day of April 1836, on the Private Life and Domestic Habits of William Penn,"

Memoirs of the Historical Society of Pennsylvania 3, part 2 (Philadelphia, 1834), p. 94.

[72]   Francis Daniel Pastorious, from "The Pennsylvania Pilgrim," trans. John G. Whittier, 1700; quoted in Oberholtzer, *Philadelphia: A History of the City and Its People*, 4:81.

4
The Curious Case of Williamsburg

[1]   Louis B. Wright, *The First Gentlemen of Virginia* (Charlottesville, 1964); Thomas J. Wertenbaker, *The Planters of Colonial Virginia* (Princeton, 1922).

[2]   Beauchamp Plantagenet, "A Description of the Province of New Albion: and a Direction for Adventurers with small stock to get two for one, and good land freely, etc.," in Peter Force, ed., *Tracts and Other Papers, relating principally to the Origin, Settlement and Progress of the Colonies in North America, from the Discovery of the Country to the Year 1776*, vol. 2 (Washington, 1838); Nathaniel Shrigley, "A True Relation of Virginia and Maryland: With the Commodities Therein," in Force, ed., *Tracts*, vol. 3; Howard Mumford Jones, *O Strange New World: American Culture; The Formative Years* (New York, 1970), p. 69 and passim.

[3]   Francis Nicholson was cautioned "to take care to provide Cages, with suitable diet, and other conveniences: and not put too many of them together nor on board the same ship." Francis Nicholson to the Sheriffs of James City County, 1 March 1699, in Nicholson Papers, Colonial Williamsburg Foundation, Williamsburg, Va.

[4]   Richard Slotkin, *Regeneration through Violence: The Mythology of the American Frontier, 1600–1860* (Middletown, Conn., 1973); Roderick Nash, *Wilderness and the American Mind* (New Haven, 1973).

[5]   Sir Thomas Smith quoted in John W. Reps, *Tidewater Towns: City Planning in Colonial Virginia and Maryland* (Charlottesville, 1972), p. 10; Nicholas P. Canny, "The Ideology of English Colonization: From Ireland to America," *William and Mary Quarterly*, 3rd ser., no. 4 (Oct. 1973) 575–596; Reps, *Tidewater Towns*, p. 46.

[6]   "Virginia's Cure: or An Advisive Narrative Concerning Virginia: Discovering the True Ground of that Churches Unhappiness, and the only true Remedy," pp. 5–7, in Force, ed., *Tracts*, vol. 3.

7 Stephen Saunders Webb, "Army and Empire: English Garrison Government in Britain and America, 1569 to 1763," *William and Mary Quarterly*, 3rd ser., 34, no. 1 (Jan. 1977), p. 6 and passim.

8 Leonard Woods Labaree, ed., *Royal Instructions to British Governors, 1670–1776*, 2 vols. (New York, 1935), 2:580.

9 Order to "Establish Townships in New Provinces" in Labaree, *Royal Instructions*, 2:544.

10 Order to "Establish Townships in New Provinces," in ibid., 2:538.

11 Order to "Establish Townships on New Hampshire Frontier" and "Rights and Priveleges of South Carolina Townships," in ibid., 2:542–544.

12 Order to "Establish Townships in New Provinces" and "Rights and Priveleges of South Carolina Townships," in ibid., 2:538, 540.

13 Labaree, *Royal Instructions*, 2:528–530.

14 Edward M. Riley, "The Town Acts of Virginia," *Journal of Southern History* vol. 16, no. 3 (Aug. 1950); Edmund S. Morgan, *American Slavery, American Freedom: The Ordeal of Colonial Virginia* (New York, 1975), pp. 181–191, 283–288, and passim; John C. Rainbolt, *From Prescription to Persuasion: Manipulation of Eighteenth Century Virginia Economy* (New York, 1974), passim.

15 Riley, "The Town Acts of Virginia," pp. 312–313, 321–322.

16 Morgan, *American Slavery, American Freedom*, pp. 190–191, 279–280; Herman Wellenreuther, "Urbanization in the Colonial South: A Critique," *William and Mary Quarterly*, 3rd ser., vol. 31, no. 4 (Oct. 1974); Richard Beale Davis, ed., *William Fitzhugh and His Chesapeake World, 1676–1701: The Fitzhugh Letters and Other Documents* (Chapel Hill, 1963), pp. 82–83ff.

17 Morgan, *American Slavery, American Freedom*, pp. 82, 187.

18 Henry Hartwell, James Blair and Edward Chilton, *The Present State of Virginia, and the College*, ed. Hunter Dickinson Farish (Williamsburg, 1940), pp. 4–5, 11. Blair's report was written in 1697 as a "white paper" for the Board of Trade whose membership then included John Locke. Blair's political interest in the report is discussed in Robert A. Bain, "The Composition and Publication of *The Present State of Virginia, and the College*." *Early American Literature* vol. 6, no. 1 (Spring 1971). See also Michael G. Kammen, ed. "Virginia at the Close of the

Seventeenth Century: An Appraisal by James Blair and John Locke," *The Virginia Magazine of History and Biography* vol. 74, no. 2 (Apr. 1966).

[19]   Francis Makemie, "A Plain & Friendly Persuasive to the Inhabitants of Virginia and Maryland For Promoting Towns & Cohabitation," *Virginia Magazine of History and Biography* 4, no. 3 (Jan. 1897), 252–254.

[20]   Rainbolt, *From Prescription to Persuasion*, p. 145.

[21]   "Speeches of Students of the College of William and Mary, Delivered May 1, 1699," *William and Mary Quarterly*, 2nd ser., 10, no. 4 (Oct. 1930), 329, 332–333.

[22]   "The Statutes of the College of William and Mary in Virginia," in Edgar W. Knight, ed., *A Documentary History of Education in the South before 1860*, 5 vols. (Chapel Hill, 1949) 1:501–507.

[23]   Richard Beale Davis, *Intellectual Life in Jefferson's Virginia, 1790–1830* (Chapel Hill, 1964), p. 50.

[24]   "An Act Continuing the Act directing the Building the Capitol and the City of Williamsburg; with Additions" (Oct. 1705), in William Waller Henig, ed., *The Statutes at Large: Being A Collection of all the Laws of Virginia* 3 (New York, 1819–1823), 419.

[25]   For a brief discussion of Nicholson's career as urban designer and Wren's proposal for the rebuilding of London after the Great Fire of 1666, see John W. Reps, *The Making of Urban America; A History of City Planning in the United States* (Princeton, 1965), pp. 103–110, 15–19. The political interests that may have underlain Nicholson's support of the College and the new capital at Middle Plantation are suggested in Stephen Saunders Webb, "The Strange Career of Francis Nicholson," *William and Mary Quarterly*, 3rd ser., vol. 22, no. 4 (Oct. 1966). See also "Sir Francis Nicholson," *Dictionary of National Biography* (1921), vol. 14, pp. 457.

[26]   Henig, *Statutes at Large*, 3:419–423.

[27]   Reprinted and discussed in Reps, *The Making of Urban America*, pp. 112–113.

[28]   The only precedent for such a street arrangement is John Evelyn's plan for London, published in 1756, and his *The Compleat Gard'ner*, a copy of which Nicholson owned. Reps, *Tidewater Towns*, p. 170. Hugh Jones wrote that

Nicholson "laid out the city of Williamsburgh (in the form of a cypher made of W and M)." Hugh Jones, *Present State of Virginia,* ed. Richard L. Morton (Chapel Hill, 1956), p. 66.

[29]   Leone Battista Alberti, *Ten Books on Architecture,* from the Italian trans. of Cosimo Bartoli (1755; reprint ed., New York, 1966), Book IV, chap. 4, p. 75.

[30]   Arthur A. Shurcliff, "The Ancient Plan of Williamsburg," *Landscape Architecture* 28, no. 2 (Jan. 1938), 87–102.

[31]   P. H. Scholfield, *The Theory of Proportion in Architecture* (Cambridge, 1958), p. 55 and passim; Rudolf Wittkower, *Architectural Principles in the Age of Humanism* (London, 1952).

[32]   William H. Pierson, Jr., *American Buildings and Their Architects* (New York, 1970), pp. 70–110; Marcus Whiffen, *The Public Buildings of Williamsburg* (Williamsburg, 1958), passim; Sabastian Serlio, *The Book of Architecture* (1611; reprint ed, New York, 1970), pp. 13–15.

[33]   Whiffen, *The Public Buildings of Williamsburg,* pp. 24, 77–83, 100–108, 152–160; Marcus Whiffen, *The Eighteenth-Century Houses of Williamsburg* (Williamsburg, 1960), pp. 56–59.

[34]   Helen Park, "A List of Architectural Books Available in America before the Revolution," *Journal of the Society of Architectural Historians* 20, no. 3. (Oct. 1961), 126–130.

[35]   William Halfpenny, *Practical Architecture, or a Sure Guide to the true working according to the Rules of that Science* (London, 1730), preface.

[36]   Robert Morris, *Lectures on Architecture* (London, 1734), p. 81.

[37]   Ibid., p. 94.

[38]   "The Monitor," no. 10, *The Virginia Gazette,* no. 12, Oct. 15–22, 1736 (Williamsburg).

[39]   A. L. Rowse, *The England of Elizabeth: The Structure of Society* (New York, 1951), pp. 196–211; F. J. Fisher, "The Development of London as a Centre of Conspicuous Consumption in the Sixteenth and Seventeenth Centuries," *Transactions of the Royal Historical Society,* 4th ser., 30 (London, 1948), 37–50; George Rudé, *Hanoverian London, 1714–1808* (Berkeley, 1971), chap. 4, pp. 64–81.

[40]   Robert Carter of Nomini Hall, *Letterbook II,* 25 Mar. 1765, Colonial Williamsburg Foundation, Williamsburg, Va.

[41]   Ibid., 23 May 1764.

[42]   Robert Wormeley Carter to Landon Carter, 16 Nov. 1764, in Landon Carter Papers, Alderman Library of the University of Virginia.

[43]   Robert Beverley, *The History and Present State of Virginia,* ed. Louis B. Wright (Chapel Hill, 1947), p.xxii.

[44]   Robert Carter to John Pemberton, 14 Feb. 1720, in Louis B. Wright, ed., *Robert Carter, 1720–1727: The Commercial Interests of a Virginia Gentleman* (San Marino, 1940), p. 77.

[45]   William Fitzhugh to George Mason, 21 July 1698, in Davis, ed., *William Fitzhugh and His Chesapeake World,* p. 361.

[46]   Robert Carter to William Dawkins, 23 Feb. 1720/21, in Wright, ed., *Letters of Robert Carter, 1720–1727,* pp. 81–82.

[47]   Hugh Jones, *The Present State of Virginia,* pp. 18, 71, 80.

[48]   *The Virginia Gazette,* no. 34, Mar. 18–25, 1737 (Williamsburg).

[49]   Ibid., no. 16 Nov. 12–19, 1736 (Williamsburg).

[50]   Ibid., no. 17 Nov. 19–26, 1737; Davis, *William Fitzhugh and His Chesapeake World,* p. 49.

[51]   *The Virginia Gazette,* no. 26, Jan. 21–28, 1736 (Williamsburg).

[52]   Louis B. Wright, "The Prestige of Learning in Early America," *Proceedings of the American Antiquarian Society* 83, part 2 (Apr. 1973), 18.

[53]   Edmund S. Morgan, *Virginians at Home: Family Life in the Eighteenth Century* (Charlottesville, 1963), pp. 80–83 and passim.

[54]   William Gooch to the Bishop of London, 26 May 1728, Official Correspondence of Governor William Gooch, Colonial Williamsburg Foundation, Williamsburg, Va.

[55]   Hunter Dickinson Farish, ed., *Journal and Letters of Philip Vickers Fithian, 1773–1774* (Williamsburg, 1943), pp. 11, 35.

56 Ibid., 30 Aug. 1773, 13 Dec. 1773, Fithian to the Rev. Enoch Green, 1 Dec. 1773, pp. 11, 39, 35.

57 Ibid., 27 Dec. 1773, 21 Dec. 1773, 30 Dec. 1773, 17 Dec. 1773, pp. 56, 48, 58, 43.

58 Wright, *The First Gentlemen of Virginia*, p. 14.

59 Richard M. Gunmere, *The American Colonial Mind and the Classical Tradition* (Cambridge, 1963), pp. 84–90.

60 Richard Beale Davis, "William Byrd: Taste and Tolerance," in Everett Emerson, ed., *Major Writers of Early American Literature* (Madison, 1972), pp. 152–156; Pierre Marambaud, *William Byrd of Westover, 1674–1744* (Charlottesville, 1971), pp. 92, 99, 105 and passim.

61 William Byrd II, "Inamorato L 'Oiseaux," in Maude H. Woodfin and Marion Tinling, eds., *Another Secret Diary of William Byrd of Westover, 1739–1741, and Literary Exercises, With Letters, 1696–1726* (Richmond, 1942), pp. 276–281.

62 Louis B. Wright and Marion Tinling, eds., *William Byrd: The London Diary (1717–1721) and Other Writings* (New York, 1958), p. 38.

63 For a description see Reps, *Tidewater Towns*, p. 267.

64 Marambaud, *William Byrd of Westover*, p. 92 and passim.

65 William Byrd, *The Prose Works of William Byrd of Westover*, ed. Louis B. Wright (Cambridge, Eng., 1966), "The Secret History of the Dividing Line," p. 55; Wright and Timlin, eds., *William Byrd: The London Diary (1717–1721) and Other Writings*, p. 38.

66 Henry Peacham, *The Art of Living in London*, with *The Complete Gentleman* and *The Truth of Our Times*, ed. Virgil B. Heltzel, (Ithaca, 1962), pp. 245–250.

67 Raymond Williams, *The Country and the City* (New York, 1973), passim. Farish, ed., *Journal of Philip Vickers Fithian*, 20 Dec. 1773, p. 46.

68 *The Ladies Complete Letter-Writer* (London, 1763), pp. 161, 239.

69 Ibid., p. 235.

70 Ibid., p. 253.

71   Alexander Spotswood to John Spotswood, 17 Aug. 1710; 20 Mar. 1710/11, in Alexander Spotswood Papers, Colonial Williamsburg Foundation, Williamsburg, Va.

72   Peyton Randolph to Landon Carter, 7 Mar. 1767, in Emmet Collection, New York Public Library, New York, N. Y.

73   Thomas J. Wertenbaker, *The Golden Age of Colonial Culture* (New York, York, 1942), "Williamsburg"; James A. Soltow, *The Economic Role of Williamsburg* (Williamsburg, 1965); Carl Bridenbaugh, *Seat of Empire: The Political Role of Eighteenth-Century Williamsburg* (Charlottesville, 1958), pp. 24–31 and passim; Thad W. Tate, Jr., *The Negro in Eighteenth-Century Williamsburg* (Charlottesville, 1960).

74   Such familiar "FFV" surnames as Byrd, Bland, Bolling, Burwell, Cary, Chew, Ludlow, Fitzhugh, and Mason belonged to families well connected with London commercial and governmental circles. Bernard Bailyn, "Politics and Social Structure in Virginia," in James Morton Smith, ed., *Seventeenth-Century America* (Chapel Hill, 1959), pp. 98–100; Wright, *First Gentlemen of Virginia*, chap. 2, passim.

75   Diary of Landon Carter, Landon Carter Papers, Alderman Library of the University of Virginia; Bailyn, "Politics and Social Structure in Virginia," pp. 107–111.

76   U. S. Bureau of the Census, *Historical Statistics of the United States, Colonial Times to 1957* (Washington, D.C., 1960), p. 769; Winthrop D. Jordan, "Enslavement of Negroes in America to 1700," in Stanley N. Katz, ed., *Colonial America: Essays in Politics and Social Development* (Boston, 1976), p. 250.

77   Morgan, *American Slavery, American Freedom*, pp. 338–362.

78   Ibid., pp. 341–346.

79   Gideon Sjoberg has argued that the formation of a literate elite is a specially urban phenomenon, for localization in urban areas enables "dominant elements" to concentrate their power while the urban economy releases them from the drudgery of rural labor and provides the material support necessary for their existence. Sjoberg is careful to distinguish the pre-industrial urban elite from the larger "leisure class" of the industrial city; only in the later instance is technological develpment sufficient to free significant numbers from manual labor. *The Preindustrial City: Past and Present* (New York, 1960). In the case of Virginia it was not an urban economy but slavery which released the aspiring elite from the "drudgery of rural labor" and provided the material support for their ascendancy.

5
Savannah: The City in the Country

1   John Percival to George Berkely, 23 Dec. 1730; William Byrd to John Percival, 10 June 1729, in Benjamin Rand, ed., *Berkeley and Percival: The Correspondence of George Berkeley, afterwards Bishop of Cloyne, and Sir John Percival, afterwards Earl of Egmont* (Cambridge, 1914). Berkeley had been given the patent for the Deanery of Derry in 1724.

2   Percival to Byrd, 3 Dec. 1730; Percival to Berkeley, 23 Dec. 1730, ibid.

3   For a fuller account of Trusteeship Georgia than we will attempt here see: James Ross McCain, *Georgia as a Proprietary Province: The Execution of a Trust* (1917; reprt. Boston, 1972); Leslie F. Church, *Oglethorpe: A Study of Philanthropy in England and Georgia* (London, 1932); E. Merton Coulter, *Georgia: A Short History* (Chapel Hill, 1960), chaps. 2–7; Trevor Richard Reese, *Colonial Georgia: A Study in British Imperial Policy in the Eighteenth Century* (Athens, 1963); Paul S. Taylor, *Georgia Plan: 1732–1752*, Institute of Business and Economic Research, Graduate School of Business Administration, University of California (Berkeley, 1972); Harold E. Davis, *The Fledgling Province: Social and Cultural Life in Colonial Georgia, 1733–1776* (Chapel Hill, 1976); and Kenneth Coleman, *Colonial Georgia: A Short History* (New York, 1976).

4   J. G. A. Pocock, *The Machiavellian Moment: Florentine Political Thought and the Atlantic Republican Tradition* (Princeton, 1975), pp. 349–360.

5   Ibid., pp. 383–395.

6   The anatomy of "Country" ideology, variously referred to as "Old Whig," "Independent Whig," or "Commonwealth" thought, is explored in Pocock, *Machiavellian Moment*, chap. 10–14, passim; Caroline Robbins, *The Eighteenth-Century Commonwealthman: Studies in the Transmission, Development and Circumstance of English Liberal Thought from the Restoration of Charles II until the War with the Thirteen Colonies* (New York, 1968), and J. G. A. Pocock, "Machiavelli, Harrington and English Political Ideologies in the Eighteenth Century," in *Politics, Language and Time: Essays on Political Thought and History* (New York, 1960, reprt. 1973). See also Isaac Kramnick, *Bolingbroke and His Circle: The Politics of Nostalgia in the Age of Walpole* (Cambridge, Mass., 1968).

7   The most active members in carrying out the work of the Georgia Corporation were the Hon. James Vernon, Esq., John Percival, Earl of Egmont, Henry L 'Apostre, the Rev. Samuel Smith, Thomas Towers, Esq., John Laroche, Esq., Robert Hucks, Esq., the Reverent Stephen Hales, James Edward Oglethorpe,

Anthony Ashley, fourth Earl of Shaftesbury, Adam Anderson, Thomas Coram, John, Lord Viscount Tyrconnel, George Heathcote, and Sir William Heathcote. Brief sketches of these men and their roles in the Trust are included in McCain, *Georgia as a Proprietary Province*, pp. 30–56.

[8] Ruth and Albert Saye, "John Percival, First Earl of Egmont," in Horace Montgomery, ed., *Georgians in Profile: Historical Essays in Honor of Ellis Merton Coulter* (Athens, 1958), p. 7; Paul Langford, *The Excise Crisis: Society and Politics in the Age of Walpole* (Oxford, 1975), p. 343 and passim; John Percival, first Earl of Egmont, *Diary of Viscount Percival, First Earl of Egmont*, 3 vols., Historical Manuscripts Commission (London, 1923), 1:85–86.

[9] James Boswell, *Boswell's Life of Johnson*, ed. George Birkbeck Hill, 6 Vols, (Oxford, 1934), 3:282. For Oglethorpe's background see Henry Bruce, *Life of General Oglethorpe* (New York, 1890); Church, *Oglethorpe;* and Amos A. Ettinger, *James Edward Oglethorpe: Imperial Idealist* (Oxford, 1936).

[10] Saye, "John Percival, First Earl of Egmont," in *Georgians in Profile*, p. 9; Egmont, *Diary*, 39 Apr. 1732, 1:264.

[11] J. H. Plumb, *England in the Seventeenth Century* (Baltimore, 1972), pp. 11–20; George Rudé, *Hanoverian London, 1714–1808* (Berkeley, 1971), chap. 5, pp. 82–99.

[12] William Penn, *Some Account of the Province of Pennsylvania* (London, 1681), pp. 3–4.

[13] Quoted in Christopher Hill, *The Century of Revolution, 1603–1714* (Edinburgh, 1961), p. 296.

[14] Benjamin Martyn, "A New and Accurate Account of the Provinces of South Carolina and Georgia," in Peter Force, ed., *Tracts and Other Papers, Relating Principally to the Origin, Settlement and Progress of the Colonies of North America* (New York, 1947), 1:31.

[15] H. B. Flant, "Financing the Colonization of Georgia," *Georgia Historical Quarterly* vol. 20, no. 1 (Spring, 1936), passim; Geraldine Meroney, "The London Entrepôt Merchants and the Georgia Colony," *William and Mary Quarterly*, 3rd ser., vol. 25, no. 2 (Apr. 1968), passim.

[16] Martyn, "A New and Accurate Account," in Force, ed., *Tracts*, pp. 50–51.

[17] George Watts, "A Sermon Preached before the Trustees for Establishing the Colony of Georgia in America, at their Anniversary Meeting in the Parish Church

of St. Bridget, alias St. Brede, in Fleetstreet, London, on Thursday, Mar, 18, 1735" (London, 1736), p. 14.

18   Vernon W. Crane, *The Promotion Literature of Georgia* (Cambridge, 1925); Trevor Richard Reese, "Benjamin Martyn, Secretary of the Trustees of Georgia," *Georgia Historical Quarterly* vol. 38, no. 2 (June 1954); Phinizy Spalding, "Some Sermons before the Trustees of Colonial Georgia," *Georgia Historical Quarterly* vol. 57, no. 3 (Fall 1973); Allen D. Candler, ed., *The Colonial Records of the State of Georgia* (Atlanta, 1904), 1:11–21.

19   Samuel Smith, "A Sermon Preached Before the Trustees for Establishing the Colony of Georgia in America, and before the Associates of the late Rev. Dr. Bray . . . Tuesday, February 23, 1730–31" (London, 1733), p. 22.

20   Philip Bearcroft, "A Sermon Preached Before the Honorable Trustees for Establishing the Colony of Georgia in America . . . March 16, 1737–38" (London, 1738), p. 6.

21   William Berriman, "A Sermon Preach'd Before the Honorable Trustees for Establishing the Colony of Georgia in America" (London, 1739), p. 9.

22   Lewis Bruce, "The Happiness of Man the Glory of God: A Sermon Preached before the Trustees for Establishing the Colony of Georgia in America . . . March 15, 1743" (London, 1744), pp. 26–28.

23   Jack Crowley has explored the anticommercial bias of the economic attitudes behind the Georgia plan in *This Sheba, Self: The Conceptualization of Economic Life in Eighteenth–Century America* (Baltimore, 1974), pp. 16–34.

24   Caroline Robbins, "The 'Excellent Use' of Colonies: A Note on Walter Moyle's Justification of Roman Colonies, ca. 1699," *William and Mary Quarterly*, 3rd ser., vol. 23 no. 4 (Oct. 1966), passim. See also Kramnick, *Bolinbroke and His Circle*, pp. 243–256 and passim.

25   Bearcroft, "Sermon," p. 8.

26   Pocock, *Machiavellian Moment*, pp. 381–393 and passim.

27   Candler, ed., *Colonial Records*, 1:16–17.

28   Saye, "John Percival, First Earl of Egmont," p. 4.

29   "Rules for the Year 1735," included with "An Account Shewing the Progress of the Colony of Georgia, in America, from its first establishment," published per

order of the Honorable Trustees (London, 1741), pp. 40–41, in Force, ed., *Tracts*, vol. 1. For a discussion of the Trustees' land policy see Milton L. Ready, "Land Tenure in Trusteeship Georgia," *Agricultural History* vol. 48, no. 3 (July 1974).

[30] "Rules for the Year 1735," p. 40, in Force, ed., *Tracts*.

[31] This policy, originally intended to assure a number of "Soldiers, equal to the Number of Lots of Lands," was soon abandoned. The Trustees entertained applications for licenses to alienate lands, and by the end of the decade, "when the succession of Females became less dangerous to the Province, by the growing strength and increase of the People, and by the Security provided for it by his Majesty's Forces there, the Trustees resolved to enlarge the Tenures of the Lands to Estates in Tail general." "An Account Shewing the Progress of the Colony of Georgia, in America," pp. 5, 7, in Force, *Tracts*, vol. 1.

[32] Jefferson Randolph Anderson, "The Genesis of Georgia," *Georgia Historical Quarterly*, 13 (1929), 267–274; "An Account Shewing the Progress of the Colony of Georgia in America," p. 5, in Force, ed., *Tracts*. Shortly after Oglethorpe, who had served as a commissioned officer in the War of the Spanish Succession, set sail for Georgia on November 17, 1732, he was commissioned to appoint officers to train a militia. During his ten-year stay in Georgia he was much preoccupied with establishing a defensive ring of forts around the southern frontier. His martial enthusiasm had its opportunity during 1739–1743, when hostilities with Spain broke out on the Florida border. Oglethorpe's forces managed successfully to confine the Spanish to Florida, and with the Treaty of Aix-la-Chapelle (1748) the British boundary was finally secured.

[33] An undated and unsigned manuscript draft of "Some Account of the Design of the Trustees for Establishing Colonies in America," in the collections of the Georgia Historical Society, bears no relation to a published version under the same title included with "A Brief Account of the Establishment of the Colony of Georgia" (London, 1733) commonly attributed to Benjamin Martyn. Its many references to the Machiavelli of *The Art of War* (Florence, 1521) and Vitruvius' *Ten Books on Architecture* reflect the neoclassicism of contemporary political speculation, military "science" and aesthetics. It could have been written either by Oglethorpe, or by Martyn, who had aspirations to learning. Trevor Richard Reese, "Benjamin Martyn, Secretary of the Trustees of Georgia," *Georgia Historical Quarterly*, vol. 38, no. 2 (June 1954).

[34] The Trustees themselves were prepared to trade in any negro slaves who happened to be found in Georgia. "An Act for rendering the Colony of Georgia more Defencible by Prohibiting the Importation and use of Black Slaves or Negroes into

the same," in Candler, ed., *Colonial Records*, 1:50–51. Oglethorpe had served as deputy-governor of the Royal African Company before he became involved with the Georgia project.

[35] The other was "An Act to prevent the Importation and Use of Rum and Brandies in the Province of Georgia," in Candler, ed., *Colonial Records* 1:44–45. The Act prohibiting the use and sale of rum was repealed in 1742, while the prohibition of negro slavery was repealed in 1750. For discussions of the Trustees' labor and slavery policies see David M. Potter, Jr., "The Rise of the Plantation System in System in Georgia," *Georgia Historical Quarterly* vol. 16, no. 2 (June 1932); H. B. Flant, "The Labor Policy of the Trustees for Establishing the Colony of Georgia in America," *Georgia Historical Quarterly* vol. 16, no. 1 (Mar. 1932); and Betty Wood, "Thomas Stephens and the Introduction of Black Slavery in Georgia," *Georgia Historical Quarterly* vol. 58, no. 1 (Spring 1974).

[36] Benjamin Martyn, "Some Account of the Designs of the Trustees for Establishing the Colony of Georgia in America," p. 5, in Force, ed., *Tracts*. Martyn, "A New and Accurate Account," p. 34, in ibid.

[37] "Journal of the Trustees for Establishing the Colony of Georgia in America," in Candler, ed., *Colonial Records* 1:83, 84, 121, and passim.

[38] Flant, "Financing the Colonization of Georgia"; Richard S. Dunn, "The Trustees of Georgia and the House of Commons, 1732–1752," *William and Mary Quarterly*, 3rd, ser., vol. 11, no. 4 (Oct. 1954); Albert B. Saye, "The Genesis of Georgia Reviewed," *Georgia Historical Quarterly*, vol. 50, no. 2 (June 1966); Meroney, "The London Entrepôt Merchants and the Georgia Colony," *William and Mary Quarterly;* Taylor, *Georgia Plan*, pp. 31–33. Roughly one third of the settlers in Georgia during the first ten years were brought by private investment. Taylor, *Georgia Plan*, pp. 99–100.

[39] There was also a yearly rental of twenty shillings per hundred acres, beginning after the first ten years of the grant. "Rules for the Year 1735." p. 43, in Force, ed., *Tracts*.

[40] Holders of fifty-acre grants were required to pay a two shilling rent per annum on each fifty acres beginning after the first ten years of the grant. "Rules for the Year 1735," p. 41.

[41] "A New and Accurate Account," p. 50; "Some Account of The Designs of the Trustees," p. 5.

[42] Quoted in Taylor, *Georgia Plan*, p. 15.

[43] Wesley, however, proved a frail reed and left within three months. Charles remained, to the utter dismay of the Trustees. He had refused in pique the sacrament to a young female parishioner who had spurned his overtures in order to marry another Georgian unless, reported Thomas Stephens, "she had first conferr'd with him in private." An uproar ensued since the young woman was the niece of Thomas Causton, highly influential as the Trustees' storekeeper in Savannah, whereupon Wesley skipped town in 1737 under cover of night with the help of three of the more "obnoxious" rogues in the colony. The Board revoked his commission "with great pleasure, he appearing to us to be a very odd mixture of a man, an enthusiast and at the same time a hypocrite, wholly distasteful to the greater part of the inhabitants, and an incendiary of the people against the magistracy." William Stephens, "A Journal of the Proceedings in Georgia, Beginning October 20, 1737," in Candler, ed., *Colonial Records,* 4:37–41; Egmont, *Diary,* 26 Apr. 1738, 2:481.

[44] Martyn, "Some Account of the Designs of the Trustees," p. 6, in Force, ed., *Tracts.*

[45] Only Anglicanism was actively supported by the Trustees, who asked The Society for the Propagation of the Gospel in Foreign Parts to support a minister in Georgia. Candler, ed., *Colonial Records* 1:87.

[46] The Salzburgers were especially devoted to Oglethorpe and it was said by several that the settlers responded willingly to his summonses to work at such tasks as clearing fields. "An Extract of the Journals of Mr. Commissary Von Reck and of the Reverend Mr. Bolzius, One of their Ministers" (London, 1734), p. 13, in Force, ed., *Tracts,* vol. 4; "Extract of a Letter from South Carolina Gazette dated at Charles-Town, 22d. March 1732," p. 37, in Force, ed., *Tracts,* vol. 1; William Stephens, "Journal of the Proceedings in Georgia, Beginning October 20, 1937," in Candler, ed., *Colonial Records,* 17 Oct. 1739, 4:433.

[47] E. Merton Coutler, *Georgia: A Short History* (Chapel Hill, 1960), p. 74.

[48] Quoted in Taylor, *Georgia Plan,* pp. 14–15.

[49] Egmont, *Diary,* 1. Nov. 1732, 1:295.

[50] Candler, ed., *Colonial Records,* 1:17–19; Coulter, *Georgia: A Short History,* p. 20. The true nature of the Trustees' intentions is best demonstrated by the fact that when it appeared in 1751 that they would be giving up the charter, they hastily established a representative assembly so that the Crown, in taking over the colony, could not readily deny the Georgians self-government. Coulter, ibid., pp. 76–77; "Minutes of the Common Council of the Trustees for establishing the

colony of Georgia in America," in Candler, ed., *Colonial Records*, 19 Mar. 1749/50, 2:498–500.

[51] Coulter, *Georgia: A Short History*, pp. 19–20; Egmont, *Diary*, 17 June 1731, 26 Nov. 1731, 1:193, 209.

[52] James Edward Oglethorpe to the Trustees, 13 Feb. 1736, in "Letters from General Oglethorpe to the Trustees of the Colony and Others, from October 1735 to August, 1744," Georgia Historical Society, *Collections* (Savannah, 1873), 3:13.

[53] Martyn, "A New and Accurate Account," p. 28, and "Some Account of the Designs of the Trustees," pp. 5–6, in Force, ed., *Tracts*.

[54] "A Brief Account of the Establishment of the Colony of Georgia, Under James Oglethorpe, 1 February, 1733," p. 10, in Force, ed., *Tracts*, vol. 1. Oglethorpe to the Trustees, 10 Feb. 1733, in "Reasons for Establishing the Colony of Georgia," Georgia Historical Society, *Collections* (Savannah, 1840), vol. 1; Thomas Gamble, "Col. William Bull—His Part in the Founding of Savannah," *Georgia Historical Quarterly* vol. 17, no. 2 (June 1933).

[55] Gordon's map is discussed in John W. Reps, "Town Planning in Colonial Georgia," *Town Planning Review* 30, no. 4 (Jan. 1960), 274.

[56] Ibid., p. 278.

[57] "Rules for the Year 1735," p. 40, in Force, ed., *Tracts*.

[58] Francis Moore, "A Voyage to Georgia Begun in the Year 1735," Georgia Historical Society, *Collections* (Savannah, 1840), 1:97–98. Reps rightly points out that Moore's assurance of safety for villages within the towns may have been a promotional device to allay the fears of prospective settlers; *The Making of Urban America: A History of City Planning in the United States* (Princeton, 1965), p. 198. That Moore's explanation for the wards as primarily military in purpose is implausible is suggested by Frederic R. Stevenson: "it is hard to imagine any defensive strategy based on holding so much ground once the fortified town wall was broken through. A stand would then have had to be made on the river bank, using perhaps the nearest row of houses as a rampart and manning the ships in the harbour." "Charleston and Savannah," *Journal of the Society of Architectural Historians* vol. 10, no. 4 (Dec. 1951).

[59] Reps, "Town Planning in Colonial Georgia," pp. 277–279.

[60] "An Extract of the Journals of Mr. Commissary Von Reck and of the Reverend

Mr. Bolzius," p. 11; *London Magazine* (1745), quoted in Reps, "Town Planning in Colonial Georgia," p. 279; "An Account, Shewing the Progress of the Colony of Georgia," p. 32.

[61]   *A True and Historical Narrative of the Colony of Georgia, by Pat. Tailfer and others. With Comments by the Earl of Egmont*, ed. Clarence L. Ver Steeg (Athens, 1960), p. 140.

[62]   Turpin C. Bannister, "Oglethorpe's Sources for the Savannah Plan," *Journal of the Society of Architectural Historians* 20, no. 2 (May 1961), 58–62.

[63]   *Ibid.*, p. 48; Reps, *The Making of Urban America*, p. 192.

[64]   "An Account, Shewing the Progress of the Colony of Georgia," p. 21.

[65]   Von Reck and Bolzius, "Journals," p. 11; Peter Graham et al., "A State of the Province of Georgia, Attested upon Oath, in the Court of Savannah," p. 4; "An Account, Shewing the Progress of the Colony of Georgia," p. 32; "A Description of Georgia, by a Gentleman who has resided there upwards of Seven Years and was One of the First Settlers," p. 5; all in Force, ed., *Tracts*.

[66]   Robert Mountgomery, Baronet, "A Discourse Concerning the Designed Establishment of a New Colony to the south of Carolina, in the Most Delightful Country in the Universe," pp. 9–13, in Force, ed. *Tracts*, vol. 1.

[67]   Ibid., p. 11.

[68]   Reps, "Town Planning in Colonial Georgia," p. 282.

[69]   Reps, *The Making of Urban America*, pp. 12–15; Gilbert Gamblin, *The Town in Ulster: An Account of the Origin and Building of Towns of the Province and the Development of Their Rural Setting* (Belfast, 1951), pp. 17–48.

[70]   Newcourt's plan is discussed in Reps, *The Making of Urban America*, pp. 15, 165.

[71]   Donald J. Olson, *Town Planning in London: The Eighteenth and Nineteenth Centuries* (New Haven, 1964); Reps, "Town Planning in Colonial Georgia," p. 282.

[72]   "Journal of the Trustees for Establishing the Colony of Georgia in America," 8 Jan. 1752, in Candler, ed., *Colonial Records*, 1:571.

73 E. Merton Coulter and Albert B. Saye, eds., *A List of the Early Settlers of Georgia* (Athens, 1949), p. xi.

74 Egmont, *Diary*, 29 April and 7 June, 1739, 3:56–66, 2:317–318, and passim.

75 For background on the "malcontents" and their version of the Georgia enterprise, with Percival's comments on their allegations, see Tailfer, *A True and Historical Narrative*, with comments by Egmont. Oglethorpe to the Trustees, 16 July 1739, "Letters from General Oglethorpe to the Trustees," pp. 79–80; Stephens, *Journal*, Mar. 25, 27, 1738, 22 Jan. 1739, Dec. 30, 1737, Feb. 18, 1740. Although Stephens was in the employ of the Trustees, in his manner of investigation and entries to his *Journal* he sought to give as balanced and full account as possible "so the full Truth and Causes" might be "laid open." For a brief biography of Stephens see Natalie F. Bocock, "William Stephens," *Georgia Historical Quarterly* vol. 17, no. 4 (Dec. 1933).

76 Egmont, *Diary* vol 2, 27 Feb. 1735, p. 159; 26 Feb. 1736, p. 239; 6 February 1737, p. 341.

77 Ibid., 21 Jan. 1741, p. 180; Candler, ed., *Colonial Records*, 1:363.

78 For example, the Trustees were assured throughout the period by London silk dealers and weavers as well as Georgians that Georgia silk was of high quality, competitive with what was produced in the Piedmont. Egmont, *Diary* vol. 3, p. 27 Mar. 1740, p. 117; 16 Jan. 1740, p. 100; 7 June 1739, p. 66; 2 Nov. 1739, p. 86; II, 9 Apr. 1735, p. 168; Stephens, "Journal," 30 Apr. 1741, p. 6; 8 May 1741, p. 7; 11 June 1741, p. 7. The Trustees were led by reports they received to except mulberry, indigo, cotton, wine, cochineal, and all manner of other crops to "thrive" in the colony; "Journal of the Trustees," 16 Jan. 1739/40; 23 Jan. 1739/40; 3 March 1741/42; 11 Feb. 1743/44; 18 May 1751. Any assessment of the economic viability of silk culture in Georgia must be tenuous at best, for it depended upon inadequately known climatic conditions of the period as well as labor attitudes and skills of which we can have only an imperfect picture. Furthermore, the question of the economics of negro slave labor, officially introduced into Georgia in 1752, must greatly complicate any effort to strike a financial balance sheet for the colony in the eighteenth century. In spite of these difficulties, an attempt to do just that has been made by Milton Ready, "An Economic History of Colonial Georgia, 1732–1754" (Ph. D. diss., University of Georgia, 1970), passim.

79 Reese, *Colonial Georgia*, pp. 7, 37–38. One explanation of Georgia's financial difficulties, aside from the irregularity of parliamentary subsidies, comes from Oglethorpe himself. In his letters to the Trustees he complained that colonial merchants, from whom the Trust purchased supplies, overcharged them for goods

that were bad or never arrived. This problem became especially acute when, during the border crisis with Spain in 1738, which cost the colony a year's harvest, the Trust had to buy virtually all supplies and foodstuffs from northern merchants. Compounding this setback was storekeeper Thomas Causton's failure to keep adequate records of the Trust's indebtedness and his understandable readiness to dispense supplies on credit. "Letters from General Oglethorpe to the Trustees," 19 Sept. 1738, 7 Oct. 1738, 19 Oct. 1738, and passim.

[80] Taylor, *Georgia Plan*, p. 211.

[81] Clarence L. Ver Steeg, *Origins of a Southern Mosaic* (Athens, 1975), pp. 69–90.

[82] See, for example, Daniel J. Boorstin, *The Americans: The Colonial Experience* (New York, 1958), pp. 95–96. Several Georgia historians have struggled against the notion that early Georgia was particularly utopian or even philanthropic in design. Chief among these is Albert B. Saye, whose opening essays in *New Viewpoints in Georgia History* (Athens, 1943) refute the view that Georgia was a haven for debtors, or even intended to be. Jefferson R. Anderson, in his "Genesis of Georgia," argued with single-minded determination that Georgia was the product of James Edward Oglethorpe's ambition for military fame in concert with the Crown's imperial struggle with Spain. More balanced attempts to assess the Georgia enterprise in the context of eighteenth-century British imperialism can be found in Trevor Reese, *Colonial Georgia*, and Larry E. Ivers, *British Drums on the Southern Frontier: The Military Colonization of Georgia, 1733–1749* (Chapel Hill, 1974), passim. Most recently, Paul S. Taylor has defended the essential viability of the Georgia plan, attributing its failure to the campaign against the Trustees waged by those Georgians desiring the legalization of negro slavery, and to the unwillingness of Parliament to provide adequate and ongoing financial support; *Georgia Plan*.

[83] Lowell, Massachusetts, and the careers of Charles Loring Brace and Frederick Law Olmsted provide the "case studies" of nineteenth century urban conceptualizations explored in Thomas Bender's *Toward an Urban Vision: Ideas and Institutions in Nineteenth-Century America* (Lexington, 1975).

[84] Jane Jacobs, *The Death and Life of Great American Cities* (New York, 1961), pp. 16–25; Nathan Glazer, "Why City Planning is Obsolete," *Architectural Forum* 109 (July 1958), 96–98.

A Note on
Method and Sources

✣

The preceding chapters have attempted, admittedly incompletely and tentatively, to explore a facet of experience common to a significant number of men and women who settled the North American colonies in terms of the varied perceptions and expectations they may have held of that experience. Our interest has been in what the city signified to those who became engaged in erecting cities in the midst of a rural landscape. We have not premised a single "idea" of the city that was our business to detect; nonetheless the urban and the rural experience held some meaning for these men and women. Perceptions of the landscape, whether urban, rural, or suburban, were informed by convictions and apprehensions derived from both contemporary and inherited political, social, and moral preoccupations. Those perceptions were expressed in a variety of forms—correspondence, religious and political discourse, and, of course, promotional literature. No single text, or category of texts, could alone reveal the nuances and associations that together constituted the various meanings of the city for the founders of colonial America's principal towns.

Moreover, the city was not only an abstraction, but a real place, and it was portrayed in line and form as well as in words. Thus this investigation into the history of urban conceptions has of necessity drawn upon graphic sources as well as texts. The use of town plans as a source for the exploration of ideas of the city, however, presents special problems. At the simplest level, the historian's interpretation of particular arrangements of space on the landscape may differ from the perception of space held by the individual who initially diagrammed those arrangements; indeed the interpretation can vary sharply between historians. One pedestrian's enlivening diversity can be another's disorienting chaos. The second problem is raised by the question of what kind of art form an urban plan is, if in

205

fact it is an art form. Related to that question is another problem: whose perception of the city is being reflected in the plan?

The town plan of the seventeenth and early eighteenth centuries was not, like the Florentine painting of the quattrocento, let us say, the product of a distinct cultural group. Thus its appearance or meaning can not be explained entirely by social analysis. Towns were laid out first of all by those who were capable of surveying, and the early surveyors—with the exception of Thomas Holme and James Edward Oglethorpe—who laid out the colonies' first towns, remain, for the most part, anonymous. That both Holme and Oglethorpe had been military men, and that surveying was a skill expected of military engineers, would seem to lend credence to the view that town planning during the period was generally governed by a tradition of military encampment. But others besides military men had been engaged in city planning. Leonardo da Vinci sketched out a plan for the redesign of Florence; Sir Christopher Wren was trained as a mathematician; and some landowners of substance who managed their own properties mastered the art of surveying by practical necessity. William Byrd II and Thomas Jefferson, for examples, both surveyed and both favored grid plans which are deceptively similar to the rectilinear plan of the Roman military camp.

If there was a single group which by profession possessed the mathematical skills necessary to the surveyor it was the mathematical practitioners of the seventeenth and early eighteenth centuries. This was a broad group indeed, which included astronomers, draftsmen, architects, instrument makers, surveyors, military engineers, computers of navigational and astronomical tables, navigators, school masters, and an occasional lecturer in "natural philosophy" at Cambridge or Oxford.* In addition, anyone who had studied in the classical liberal arts curriculum might have the mathematical knowledge necessary to the surveyor. The difficulty that arises in attempting to interpret the intended function of any particular town plan in an era preceding that which saw the development of civil engineering as a profession is thus one of attempting to characterize the perceptions of those responsible for a plan in terms of a single occupational or social group. That difficulty is compounded by the presence of patterns for town plans that may be less practical than iconographical in origin, as we have seen in the instance of Puritan town planning.

The historian then has, it would seem, two choices. He can abandon the effort entirely of turning to graphic materials as offering possible clues

---

* Eva G. R. Taylor, *The Mathematical Practitioners of Tudor and Stuart England* (Cambridge, Eng., 1954), and *The Mathematical Practitioners of Hanoverian England, 1714–1840* (London, 1966).

to the meaning of the city for those who erected cities, contenting himself with the use of town plans as illustrations to be made of what his audience wills. Or he can regard the town plan in the same way that we have come to regard language in the history of ideas. Certain designs, like certain vocabularies, will have special connotations derivative of the contexts in which they occurred. The task then becomes one of uncovering those contexts and only then attempting to ascertain the elocutionary, or symbolic, as well as practical intent of a given plan.

Since we have indicated in the annotations to the preceding chapters the various sources used in the support of their conclusions, we shall attempt here only to highlight those sources which should prove especially helpful to those who might wish to investigate further the conception of the city in early America. For the colonial background of the foundings of Philadelphia, Williamsburg, and Savannah, as well as the early histories of those cities, see: James T. Lemon, *The Best Poor Man's Country: A Geographical Study of Early Southeastern Pennsylvania* (Baltimore, 1972); Sam Bass Warner, Jr., *The Private City: Philadelphia in Three Periods of Its Growth* (Philadelphia, 1968); E. P. Oberholtzer, *Philadelphia: A History of the City and Its People* (Philadelphia, 1911); Edwin B. Bronner, *William Penn's "Holy Experiment": The Founding of Pennsylvania, 1681–1726* (Princeton, 1968); James Ross McCain, *Georgia as a Proprietary Province: The Execution of a Trust* (Boston, 1917, 1972); Paul S. Taylor, *Georgia Plan: 1732–1752* (Berkeley, Cal., 1972); Albert B. Saye, *New Viewpoints in Georgia History* (Athens, 1943); Harold E. Davis, *The Fledgling Province: Social and Cultural Life in Colonial Georgia, 1733–1776* (Chapel Hill, 1976); Carl Bridenbaugh, *Seat of Empire: The Political Role of Eighteenth Century Williamsburg* (Charlottesville, 1963); Joseph A. Osborne, *Williamsburg in Colonial Times* (Richmond, 1935);Philip A. Bruce, *Institutional History of Virginia in the Seventeenth Century*, 2 vols. (New York, 1910); Thomas J. Wertenbaker, *The Planters of Colonial Virginia* (Princeton, 1922); and Edmund S. Morgan, *American Slavery, American Freedom: The Ordeal of Colonial Virginia* (New York, 1975).

Ideas of the city in early America occurred, of course, within the context of colonial urbanization. Still essential to an appreciation of this background are Carl Bridenbaugh's *Cities in the Wilderness: The First Century of Urban Life in America, 1625–1742* (New York, 1938, 1966) and Thomas J. Wertenbaker, *The Golden Age of Colonial Culture* (New York, 1942), which is urban in focus. The study of the New England town is seemingly tireless and continues to produce a variety of interpretations. For basic studies one should consult Sumner Chilton Powell, *Puritan Village: The Formation of a New England Town* (New York, 1965); Kenneth A. Lockridge, *A New England Town: The First Hundred Years* (New

York, 1970); Michael Zuckerman, *Peaceable Kingdoms: New England Towns in the Eighteenth Century* (New York, 1970); Robert E. Wall, Jr., *Massachusetts Bay: The Crucial Decade, 1640–1650* (New Haven, 1972); Kenneth A. Lockridge and Alan Kreider, "The Evolution of Massachusetts Town Government, 1640–1740," *William and Mary Quarterly,* 3rd ser. (Oct. 1966); Darrett B. Rutman, *Winthrop's Boston: A Portrait of a Puritan Town, 1630–1649* (Chapel Hill, 1965); Justin Winsor, *The Memorial History of Boston,* 4 vols. (Boston, 1882); and Walter Muir Whitehill, *Boston: A Topographical History* (Cambridge, Mass., 1959).

In addition to the various manuscript collections available at the Historical Society of Pennsylvania, the Massachusetts Historical Society, the Georgia Historical Society, the University of Georgia at Athens, and the Colonial Williamsburg Foundation, a number of published collections contain contemporary accounts of the colonies which include passages descriptive of the foundings of Boston, Philadelphia, and Savannah and the early years of those towns. These include Peter Force, ed., *Tracts and Other Papers, Relating Principally to the Origin, Settlement, and Progress of the Colonies in North America, from the Discovery of the Country to the Year 1776* (Washington, 1838, 1844; New York, 1947); Alexander Young, *Chronicles of the First Planters of the Colony of Massachusetts Bay, from 1623 to 1636* (Boston, 1846); Massachusetts Historical Society, *Collections* (Boston, 1792–   ); Massachusetts Historical Society, *Proceedings* (Boston, 1879–   ); Albert Cook Myers, ed., *Narratives of Early Pennsylvania, West New Jersey, and Delaware, 1630–1707* (New York, 1912); John F. Watson, *Annals of Pennsylvania, from the Discovery of the Delaware* (Philadelphia, 1850); Samuel Hazard, *Annals of Pennsylvania, From the Discovery of the Delaware* (Philadelphia, 1850); *Colonial Records of Pennsylvania* (Philadelphia, 1852–   ); F. D. Lee and J. L. Agnew, *Historical Record of the City of Savannah* (Savannah, 1869); Georgia Historical Society, *Collections* (Savannah, 1840–1916); Allen D. Chandler, *The Colonial Records of the State of Georgia* (Atlanta, 1904–   ); and Virginia Historical Society, *Collections* (1882–1892).

Statutes relating to the founding of Boston, Philadelphia, Williamsburg, and Savannah, as well as the establishment of towns in the colonies, are occasionally contained in the above collections. But one should also consult Leonard Woods Labaree, ed., *Royal Instructions to British Governors, 1670–1776,* 2 vols. (New York, 1935); Nathaniel B. Shurtleff, ed., *Records of the Governor and Company of Massachusetts Bay in New England,* 5 vols. (Boston, 1853); *The Statutes at Large of Pennsylvania, 1682–1801* (Harrisburg, 1896); Staughton George, ed., *Charter to William Penn, and Laws of the Province of Pennsylvania* (Harrisburg, 1879); and William Walter Henig, *The Statutes at Large: Being a Collection of all the Laws of Virginia,* 13 vols. (New York, 1819–1823).

While the literature of American attitudes toward the city since the end of the eighteenth century is growing in volume and quality (see the Preface), studies of urban perceptions contemporary with and prior to the founding of the English colonies in America are often interwoven with analyses of seventeenth- and eighteenth-century English literature and politics. See, for example, Perez Zagorin, *The Court and the Country: The Beginnings of the English Revolution* (New York, 1970); Isaac Kramnick, *Bolingbroke and His Circle: The Politics of Nostalgia in the Age of Walpole* (Cambridge, Mass., 1968); T. H. Breen, "Persistent Localism: English Social Change and the Shaping of New England Institutions," *William and Mary Quarterly*, 3rd ser. (Jan. 1975); and Maynard Mack, *The Garden and the City: Retirement and Politics in the Later Poetry of Pope, 1731–1743* (Toronto, 1969). Brief but perceptive attempts to define the idea of the city in European thought can be found in Sylvia L. Thrupp, "The City as the Idea of Social Order," in Oscar Handlin and John Burchard, eds., *The Historian and the City* (Cambridge, Mass., 1963), and in Carl E. Schorske, "The Idea of the City in European Thought," also in the Handlin and Burchard volume. Raymond Williams' *The Country and the City* (Oxford, 1973) is a personal but highly literate and instructive interpretation of the views of the country and the city in English literature.

There are, in addition, a number of treatises published in England contemporaneously with the first phase of English colonization which offer suggestions of the possible meanings of "city" to the first generations of Englishmen in America. Giovanni Botero's *Treatise Concerning the Causes of the Magnificence and Greatness of Cities* (London, 1606) was an Italian treatise which should be read in conjunction with Leo Battista Alberti's *Ten Books on Architecture*, trans. James Leone, from the Italian translation of Cosimo Bartoli (London, 1755), as expressive of Renaissance views of the city. John Stow's *A Survey of London*, 2 vols. (London, 1598, 1603) contains numerous passages which attempt an anatomy of the city and of urban life. A modern reprint of Thomas Blenerhasset's *The Plantation in Ulster: A Direction for the Plantation in Ulster* (London, 1610; New York, 1972) is among the scarce sources available to us for the principles which might have governed the placement of the surveyor's rod in the settlement of the earliest English colonies.

Perceptions of the city in early America are mirrored in contemporary descriptions and accounts of the first colonial cities reprinted in the general source collections cited above and noted in the annotations to the preceding chapters. In reading such descriptions one must assume, failing contrary evidence, that their authors were describing what they saw. And yet the kinds of things their authors mention, or fail to mention, suggest more than objective reality; they suggest as well an angle of vision or point of view with respect to that which is being described. In reading such accounts the historian must be sensitive to the character of adjectives and phrases being used. When "one hundred and twenty dwellings" becomes "one hundred and twenty comely houses" or "one houndred and twenty prosperous houses," something more is being inferred of the seen landscape than the number of structures erected within it.

Expectations of the city are, again, mirrored in a variety of sources. The expectations of the founders of Boston, Philadelphia, Williamsburg, and Savannah can be detected in their correspondence and diaries, much of which, like the *Diary of the First Earl of Egmont* (London, 1923) or the papers of John Winthrop, are available in published form. The William Penn Papers at the Historical Society of Pennsylvania are in the process of preparation for publication as of this writing, but have been available to scholars. Even more valuable is the promotional literature generated by the founders of these cities and their supporters, for such documents express the expectations, desires, and anxieties which their authors presumed—surely more accurately than we can judge—would be received sympathetically by their audiences. What can legitimately be regarded as promotional literature varies from colony to colony, as did the circumstances of their establishment. In the case of Boston and Massachusetts Bay, for example, many a sermon was in part if not wholly promotional in intent, as was Edward Johnson's *Wonder-Working Providence of Sions Savior in New England,* ed. J. Franklin Jameson (New York, 1910), or William Wood's *New England's Prospect: A True, Lively, and Experimentall Description of that part of America commonly called New England* (London, 1634; New York, 1965).

The various appeals that emanated from the Virginia House of Burgesses and were penned by visitors calling for Royal support of, if not at least cooperation in, the establishment of towns in Virginia form a body of promotional literature which can be analyzed in terms of the expectations of urban life reflected in their arguments. In the case of the founding of Pennsylvania and Philadelphia, and Georgia and Savannah, promotional efforts were more explicit. William Penn himself authored several "accounts," annotated in the chapter on Philadelphia, intended to justify his proprietary enterprise and to attract settlers and financial backers. The Georgia Trust produced probably the largest single body of promotional literature. Its secretary Benjamin Martyn, as well as James Edward Oglethorpe, wrote numerous "accounts" and "descriptions" designed both to lure planters and to persuade Parliament to be generous with its annual apportionments. Examples of these have been cited in the chapter on Savannah. No less revealing are the sermons delivered by London clergymen to the members of the Georgia Trust during their annual meetings. Some of these have been reprinted; all are now available in micro-card form in the Charles Evans *Early American Imprint* series.

The history of town planning in America has been explored with careful and sensitive mastery by John W. Reps in *The Making of Urban America: A History of City Planning in the United States* (Princeton, 1965). In addition to several articles discussing city planning in colonial Philadelphia and Georgia, Reps has also discussed town planning in the colonial Tidewater in *Tidewater Towns: City Planning in Colonial Virginia and Maryland* (Charlottesville, 1972). Colonial town planning is also treated in Dan Stanislawski, "Early Spanish Town Planning in the New World," *Geographical Review* vol. 47 (Jan. 1947); Roy Hidemichi Akagi, *The Town Proprietors of the New England Colonies* (Philadelphia, 1924); Marshall Harris, *Origin of the Land Tenure System in the United States* (Ames, Ia., 1953); William Haller, *The Puritan Frontier: Town-Planning in New England Colonial Development, 1630–1660* (New York, 1951); and Anthony N. B. Garvan, *Architecture and Town Planning in Colonial Connecticut* (New Haven, 1951).

The first chapter in Reps' *Making of Urban America*, "European Planning on the Eve of Colonization," provides a useful summary of European precedents in town planning history, but can be supplemented with C. A. Doxiadis, *Architectural Space in Ancient Greece* (Cambridge, Mass., 1972); Ferdinando Castagnoli, *Orthogonal Town Planning in Antiquity* (Cambridge, Mass., 1971); Dan Stanislawski, "The Origin and Spread of the Grid-Pattern Town," *Geographical Review* (1946); R. E. Wycherley, *How the Greeks Built Cities* (Garden City, N.Y., 1969); Gilbert Camblin, *The Town in Ulster: An Account of the Origin and Building of Towns of the Provinces and the Development of Their Rural Setting* (Belfast, 1951), especially chapters 1–3; Thomas Harold Hughes and E. A. G. Lamborn, *Towns and Town Planning, Ancient and Modern* (Oxford, 1923); Thomas W. Mackesey, *History of City Planning: A Bibliography*, ed. Rolland W. Mills (Oakland, Cal., 1961); A. E. J. Morris, *History of Urban Form: Prehistory to the Renaissance* (New York, 1974); and the titles in the Planning and Cities series edited by George R. Collins and published by George Braziller. The iconographical representation of cities in European history has not received the attention it deserves. But a valuable introduction to this subject is Helen Resenau's *The Ideal City in Its Architectural Evolution* (London, 1959), while a discussion of exegetical descriptions of the cities of the Old and New Testaments forms a part of John Archer's "Puritan Town Planning in New Haven," *Journal of the Society of Architectural Historians* (May 1975).

Most state historical societies house collections of surviving prints and maps descriptive of their towns and counties. Especially rich collections pertaining to the English colonies are owned by the Library Company of Philadelphia, the Historical Society of Pennsylvania, the New York Public Library, and the New York Historical Society. The Prints and Maps Division of the Library of Congress contains good collections, as do the Boston

Public Library and the Cornell University Libraries. For catalogues and published views and maps of early American towns and cities one might consult: Graydon LaVerne Freeman, ed., *Historical Prints of American Cities* (Watkins Glen, 1952); Daniel C. Haskell, *American Historical Prints: Early Views of American Cities, etc.* (New York, 1927); and I. N. Phelps Stokes and D. C. Haskell, comps., *American Historical Prints: Early Views of American Cities* (New York, 1932). The "Note on Cartographic Research Methods" and "Selected Bibliography of Sources Consulted" at the end of Reps' *Making of Urban America* provide useful guides to further research using American town plans as a source. For plans of the English towns and cities with which the English settlers in North America might have been familiar, one should consult John Speed's *The Theatre of the Empire of Great Britain,* published in London in several editions beginning in 1611. This handsomely illustrated atlas offers descriptions and maps in color of the principal towns of the various English counties.

Index